18495₀

D1590453

11/28/06-c

B.C.

LIBRARY OF THE HISTORY OF IDEAS

VOLUME IV

Hume as Philosopher of
Society, Politics and History

LIBRARY OF THE HISTORY OF IDEAS

ISSN 1050–1053

Series Editor: JOHN W. YOLTON

HUME AS PHILOSOPHER OF SOCIETY, POLITICS AND HISTORY

Edited by

DONALD LIVINGSTON

&

MARIE MARTIN

The King's Library

UNIVERSITY OF ROCHESTER PRESS

This collection first published 1991

University of Rochester Press
200 Administration Building, University of Rochester
Rochester, New York 14627, USA
and at PO Box 9, Woodbridge, Suffolk IP12 3DF, UK

ISBN   1 878822 03 9

British Library Cataloguing-in-Publication Data
Hume as philosopher of society, politics and history. –
(Library of the history of ideas ; 1050–1053 ; 4)
    I. Livingston, Donald W.   II. Martin, Marie
    III. Series
    192
    ISBN 1–878822–03–9

This publication is printed on acid-free paper

Printed in the United States of America

TABLE OF CONTENTS

ACKNOWLEDGEMENTS

The articles in this volume first appeared in the *Journal of the History of Ideas* as indicated below, by volume, year and pages, in order.

Berry, Christopher J., "From Hume to Hegel: The Case of the Social Contract", 38 (1977) 691–703.

Cottle, Charles E., "Justice as Artificial Virtue in Hume's *Treatise*", 40 (1979) 457–66.

Force, James E., "Hume and Johnson on Prophecy and Miracles: Historical Context", 43 (1982) 463–75.

Grene, Marjorie, "Hume: Sceptic and Tory?", 4 (1943) 333–48.

Hundert, E. J., "The Achievement Motive in Hume's Political Economy", 35 (1974) 139–43.

Lyon, Robert, "Notes on Hume's Philosophy of Political Economy", 31 (1970) 457–61.

McRae, Robert, "Hume as a Political Philosopher", 12 (1951) 285–90.

Mossner, Ernest Campbell, "Was Hume a Tory Historian? Facts and Reconsiderations", 2 (1941) 225–36.

Siebert, Donald T., "Hume on Idolatry and Incarnation", 45 (1984) 379–96.

Venning, Corey, "Hume on Property, Commerce, and Empire in the Good Society: the Role of Historical Necessity", 37 (1976) 79–92.

Wallech, Steven, "The Elements of Social Status in Hume's *Treatise*", 45 (1984) 207–18.

Werner, John M., "David Hume and America", 33 (1972) 439–56.

Wertz, S. K., "Hume, History, and Human Nature", 36 (1975) 481–96.

I

INTRODUCTION

By Donald Livingston

The first critical examinations of Hume's philosophy were contained in Thomas Reid's *Inquiry into the Human Mind* (1764) and in James Beattie's *The Nature and Immutability of Truth, In Opposition to Sophistry and Scepticism* (1770). Beattie interpreted Hume as a nihilistic skeptic, and Reid, more charitably, treated him as a philosopher whose skepticism was the result of following the Cartesian "way of Ideas" to the bitter end. In neither case was Hume thought to have had anything positive of his own to teach. Kant had a much higher opinion of Hume's merit as a philosopher than Reid or Beattie, but, like them, he found little in Hume that was positive. Aside from giving Hume credit for having awakened him from his dogmatic slumbers, Kant suggested that Hume was on the way to discovering the principles of his own "transcendental" or "critical" philosophy and would, perhaps, have done so had he not been confused in thinking that mathematical propositions are analytic. But here Kant and many since have been mistaken. Hume, in fact, did not believe that mathematical propositions are analytic. Indeed, he held a doctrine similar to Kant's that they are both necessarily true and have empirical content. But this insight is lodged in a conception of philosophy quite different from Kant's transcendental philosophy.[1] The question of what this philosophy is is still a matter of debate. But that Hume has a positive philosophy with doctrines of its own to teach can no longer be easily dismissed.

Norman Kemp Smith was the first to offer a systematic refutation of the negative, skeptical reading of Hume. In *The Philosophy of David Hume* (1941), he argued that Hume is a naturalist, not a skeptic. Hume used skeptical arguments merely to refute rationalism and to establish the proposition that beliefs are determined not by reason but by sentiment. Although Smith made it possible to view Hume as a naturalist, he did not systematically explore Hume's naturalism, nor did he give an entirely convincing account of how naturalism could be grafted onto the apparently devastating skepticism that had so impressed early commentators. And like his philosophical predecessors, Smith had treated Hume mainly as an epistemologist, despite the fact that he had introduced the novel

---

[1] I discuss this in *Hume's Philosophy of Common Life* (Chicago: University of Chicago Press, 1984), pp. 49–59.

thesis that Hume's epistemology was built upon his moral philosophy
and not the other way around. One reason for this is that epistemology
and problems in the philosophy of science have dominated Anglo-
American philosophy, and so it is not surprising that those interests
would be reflected in commentaries on Hume's philosophy.

But very little of Hume's writings, taken as a whole, are devoted to
epistemological subjects. Over half of what he wrote was in history, and
most of the rest of it was in ethics, aesthetics, philosophy of religion, and
what today would be called the social sciences. Only Book I, entitled "Of
the Understanding" in *A Treatise of Human Nature* (1739) and recast as
An Enquiry Concerning Human Understanding (1748), deals exclusively
with epistemological issues. And Hume makes it clear, in Book I of the
Treatise, that the main object of the work as a whole is the study of the
passions, out of which the world of human culture is generated.[2] That
topic is the subject of the remaining two Books, "Of the Passions" and
"Of Morals." The epistemology of Book I is necessary only to provide a
framework for a science of human culture.

The *Treatise* was published anonymously in 1739–40. It proved to be
a failure mainly because the skeptical arguments Hume so vigorously
deployed in Book I to distinguish between true and false philosophical
inquiry seemed to capture the *Treatise* itself and to undermine the very
possibility of a science of human culture. Undaunted, Hume immediately
set about recasting the philosophy of the *Treatise* in the more readable
form of essays, discourses, inquiries, and dialogues. The *Philosophical
Essays* (1741) was the first work to bear Hume's name and also the first
to make his reputation. The 1748 edition of the *Essays* attracted a letter of
appreciation from Montesquieu which was much welcomed by the obscure Hume. The essay form proved a successful medium for the expression of the philosophy of the *Treatise*, and most of his later writing
took this form. In 1753, Hume collected his philosophical writings (ex-
cluding the *Treatise*) and published them under the title *Essays and
Treatises on Several Subjects*. In an "advertisement" prefixed to the
second volume of the posthumous edition of this collection, Hume
sought to disarm the nihilistic interpretation of the *Treatise*, presented by
Reid and Beattie, by publicly disowning it as a juvenile work. His
readers were henceforth to consider the *Essays and Treatises on Several
Subjects* as the mature and definitive expression of his philosophy. This
included *An Enquiry Concerning Human Understanding* (first published
in 1748 as *Philosophical Essays on Understanding*); *An Enquiry Con-*

---

[2] David Hume, *A Treatise of Human Nature*, ed. Selby-Bigge (Oxford: Clarendon
Press, 1978), p. 8.

cerning the Principles of Morals; *A Dissertation on the Passions*; *The Natural History of Religion*; and *Essays, Moral, Political, and Literary.*

Philosophers are not in the habit of regarding the *Essays and Treatises on Several Subjects* as constituting Hume's philosophy. And they have been even less inclined to regard *The History of England* as an extension of Hume's philosophical work. The conception of Hume as a nihilistic skeptic has led to the view, as Collingwood put it, that Hume "deserted philosophical studies in favor of historical at about the age of thirty five."[3] And it is still common to think that Hume's motive for writing history was not desire for truth but literary fame and notoriety. This was John Stuart Mill's understanding: "Hume possessed powers of a very high order; but regard for truth formed no part of his character. He reasoned with surprising acuteness; but the object of his reasoning was, not to obtain truth, but to show that it is unattainable. His mind, too, was completely enslaved by a taste for literature . . . that literature which without regard for truth or utility, seeks only to excite emotion."[4] But, as E. C. Mossner argues in an essay of this volume, from the beginning of his career Hume had formed the plan of writing history, and he considered *The History of England* part of his philosophical system.

During his lifetime Hume achieved fame as a historian and as a philosophical essayist. His *History of England* was the standard work on the subject for a century, passing through at least 167 posthumous editions. Hume has a secure place as one of the four great historians of the eighteenth century, along with Gibbon, Voltaire, and Robertson. And he is unique in the history of philosophy, for no philosopher of Hume's stature can claim the status he has as a historian. Indeed with a few exceptions, such as Collingwood, one would be hard pressed to find a philosopher of note who had made any contribution to history. The western philosphical tradition has been, on the whole, profoundly ahistorical. Philosophy as an inquiry into ultimate reality is about the universal and the timeless, not the particular and narrative. This ahistorical outlook has dominated the Anglo-American philosophical tradition from which most commentary on Hume has arisen. A contemporary philosopher has remarked on the ahistorical characteristic of this tradition and has taken Hume to be a paradigm of it: "The divergence between history and philosophy in England and America is perhaps best personified by David Hume, a philosopher and a historian but not both at once. His principal ideas in philosophy did not stem from his concern with history;

---

[3] R. G. Collingwood, *The Idea of History* (Oxford: Clarendon Press, 1962), p. 73.
[4] John Stuart Mill, review of Brodie, *History of the British Empire*, in *The Westminster Review* 2 (1824), p. 34.

rather, when he turned to history, he had already completed his philosophical system."[5] Such a view has kept Hume's *History* safely removed from his philosophy and has construed his "philosophy" as being narrowly concerned with epistemological issues. But Hume always considered the *History* to be an expression of his philosophy. The reason for this is that Hume's conception of philosophy requires a rapprochement with history. Hume taught that "Philosophical decisions are nothing but the reflections of common life methodized and corrected."[6] By "common life" he meant man as a social being in historical time. The task of philosophy is both to reflect concrete social and historical conditions and to "methodize and correct" them. This is a profoundly historical conception of philosophy, and, indeed, cannot be carried out without doing historical work. Of all Hume's philosophical writings, this conception of philosophy is best exemplified in the philosophical essays which Hume grouped together under the title *Essays, Moral, Political and Literary*. This volume of some 600 pages ranges over the entire domain of human culture. History and philosophical reflection move easily together and merge in a form of criticism that is peculiarly Humean. Yet this most important expression of Hume's philosophy is, of all his philosophical writings, the most neglected by philosophers.

It is remarkable that during his lifetime Hume was known mainly as the author of the *History* and the *Essays*. Until very recently both have been neglected. The *History of England* went out of print in 1894 and did not appear again until 1983 when Liberty *Classics* produced a handsome inexpensive edition. A critical edition of the *Essays, Moral, Political, and Literary* was published in *The Philosophical Works of David Hume* (1874–75), edited by T. H. Green and T. H. Grose. Except for occasional reprints of this expensive four-volume set, no critical edition of the *Essays* was available until 1985 when Liberty *Classics* published a new critical edition, edited by Eugene Miller. During the last decade a handful of books have appeared which have recognized the importance of the *History* and the *Essays* and have begun to open up the rich domain of culture which Hume explored. It is remarkable that during the period when Anglo-American philosophy was obsessed with epistemology and in the grip of an ahistorical conception of philosophy which left little room for Hume's social and historical conception of human nature, it was the *Journal of the History of Ideas*, not specialized philosophy journals, which published essays on Hume as philosopher of culture. Indeed,

[5] Haskell Fain, *Between Philosophy and History* (Princeton: Princeton University Press, 1970), p. 9.
[6] David Hume, *An Enquiry Concerning Human Understanding*, ed. Selby-Bigge (Oxford: Clarendon Press, 1975), p. 162.

throughout its history most of the essays on Hume, published by the
journal, were on these topics. The essays selected for this volume range
back as far as 1941, but they are as interesting as when they first appeared. Indeed, given the recent interest in Hume as a philosopher of
society, politics, and history, they may be viewed as more timely than
ever.

In "Hume as a Political Philosopher," McRae suggests that Hume's
political philosophy combines, in an interesting way, the Aristotelian
doctrine that politics is an art with the modern doctrine that politics is an
applied theoretical science. Hume is modern in holding that politics is
grounded in theory. But what theory uncovers is the psychological origin
of politics: that the political world is an order of artifice made by men to
satisfy human needs. But this "making" is not that of an engineer who
applies theoretical principles to the world. It is the sort of making involved in the formation of languages which are the work of many generations and the slow product of time and custom. As no one did or could
have consciously intended the formation of the English language, so no
one can contrive a political order. What Hume's theoretical science of
politics shows is that men, as social-historical beings, are creatures of
custom. Humean political science aims at understanding the rationale of
existing customs and at reforming them, but such reformation must be
made, not from the standpoint of a theoretical spectator engaged in
applied science, but from that of a self-acknowledged participant in
custom engaged in rhetorical speech with other participants. So, in its
own special way, Hume's political science retains something of the Aristotelian doctrine that politics is an art that one learns by practice. Hobbes
had explicitly rejected this, holding, in a memorable metaphor, that politics is more like applied mathematics than tennis. Hume's political
science shows that politics is like tennis, with the difference that no one
can escape the game and one finds that the rules insensibly change over
time.

Hume's conception of man as a social-historical being rooted in evolv-
ing custom is recognized by Charles Cottle, who explores its implications
for the philosophy of law in "Justice as Artificial Virtue in Hume's
Treatise." Cottle argues that commentators have tended to collapse the
distinction Hume makes between artificial virtue (such as justice) and
natural virtues (such as benevolence). Although Hume holds that an
artificial system such as justice is natural in that it is found in all men, the
system of justice has certain features which bring it into conflict with
natural virtues. The rules of justice are like the constitutive and regulative rules of games: they are applied deductively to achieve certainty;
they admit of no degrees; they are inflexible; and they require in their

application a radical sort of impartiality not required by the natural virtues. The impartiality of natural virtue demands that one's self interest be suppressed but also requires a sympathetic identification with the interests of others. The artificial system of justice, however, frequently fails to attend to the interests of anyone, including the public. Systems of jurisprudence, such as legal positivism, and those based on the utilitarian principle, such as Bentham's, may be viewed as Hume's artificial system of justice writ large. But Hume is not a positivist, and despite Bentham's claim to have discovered the utilitarian principle in Hume, he never used the greatest happiness for the greatest number as a criterion of what makes an act moral or just. Hume recognized that the artificial system of justice could come into conflict with the natural system of moral judgment and that in such cases the latter would have the authority to discipline the former. Hume's theory of justice gives special place to the origins of law as it arises out of the life of society. Hume's "sociological jurisprudence," Cottle argues, is similar to the American "realist" school which denies that deduction is the model for bringing particulars under rules, and has more in common with the jurisprudence of Justice Holmes, Jerome Frank, and John Dewey than with the utilitarian and positivistic schools with which it is often identified.

In "From Hume to Hegel: The Case of the Social Contract," Christopher Berry argues that although Hume and Hegel both reject the rationalist contract theory of political obligation, there is a great gulf between their positions because they presuppose totally different conceptions of human nature. According to Berry, Hume's argument presupposes the very ahistorical conception of human nature held by his rationalist opponents. Hegel inherited from Herder the idea that man is essentially a cultural being: the individual is his culture. Hegel sought to avoid the relativism and romanticism this implies with the doctrine that there is an absolute meaning in cultural diversity. The human mind is one, and its *telos* is to complete itself as a self-comprehending totality. The historical process is a rational process in that it is a succession of stages in the necessary process of the human mind's attempt to gain philosophical self-comprehension. In another essay of this volume, Spencer Wertz provides a challenge to the view that Hume's conception of human nature is ahistorical. The problem of what it means to say that human nature is or is not historical and what historicity itself is may be left to the reader. In the meantime, Berry's comparative study of Hume and Hegel is a fruitful one. Both were thinkers who sought a rapprochement between philosophy and history; both made contributions to history; both worked out a theory of human culture which was placed firmly in a prior critique of the nature and limits of philosophy. And it is from their different critiques of philosophy that fundamentally different paths emerge. Hume argued that the traditional conception of philosophy, as a radically autonomous form of reflection, independent of custom, is self-deceptive. True philosophical consciousness recognizes the autonomy of custom and denies any universal rational meaning to history. Hegel argued that custom itself is philosophically spiritualized, and so he could see the totality of history as a concrete expression of philosophical consciousness seeking self-comprehension. Given the mutually illuminating study Berry has opened up, it is no longer possible to see Hume and Hegel as virtually incommensurable thinkers.

In 1752, Hume published a set of essays under the title *Political Discourses*. Nine of the essays, totaling over a hundred pages, were on economic theory. Robert Lyon discusses Hume's contribution to this field in "Notes on Hume's Philosophy of Political Economy." He finds two contributions that are especially original to Hume. One is the variable of time in economic analysis (the differentiation of the short run from the long run), a notion which, he thinks, was not exploited until J. M. Keynes took it up in *The General Theory of Employment, Interest, and Money* (1936). The second contribution is Hume's emphasis on psychological factors as part of economic and political data and problems of money and trade. In an effort to make economics more "scientific," classical economists made economics more abstract and autonomous. Hume, however, sought to integrate economics into the other human sciences. The subject of political economy for him was not an abstraction called "cost" or "price," but man as a creature of custom and history.

In "The Achievement Motive in Hume's Political Economy," E. J. Hundert develops Lyon's observation about the importance of psychological factors in economic theory. He argues that Hume posits an "achievement motive" in individuals as the source of their economic activity and, in what was an original move, extends this motive to include the working class. It was commonly held that workers, if not constrained, would be idle and destructive to themselves and the public. Hume did not deny that this was in fact the condition of many workers but insisted that it was due to lack of opportunity to achieve. Workers could lead a rational and virtuous existence if opportunities for gratification were held out to them rather than punishment. Hume led the way for Adam Smith's vision of a society of achieving psychic equals.

Steven Wallech's "The Elements of Social Status in Hume's *Treatise*" may be viewed as expanding Hundert's observation about the importance of property in elevating the character of the poor. Wallech shows that for Hume the self is social and historical, and he discusses the importance of property and justice in structuring the self. Contrary to

Rousseau, who saw property and civil society as dangerous to human happiness, Hume teaches that property makes personal distinction possible and brings peace, order and wealth to social life.

Donald Siebert in "Hume on Idolatry and Incarnation" discusses Hume's understanding of the importance of ritual in constituting social life. Established religion was a common enemy to the Enlightenment. Hume distinguished two forms: "superstition" (identified usually with Catholicism which stresses the sacramental character of ritual) and "enthusiasm" (identified with the puritan forms of Protestantism which reject the sacred character of ritual in favor of personal illumination from the Deity). Siebert argues that Hume tended to think, early in his career, that "enthusiasm," because it generated a love of liberty, was less destructive than "superstition," and, in time, could be made even beneficial. But in writing the history of the English Civil War, which apeared in the volumes of *The History of England* covering the reigns of James I and Charles I, Hume changed his mind. He came to see Puritan ideology as solitary, anti-social, and implacable. In this it resembled secular philosophical ideologies which conceive themselves to be independent of the authority of all custom and tradition. In writing *The History of England* (1754–63), he came to appreciate the humanizing effects of the ritual and liturgy of the Anglican Church and even of Catholicism. Hume's understanding of how art, religion, and ritual are intertwined in social life is expressed also in *The Natural History of Religion* (1757), where he affirms pagan religion over theism because of its grounding in mythical customs and traditions. Theism lends itself easily to incorporation in a philosophical system. Philosophical ideologies (whether religious or secular) are emancipated from custom and tend to sever social bonds. Mythical religions tend to celebrate and affirm them.

The essays by James Force, "Hume and Johnson on Prophecy and Miracles: Historical Context," and S. K. Wertz, "Hume, History and Human Nature," explore issues having to do with historical methodology. Force shows that Hume's famous argument against miracles in Section X of *An Enquiry Concerning Human Understanding* applies also to prophetic interpretations of history and that by the middle of the eighteenth century prophetic history had become the dominant form of justifying revealed religion. Hume's critical canons ruled out the possibility of any prophetic interpretation of history, sacred or secular. Wertz makes a compelling case against the view that Hume's conception of human nature is static and ahistorical. He argues that Hume's doctrine of the uniformity of human nature is a methodological principle which should not be confused with historical events. It functions as a limiting notion and must be understood in conjunction with Hume's theory of sympathy. So interpreted, the principle of the uniformity of human nature may be viewed as an early statement of the doctrine of *verstehen* offered by such thinkers as Dilthey and Collingwood. Wertz shows that *The History of England* is not a work designed to exhibit resemblances and uniformities in history, as the doctrine of the uniformity of human nature might lead one to suppose. On the contrary, its main purpose is to bring to light and to understand discontinuities, radical change, the novel, the extraordinary, and the remarkable.

In his autobiography (*My Own Life*), Hume says that of all the changes he made to successive editions of the *History* most of them were made to the Tory side. With that remark posterity was invited to label Hume a Tory historian, and it has not failed to do so. Yet in political philosophy, economics, and morals Hume was a liberal thinker which, if anything, should make him a Whig. In "Was Hume a Tory Historian? Facts and Reconsiderations," E. C. Mossner explores the paradox by examining the nature of party politics in eighteenth-century Britain, how the labels "Whig" and "Tory" were used, and how their meanings shifted during Hume's lifetime. He concludes that to be a Tory, on one meaning, was to have sympathy for the Stuarts in the English Civil War. In this sense Hume was a Tory, but his view of historical change was liberal. Mossner also puts to rest the interpretation that, having reached a skeptical impasse, Hume abandoned philosophy for history. Mossner shows that Hume's intention to write history was formed during the period of the *Treatise* when his philosophy was still in the making.

Marjorie Grene in "Hume: Sceptic and Tory?" argues that there is a deep sense in which Hume's philosophy itself may be said to be "Tory." Hume's *Treatise* teaches that custom is the great guide of life. There Hume showed that custom, refined by general rules, yields scientific judgments but also moral and political judgments. Hume's assessment of the Civil War in *The History of England* is simply an application of the theory of political judgment of the *Treatise*. The Puritan revolutionaries destroyed an established political order out of "enthusiasm" for abstract natural and theological "rights." The *Treatise* teaches that abstractions (whether in science, morals, or politics) unguided by custom are either empty or arbitrary. His sympathy for Charles I was not merely personal; it had a philosophical grounding as well. Charles was defending an established political order; he was willing to entertain reform but not revolution. Hume affirmed the right to revolution, but he judged that the Puritans did not have a good case. Grene's essay, published in 1943, is really the first to explore the deep philosophical connections that exist between the *Treatise* and *The History of England*.

John M. Werner in "David Hume and America" raises the question of

what influence Hume's philosophy had on the American founders. Hume
certainly had a keen interest in American affairs. He advocated complete
independence for the colonies as early as 1768, before the thought had
occurred to most Americans.[7] He maintained this position until his death
August 25, 1776, five days after the Declaration of Independence was
published in Edinburgh's *Caledonian Mercury*. Hume's position was
radical. Even after the battle of Saratoga, the "friends" of America, Pitt,
Burke, Shelburne, Barré, were unwilling to accept complete independence. Werner argues that American opinion about Hume was mixed.
A majority of the American leadership had probably read the *History* and
was familiar with the *Essays*. But Whig prejudices were strong in America, and Hume's treatment of the English Civil War was a barrier for
many, notably Jefferson and Adams. Werner shows, however, that there
were many notable Americans for whom Hume's writings in politics,
economics, and history provided inspiration. These include, among many
others, Benjamin Franklin, Thomas Paine, Samuel Adams, Benjamin
Rush, Josiah Quincy, Jr., and especially the federalists Alexander Hamilton and James Madison.

Hume did not support independence for the colonies because he
thought the Americans were right in their quarrel with Parliament. Hume
rejected the entire Whig ideological framework within which the dispute
was conducted. His mind moved in a larger philosophical sphere than
that marked out by Whig ideology. He supported independence for the
American colonies because he supported independence for all the British
colonies. Hume had come to reject the very idea of the British Empire.[8]
In "Hume on Property, Commerce, and Empire in the Good Society: The
Role of Historical Necessity," Corey Venning explores Hume's views on
macropolitical organization. Did Hume think that the high incidence of
empire in history implies its utility? Venning argues that Hume did not
think so. Property and commerce are necessary for individual happiness
as well as the public interest. In the good society as many should have
property as possible. Great concentrations of wealth in the hands of
individuals or of the state are to be avoided. Consequently, Hume thought
that empires are destructive of property, commerce, liberty, the arts and
sciences, and, in the end, of themselves. And the empires of free governments (such as Britain) tend to be more oppressive than absolute monarchies (such as France). No such institution can serve utility or the good

[7] I discuss Hume's views on the American crisis in "Hume, English Barbarism,
and the American Crisis" in *Scotland and America in the Age of the Enlightenment*,
ed. by Richard B. Sher and Jeffrey Smitten (Edinburgh: Edinburgh University Press,
1990).
[8] *Ibid.*

society. A political order is like a friendship or family, an order that exists for the sake of the association itself and not for the purpose of achieving some goal extrinsic to it. Personal and domestic values should motivate individuals, not collective values such as a nationalistic, historical "mission" or "responsibility" to advance enlightenment, the classless society, or natural rights. The best macropolitical arrangement is an order of competing states connected by the tie of commerce and where empire is prevented by a policy of the balance of power.

The image of Hume as a philospher of culture that emerges from these essays is scarcely known by most professional philosophers. Yet the philosophical foundations for this philosophy were laid in Hume's first book, and masterpiece, *A Treatise of Human Nature*. The rest of his philosophical and historical writing may be viewed as an application of the master science of human nature framed in that book. This year is the 250th anniversary of the publication of the *Treatise*. It is hoped that these essays, cultivated by *The Journal of the History of Ideas* over the years, will inspire philosophers to take a fresh look at Hume and to explore the rich philosophy of culture he drew out of the *Treatise*.

PART ONE

POLITICAL PHILOSOPHY

II

FROM HUME TO HEGEL: THE CASE OF THE SOCIAL CONTRACT

By Christopher J. Berry*

Both Hume and Hegel are concerned in their political philosophy with rejecting what they regard as the contractarian explanation and justification of political allegiance. The intent of this paper is to examine these rejections, paying special attention to the relationship between the employment and understanding of historical and philosophical arguments, in order to point up a very general (though unoriginal) interpretation of changes in the conception of "man" that occurred between the writings of these two dominating figures. In addition, this general interpretation will also serve as a perspective on their own positions on this issue.

First Hegel's argument for the dismissal of the Social Contract: this argument is centered on his depiction of the relationship between the individual, or citizen, and the State. To Hegel, "we are already citizens of the State by birth"[1] and given that the State is no mere administrative organ but "mind [*Geist*] objectified," wherein freedom is actualized, then "it is only as one of its members that the individual himself has objectivity, genuine individuality and an ethical life."[2] The wider significance of this will be taken up later but suffice it at present to declare that the "genuineness" of the "individuality" will be the nub. Here attention will be focused on how this argument bears more narrowly on the rejection of the concept of the social contract. Hegel believes that this concept has cogency only if it separates the individual from the State thus making membership of the State optional, a matter of voluntary choice. This means that the State's existence depends on the individual's capricious will through his individually given consent.[3] The consequence of such a view is that it makes the State a mere contingent agglomeration of individuals which, for Hegel, obscures the true relationship between the individual and his State, that is, the arena where the individual's freedom is manifest and where his will is universal and rational,[4] a consequence, moreover, having a practical manifestation in the French Revolution.[5]

* An earlier version of this paper was read to the History of Ideas Seminar, University of Glasgow. I am grateful to the participants and also to my colleagues, Andrew Lockyer and Geraint Parry for their comments.

[1] *Philosophy of Right,* trans. T. M. Knox (Oxford, 1952), 242 (hereafter *PR*).

[2] *PR*, 156; cf. *Philosophy of History,* trans. J. Sibree (London, 1872), 49 (hereafter *PH*); and L. J. Goldstein, "The meaning of 'State' in Hegel's *Philosophy of History,*" *Philosophical Quarterly,* 12 (1962), 60-72.

[3] *PR*, 156-57.

[4] Cf. *PR*, 59, 242; *PH*, 41; *History of Philosophy*, trans. E. Haldane and F. Simson (London, 1892), III, 402 (hereafter *HP*).

[5] Cf. *PR*, 33, 157; *PH*, 469-70; J. Hippolyte, "The French Revolution in Hegel's Phenomenology," in his *Studies on Marx and Hegel,* trans. J. O'Neil

Thus for Hegel the State is not based upon a contract since that presupposes arbitrariness in the sphere of necessity. The legitimate arena for contract is in the "moment" he terms "Abstract Right" where the relationship between the contracting parties is contingent or arbitrary. The object of such contracts is "a single external thing."[6] The contractarians have endeavored to assimilate the relationship between the individual and his State (where will is universal) to this superficial level (where will is merely "common"). By operating at the level of understanding they have misapprehended the true (dialectical) relationship of the parts to the whole.

Though these conceptions of the relationship between the individual and the State and the contrast between the merely common capricious will and rational universal will are the core of Hegel's rejection of the contractarian position, he also dismisses its companion notion, the state of nature. This notion has already been implicitly[7] rejected through Hegel's denial of the separation between the individual and the State. However, it is important to note for subsequent discussion the declaration made in the *Philosophy of Right* to the effect that the historical origins of the State are irrelevant to the philosophical treatment, or Idea, of the State. From that perspective the question of the State's origins are phenomenal ("mere appearance") and thus the concern of history.[8] This juxtaposition between the concerns of history and philosophy will be broached again later in the paper.

To turn now to Hume: his thought, to Hegel, belongs to the decadent pre-Kantian period and the philosophical value of Hume's scepticism has been overrated simply because of its historical importance in waking Kant up from his well known slumber.[9] Hume, nevertheless, like Hegel rejects the contractarian position. Hume's argument is two-pronged: historical and philosophical. Historically he rejects the idea of the social contract as the source of government because it just does not bear up under scrutiny—"first rudiments of government . . . arise from quarrels"[10]—and the history of all societies testifies to the role of force and usurpation.[11] Allegiance, moreover, was "formed from violence and submitted to from necessity"[12] and so, given the facility inherent in human nature to contract habits,[13] even the rule of usurpers acquires the attributes of authority. Furthermore, Hume

---

(London, 1969); J. F. Suter, "Burke, Hegel and the French Revolution" in P. Z. Pelcyznski, ed. *Hegel's Political Philosophy: Problems and Perspectives* (Cambridge, 1971), 52-73.

   [6] *PR,* 58.

   [7] Explicitly in *PH,* 42, where the state of nature is "one of those nebulous images which theory produces," and *PR,* 128, where it is criticized "philosophically" for associating "freedom" with the satisfaction of physical needs, which, for Hegel, omits the necessary "reflective" element in freedom; thus it is more properly a state of "savagery and unfreedom."

   [8] *PR,* 156.

   [9] *HP,* III, 361, 369.

   [10] *Treatise of Human Nature* (New York, 1961), 479 (hereafter *THN*).

   [11] *Essays: Moral Political and Literary* (Oxford, 1963), 460 (hereafter *E*).

   [12] *E,* 461.

   [13] Cf. *inter alia, E,* 37; *THN,* 382, 240, 164.

also attacks the State of Nature concomitant of the social contract. Such a condition, "an idle fiction,"[14] never existed since men were always at least familial beings through the sexual appetite and the biological fact (also adumbrated by Locke) that conception can occur whilst the existing progeny are still parentally dependent,[15] so that it is not impossible "for men to preserve society for some time, without having recourse to such an invention (government)."[16]

This historical argument is complemented however (explicitly in the essay "Of the Original Contract," a significant title as we shall see) by a "more philosophical refutation."[17] This refutation is based on the twin foundation of moral duties. There are moral duties derived from natural instincts or immediate propensities such as love, pity, and gratitude. These attitudes attain the status of morality through subsequent reflection[18] upon their beneficial social consequences. There are also moral duties of an "artificial" foundation such as, preeminently, justice but also allegiance and fidelity. These are "artificial" because they do not arise spontaneously but are the product of rules,[19] which are themselves the product of experience and reflection. These restrain natural impulses by seeing that, in the absence of such restraint, social existence would be untenable. Thus, justice is a duty without which society would dissolve. Now since fidelity, or promise-keeping, and allegiance are similarly artificial they presuppose justice and hence also presuppose society. Yet the contractarians endeavor to make promises the basis of allegiance (obligation) and thus of civil society itself. But, since fidelity and obligation are both artificial, there is no need to subordinate one to the other and, consequently, the contractarian's position is philosophically inadequate.[20]

Thus far, Hume's and Hegel's arguments in refutation of contractarianism have been briefly examined separately but now we must look at these arguments in conjunction. To anticipate, we shall see that Hume's assumptions are those that Hegel refutes in his own argument. That this is so may be illustrated by adopting a wider if albeit very generalized perspective.

The idea of the social contract fell out of favor in the eighteenth-century in so far as it was interpreted as a historical occurrence.[21] The increasing eighteenth-century awareness of history as evidence, a consequence of modified Lockianism, made many theorists disavow notions like the social con-

[14] *THN*, 445.

[15] *THN*, 438; *E*, 35; cf. *Enquiry concerning the Principles of Morals*, ed. C. Hendel (Indianapolis, 1957), 36 (hereafter *EMP*); and Locke, *Second Treatise of Government*, para. 80.

[16] *THN*, 479.

[17] *E*, 466ff.

[18] In the earlier *THN* (Bk. 3, Pt. I, Sect. 2) the *feeling* of satisfaction is designated the root of the sense of virtue; cf. *infra*, n. 32.

[19] These are included in the account of artificial virtues in *THN* 449.

[20] For the sense of "adequacy" here, cf. J. Macmurray, *The Self as Agent* (London, 1957), 39.

[21] Cf. H. V. Ogden, "The State of Nature and Decline of Lockian Political Theory in England 1760-1800," *American Historical Review*, 46 (1940), 21-44.

tract and state of nature because there was no evidence for their occurrence. The thought of Adam Ferguson is symptomatic: "If there was a time in which he (man) had his acquaintance with his own species to make . . . it is a time of which we have no record."[22] Though many writers in the seventeenth-century, not without ambiguity, held or used these notions of the state of nature and social contract as explanatory tools in arriving at a theory of the legitimate relationship between a government and its subjects, many eighteenth-century thinkers rejected them because they attributed to both ideas an historical character, partly because of this very ambiguity.[23] This is important because, as the title of Hume's essay indicates, the question of the social contract thereby collapsed into an untenable theory of the original contract of government from a pre-social state. Hence an intrinsically *de jure* theory was dismissed on *de facto* grounds.

However, given this relationship between the rejection of the social contract and the use of historical evidence we can look more closely at the eighteenth-century view of history. Here we can return to Hume and to a more general aspect of his thought where he is typical, namely, the understanding of history in terms of a constant human nature:

mankind are so much the same, in all times and places, that history informs us of nothing new or strange in this particular. Its chief use is only to discover the constant and universal principles of human nature by showing men in all varieties of circumstances and situations.[24]

In other words, man or human nature remains a constant universal in the historical process. This is a common feature of early and mid-eighteenth-century thought. With the acceptance of empiricism, the information about the practices and institutions of different cultures in the Americas, Asia and Polynesia, that had become increasingly available, had to be acknowledged.

But, this acknowledgment was not straightforward, because the "evidence"

[22] *Essay on History of Civil Society*, ed. D. Forbes (Edinburgh, 1967). Cf. my "James Dunbar and Ideas of Sociality in Eighteenth-Century Scotland," *Il Pensiero Politico*, 6 (1973), 188-201.

[23] Cf. O. Gierke, *Natural Law and the Theory of Society*, trans. E. Barker (Cambridge, 1934), I, 109. "The majority of natural law theorists regarded the original contracts which they postulated as historical facts, of which, by mere play of accident, no historical evidence had been preserved." Though both Hobbes and Locke refer to America, such references are independent of their argument; Hobbes indeed admitted that there was never "a time in which mankind was totally without society." (Quoted in J. Watkins, *Hobbes's System of Ideas* [London, 1965], 72.) For Locke's ambivalence see R. Ashcraft, "Locke's State of Nature; Historical Fact or Moral Fiction," *American Political Science Review*, 62 (1968), 898-915, and less satisfactorily, W. Batz, "The Historical Anthropology of John Locke," *JHI*, 35 (1974), 663-70. Finally, Pufendorf is explicit that the state of nature is an imaginative conception and "never actually existed." *On the Law of Nature and Nations*, trans. C. & W. Oldfather (Oxford, 1934), Bk. 2, Ch. 2, para. 2ff.

[24] *Enquiry concerning the Human Understanding*, ed. C. Hendel (Indianapolis, 1955), 93 (hereafter *EHU*).

was mediated by utilizing a number of ordering principles such as climate,[25] progress, and most importantly, "man." These principles made "sense" of the diversity. There still remained standards by which this bewildering array of social practices could be judged. In other words, despite the increase in the scale and scope of history, empiricism did not lead to relativism. Postulating human constancy, it was possible, for example, to regard Amerindian society as akin to Tacitus' descriptions of the ancient Germans.[26] Thus, in what has been judged as the most influential book in the eighteenth-century, Montesquieu's *De l'Esprit des Lois*,[27] this general issue, of the retention of standards amidst diversity, is confronted and effectively dissolved in the preface: "j'ai cru que dans cette infinie diversité de lois et de moeurs ils n'étaient pas uniquement conduits par leurs fantaisies."[28] Finally, this compromise with diversity is perhaps nowhere more apparent than in the notion of "taste," which played a central role in the aesthetic thought of the period and on which Hume himself wrote a notable essay.

To return now to our comparison of Hume and Hegel on the social contract, Hume's bifocal or two-pronged approach to the social contract idea can be seen to exhibit this general eighteenth-century characteristic of removing human nature from mutability and understanding historical phenomena through the universal constancy of human traits. Hume's two appoaches are complementary because they have their basis in a theory of constant human nature. Thus Hume explicitly states, "what would become of history had we not a dependence on the veracity of historians according to the experience we have had of mankind."[29] "We" are able to have this experience because the principles and springs of human nature are, as such, common to all and operate in a constant manner. So despite his admission that there is no record of the origin of government (it "preceded the use of writing") nevertheless, "we can trace it plainly in the nature of man."[30] Given what we know of human nature together with what is known about the various but contingent conditions of social life, reasonable conjecture is permissible. Similarly, the "philosophical" argument can only "work" in its required way because it consists of universal propositions. The convention of justice proceeds from "the concurrence of certain qualities of the human mind (selfishness, limited generosity) and the situation of external objects (scarcity)."[31] Additionally, the source of virtue, natural and artificial, is a quality of the mind that gives "the pleasing sentiment of approbation."[32] This is a relationship, the basis of which Hume makes plain when discussing its converse, namely, when he declares that the perception of crime or immorality "arises entirely from the sentiment of disapprobation which by

---

[25] Cf. my "Climate in the Eighteenth Century," *Texas Studies in Literature and Language*, 16 (1974), 281-92.

[26] Cf. *inter alia* W. Robertson, *History of America*, in *Works*, ed. D. Stewart (Edinburgh, 1840), 371-72; G. Stuart, *View of Society in Europe* (Edinburgh, 1778), 156.

[27] P. Gay, *The Enlightenment: The Science of Freedom* (London, 1970), 325.

[28] *De l'Esprit des Lois*, ed. G. Truc (Paris, 1961), I, 2.

[29] *EHU*, 99.　　　　[30] *E*, 454.　　　　[31] *THN*, 445.

[32] *EMP*, 107.

the *structure of human nature* we *unavoidably* feel an apprehension of barbarity and treachery."[33]

We can now see that Hume's arguments, both historical and philosophical, which he deployed against social contract theorists, rest on the analytical separation of (constant) man from his (variable) environment or, more generally, his culture. Not, of course, that his rejection depended on this separation because it was shared with his opponents. But it was this very separation that Hegel attacked in his argument over the social contract. Accordingly, though both Hume and Hegel reject contractarianism, there is a profound gulf between their arguments. Before proceeding with an examination of the factors responsible for this gulf it will be instructive to give a direct illustration of its presence, which is also indicative of where Hume's ideas "overlap" those of his opponents.

Hume, while rejecting the idea of an original social contract, nevertheless says originally, submission must be understood as a form of contract or voluntary consent and that when it occurs it is the "best" foundation.[34] When Hegel mentions the origins of a state he locates it in "imperious lordship on the one hand, instinctive submission on the other. But even obedience . . . in itself implies some degree of voluntary consent." Though these two positions seem similar, to Hegel, this argument only shows that since the State must be seen as a totality, as an organic whole, it cannot be understood by abstracting a part and considering it in isolation. Hence, in obedience it is not the isolated individual wills that prevail, but the "general will," the concrete cultural complex.[35] The individual cannot be separated from the State. Hume shares with his contractarian opponents the defect of operating with an abstract notion of human nature and thence of society.

The gulf between Hume and Hegel is thus occasioned by a change in the interpretation of human nature. This change will now be examined by once again adopting a wider perspective, a perspective that will also draw attention to a reformulation of the contractarian idea that took place.

This perspective may be afforded by returning to a dominant eighteenth-century view of history and seeing how it, or rather changes in it, relate to Hegel. The end of the eighteenth-century sees what has been described

---

[33] *EMP,* 111, my emphasis.

[34] "When we consider how nearly equal all men are in their bodily force, and even in their mental powers and faculties, till cultivated by education, we must necessarily allow, that nothing but their own consent could at first associate them together, and subject them to any authority. The people, if we trace government to its first origin in the woods and deserts, are the source of all power and jurisdiction, and voluntarily, for the sake of peace and order, abandoned their native liberty, and received laws from their equal and companion. . . . If this, then, be meant by the original contract, it cannot be denied, that all government is, at first, founded on a contract" (*E* 454). At *E* 455, Hume talks of "consent or rather the voluntary acquiescence."

[35] *PH* 48-49. Again the context is a critique of "reflective understanding" (*Verstand*) whereby the historical position has not been grasped philosophically, but see *infra* n. 72. Cf. *Philosophy of Mind,* trans. W. Wallace with introd. by J. Findlay (Oxford, 1971), 172 (hereafter *PM*).

as the historicist revolution.[36] The thrust of this revolution was to historicize or acculturate human nature so that the previous constant/variable distinction between human nature and the cultural environment was made redundant. In this process, whereby the diversity of the social world is recognized as *that,* the thought of Herder is important and will here be taken as illustrative of this general process; he was to Cassirer "the Copernicus of history."[37]

As a leading member of the Storm and Stress movement, Herder polemicized against the Enlightenment, especially against its smugness in its precious civilization, and its consequent typification of earlier ages and their products as primitive or barbaric, these two terms being synonyms. In the course of this polemic he declares human nature to be "not the vessel of an obsolete, unchanging and independent happiness as defined by the philosopher" but rather a "pliant clay which assumes a different shape under different needs and circumstances."[38] Crucially, Herder maintains that this is so much so that "each nation has its center of happiness within itself, just as every sphere has its center of gravity."[39] We must accordingly respect each culture and judge it on its own terms. It is the drawing of this conclusion that is the decisive step. The "primitive" is only "barbaric" in terms of "civilization" but that just shows that such a perspective is faulty.[40] All comparison is fruitless,[41] hence, contrary to the canons of neo-classicism and good taste, Herder's delight in Shakespeare and in his celebration of Ossian.

Herder's dismissal of a static ahistorical acultural essential human nature rests on a wider footing than the previous paragraph might suggest, because Herder also dismisses the prevalent conceptualization of the human mind. This dismissal is expressed clearly in Herder's writings on language. Here again he is polemicizing, this time against theories of the origin of language that would locate it in a gift from God, the development from animalistic cries, or the invention of man. Instead, for Herder, language is inseparable from man.[42] Man was not from the beginning an animal but a human being as exemplified in his possession of *Besonnenheit,* a stipulative term in Herder

[36] F. Meinecke, *Die Entstehung des Historismus* (Berlin. 1936), Introd.

[37] *The Problem of Knowledge,* as quoted by C. Hendel in his introd. to Cassirer, *Philosophy of Symbolic Forms,* trans. R. Mannheim (New Haven, 1953), I, 41.

[38] "Auch eine Philosophie der Geschichte," trans. and ed. by F. M. Barnard, *Herder on Social and Political Culture* (Cambridge, 1969), 185 [hereafter *SPC(APG)*].

[39] *SPC(APG),* 186.

[40] Cf. *Ideen zur Philosophie der Geschichte der Menschheit,* in Barnard, *op. cit.,* 313 [hereafter *SPC(Ideen)*].

[41] *SPC(APG),* 186; cf. *Ideen zur Philosophie. . .,* trans. T. Churchill, ed. F. Manuel as *Reflections in the Philosophy of the History of Mankind* (Chicago, 1968), 98 [hereafter Manuel (*Ideen*)].

[42] For discussions of Herder's theory of language: T. Sapir, "Herder's *Ursprung der Sprache,*" *Modern Philology,* 5 (1907), 109-42; R. Pascal, *The German Sturm und Drang* (Manchester, 1953); G. Heintel, "Herder's *Ursprung der Sprache,*" *Revue Internationale de Philosophie,* 21 (1967), 464-74.

10   CHRISTOPHER J. BERRY

meaning reflective mind or consciousness.[43] Language is a product of the
human mind which is itself an organic unity: "everywhere the individual mind
acts in its totality."[44] In depicting the human mind in these terms, Herder
attacks the faculty theory of the mind, predominant since Plato. Man does
not have a faculty of speech but is a speech-being so that to Herder (and
this is important), "all individual faculties of our mind . . . are nothing but
metaphysical abstractions."[45] This notion of the mind as one and as free
or creative was to prove very influential, as we shall see.

Herder's theory of language thus involves a theory of the mind and it
thereby relates implicitly to his idea of human nature, but also explicitly
to his general theory of culture: "every distinct community is a nation having
its own national culture as it has its own language (*Denn jedes Volk ist Volk:
es hat seine National-Bildung wie seine Sprache*)."[46] These interrelationships
can be seen when he writes:

In the chief dialect of Peru the two sexes are indicated in so peculiar a manner that the word "sister" referring to the sister of the brother, and the sister
of the sister, the child of the father, and the child of the mother, are termed
differently; yet this same language has no proper plural! Each of these
synonyms is closely connected with the customs, the character and the origin
of a people; and everywhere it reveals the inventive spirit of man.[47]

Thus in a radical sense all comparison is fruitless: "the progress of time has
influenced the mode of thinking (*Denkart*) of the human species."[48] Men
who speak different languages (the *Volk*) are substantively different.

Though men are different, the later Herder attempts in his theory of
history to come to terms with the relativist implications of his earlier thought.
This integration is established through his notion of *Humanität:* "man
has had nothing in view and could aim at nothing else but humanity."[49]
This aim has expressed itself in a multitude of forms; "the Muse of Time,
History, herself sings with a hundred voices, speaks with a hundred
tongues."[50] Though each nation bears "in itself the standard of its perfection,
totally independent of all comparison with that of others," yet "one century
instructs another century" so that through it all "the whole history of nations is to us a school for instructing us in the course by which we reach

[43] *Ursprung der Sprache,* in Barnard, *op. cit.,* 154 [hereafter *SPC(Sprache)*].
For a discussion of this term: F. Barnard, *Herder's Social and Political Thought*
(Oxford, 1965), 42f.; R. T. Clark, *Herder: His Life and Thought* (Berkeley,
1955), 134; H. Aarsleff, *The Study of Language in England,* 1780-1860 (Princeton, 1967), 149f.; C. Taylor, *Hegel* (Cambridge, 1975), 19ff., 82.

[44] *SPC(Sprache),* 131.   [45] *Ibid.;* cf. *SPC(Ideen),* 259.

[46] *SPC(Ideen),* 284; Herder, *Sämmtliche Werke,* ed. B. Suphan (Berlin, 1891),
XIII, 257-58 (hereafter *SW*).

[47] *SPC(Sprache),* 150.

[48] Manuel (*Ideen*), 106; *SW,* XIV, 337. Similarly, Herder notes the difficulties experienced by missionaries in communicating Christian ideas to aborigines,
SPC(Sprache), 151.

[49] Manuel (*Ideen*), 83.   [50] *Ibid.,* 107.

the lovely goal of humanity and worth."[51] Reason has been inherited and mankind has progressed; "whatever good appears in history to have been accomplished humanity was the gainer" because "the history of mankind is necessarily a whole."[52]

Much of Herder was taken up into Romanticism and subsequently Nationalism, though these were contrary to Herder's own cosmopolitan spirit. Herder was not a Romantic and it is important to note two different (amongst the many) strands in his thought. His concern to establish the intrinsic value of primitive culture (especially its poetry) led him to see in folk-songs, produced independently of any external criteria of taste or "rules," the true expression of the spirit of the people. Furthermore, Herder believed that primitive speech was of its very nature poetic, expressive, metaphorical, and imaginative.[53] That is, it embodied the very aesthetic qualities central to the Romantic movement. Thus, from the same source (not this alone of course) came the notions of cultural specificity (political Romanticism) and creative individuality (literary Romanticism).[54]

It is the first of these notions that is crucial to the context of this paper. The post-Herderian developments, especially the theorizing about language connected with the "discovery" of Sanskrit,[55] that took culture seriously, came to change the notion of man. The hitherto effectively formal notion gave way to a substantive notion of man as intrinsically a cultural being. For example, Friedrich Schlegel argues for the common root to Greek and Sanskrit but regards resemblance at that level as misleading because really significant changes have occurred through the intermixture of peoples, which sufficed "to produce an entirely new nation, stamped with a complete individuality of character."[56] This individuality is expressed, for instance, in mythology—"the most complicated structure ever devised by human intellect"—so that the meaning of Greek and Roman mythology, though

---

[51] *Ibid.*, 98, 107, 86-87.   [52] *Ibid.*, 83; *SPC(Ideen)*, 312.

[53] Cf. my "Eighteenth Century Approaches to the Origin of Metaphor," *Neuphilologische Mitteilungen*, 74 (1973), 690-713.

[54] These two notions are of course connected: "The Romanticist placed the highest value on the individual, his freedom, and his self-development and self-realization. Yet he placed an equally high value on the group, which he considered as a living organism whose laws of organization placed the constituent individuals in a relation of mutual dependence." R. W. Lougee, "German Romanticism and Political Thought," *Review of Politics*, 21 (1959), 638. The notion of "organism" is crucial here and this too is a theme seminally developed by Herder; see M. Abrams on Herder's essay on the *Human Soul* (1778): it "must be accounted a turning point in the history of ideas," *The Mirror and the Lamp* (Oxford, 1953), 204; and more generally Barnard, *op. cit.*, chs. 3 and 4. Hegel, too, as we saw above (cf. *PR*, 163, 174, 282), had an organic conception of the State but see *infra* for Hegel's difference from Romanticism.

[55] Especially the work of the Schlegel brothers and the Grimm brothers who combined work in linguistics with (respectively) Romantic aesthetics and collecting folk-tales. Cf. Aarsleff, *op. cit.*, 154ff. and R. Robins, *A Short History of Linguistics* (London, 1969), 172.

[56] "On Indian Language, Literature and Philosophy," *Aesthetic and Miscellaneous Works*, trans. E. Millington (London, 1875), 466.

usually treated together, is in fact different.[57] In sum, there no longer exists "man" outside specific cultural experience; in the words of Fichte,

those who speak the same language are joined to each other by a multitude of invisible bonds by nature herself; long before any human art begins they understand each other and have the power of continuing to make themselves understood more and more clearly; they belong together and are by nature one and an inseparable whole.[58]

We can now turn to Hegel and a brief discussion of aspects of his thought in the context of the impact of Herder and his influence.[59] In the *Phenomenology,* Hegel also rejects (in its recent Wolffian guise) the old psychology, "Observational psychology . . . discovers all sorts of faculties, inclinations and passions" such that a "miscellany of things can happen to be somehow alongside one another in the mind as in a kind of bag."[60] Positively, in other of his writings,[61] Hegel refers to the "mind's living unity" (*lebendigen Einheit des Geistes*) which is misrepresented by being divided up into a number of hypostatized faculties or activities.

More importantly, perhaps, in the present context, Hegel takes up the substantiation of man. He argues that the individual and his culture are one: "Individuality is what its world in the sense of its own world is" or perhaps less opaquely, "*What* is to have an influence on individuality, and what *sort* of influence it is to have—which properly speaking mean the same thing—depend entirely on individuality itself, to say that by such and such an influence this individuality has become this specifically determinate individuality means nothing else than saying it has been this all along."[62] The individual *is* his culture; a relationship indeed embodied in the fact of language.[63]

---

[57] *Op. cit.,* 503. Cf. Herder: "the mythology of every people is an expression of their own distinctive way of viewing nature (*Abdruck der eigentlichen Art wie es die Nautur ansah*)," *SPC(Ideen),* 300; *SW,* XIII, 307.

[58] *Addresses to the German Nation,* trans. R. Jones and G. Turnbull with revisions by G. Kelly (New York, 1968), 190. For a discussion of Fichte's relationship to August Schlegel see Xavier Léon, *Fichte et son Temps* (Paris, 1927), III, 61-78 and to Friedrich Schlegel, *ibid.,* I, 444-54.

[59] My concern here is not to argue for a direct influence, but for discussions of Hegel's relationship to Herder: *inter alia* Manuel, *op. cit.,* xiv; S. Avinieri, *Hegel's Theory of the Modern State* (Cambridge, 1972), 39; H. S. Harris, *Hegel's Development: Toward the Sunlight* (Oxford, 1972), esp. 271n; L. Spitz, "Natural Law and the Theory of History in Herder," *JHI,* 16 (1955), 475; R. Collingwood, *Idea of History* (Oxford, 1961), 113; Taylor, *op. cit.,* 13ff., 55n, 82ff., 567f.

[60] *Phenomenology of Mind,* trans. J. Baillie (New York, 1967), 332 (hereafter *Phen*).

[61] *Logic,* trans. W. Wallace (Oxford, 1892), 238; *PM,* 4: *Encyklopädie in Sämmtliche Werke,* ed. G. Lasson (Leipzig, 1923), 138, 333; cf. *PM,* 183, 189.

[62] *Phen,* 336, 334 (Hegel's emphasis).

[63] Cf. *Phen* esp. 530, and P. Riley, "Hegel on Consent and Social Contract Theory," *Western Political Quarterly,* 26 (1973), 130-61.

Moreover there is a dynamic so that this substantive human nature or the human mind itself now has a history, a history that is integral to, and at one with, the history of man's mental products, his culture. Such sentiments can now be related to the attack on the idea of the social contract.[64] As we saw, for Hegel, the contractarians operate with an abstract notion of man, who is comprehended outside his cultural complex and who, in addition, presumes to judge it. The social contract theory manifests an ahistorical abstract individualism. For Hegel, on the contrary, man is born a member of the State, and because the State is the highest moment of Ethical Life then it is, as noted above, the source of man's "genuine individuality."

What then, is the upshot of understanding Hegel in this perspective? He accepts the historicization of man and culture *but* Hegel is no Romantic. This acceptance is crucial to his rejection of Kantian formalism, but his dismissal of Romanticism, both political and aesthetic, is that *inter alia* political romanticism resists codification by mystifying custom[65] and aesthetic romanticism promotes intuition and feeling at the expense of thought or Reason.[66] It is important to stress that Hegel's notion of "individuality" possesses a dimension lacking in the Romantics. Thus, whilst Adam Müller, for example, also rejects the social contract theory for promoting the illusion that man can be thought of (in the state of nature) as a being outside the State (again, also seeing the French Revolution as a product of this illusion), and moreover regards the State as "the totality of human affairs, their union into a living whole"[67] he fails to see that the Revolution is an advance in Freedom. Müller's medievalism[68] is, for Hegel, symptomatic of his failure to appreciate that genuine individuality is to be found in the rational freedom of the *modern* State.[69] Romantic organicism did not preserve (*aufheben*) the individual but, instead, submerged him.

Nor is Hegel a relativist. There is an absolute meaning in all this cultural diversity and historical dynamism and this meaning for Hegel can only be its rationality: "that Reason is the Sovereign of the World; that the history of the world therefore presents us with a rational process" so that "the principles of the successive phases of Spirit that animate the Nations in a necessitated gradation, are themselves only steps in the development of the

[64] Cf. Riley, *op. cit.*, for discussion of the relationship between Hegel's position in *Phen* and *PR;* Judith Shklar, "The Phenomenology: Beyond Morality," *Western Political Quarterly,* **27** (1974), 597-623, esp. 615.

[65] Cf. *PR,* 135, 272.

[66] *Phen,* 71 and more generally, see Hegel's Lectures on Fine Art in *Hegel on Art, Religion and Philosophy,* trans. B. Bosanquet, ed. G. Gray (New York, 1970). For Hegel and Romanticism: R. Kroner's introd. to Hegel's *Early Theological Writings,* trans. T. M. Knox (Philadelphia, 1971), esp. 14ff.

[67] "Die Elemente der Staatskunst," *Political Thought of the German Romantics,* trans. A. Hayward, ed. H. Reiss (Oxford, 1955). 143-57.

[68] Cf. Reiss, *op. cit.,* 29.

[69] Cf. *PR,* 242, "The great advance of the State in modern times is that nowadays all the citizens have one and the same end, an absolute and permanent end; it is no longer open to individuals as it was in the Middle Ages, to make private stipulations in connexion with it."

one universal Spirit, which through them elevates and completes itself to a self-comprehending totality."[70] It is the fundamental presupposition of Hegel's entire philosophical system that the world is rational, that it has meaning, and that this rationality and meaning is to be found within the world. Accordingly, to return to Hegel's discussion of the social contract in the *Philosophy of Right*, we can see explicitly that there he is concerned with showing the inherent rationality of the modern State, a rationality that is apparent if it is looked upon rationally.[71] It is in this light that Hegel's rejection of any consideration of the origin of states as irrelevant and the true provenance of history is to be understood.

But we still need to make two observations. First, to re-emphasize the non-relativist import of Hegel's position, this association of history with the irrelevance of origins does not mean that history is irrelevant to rationality. Rather history, properly understood, exhibits, indeed *is,* the actualization of freedom ("the development of Spirit in time")[72] an actualization to be seen in the State. Hence, this particular instantiation is (notoriously) designated the "march of God."[73] Similarly, philosophy, as the highest expression of Absolute Spirit, is truly the history of philosophy since thereby "the history of philosophy is a revelation of what has been the aims of Spirit throughout its history, it is therefore world's history"[74]—a Theodicy.[75] History and philosophy are thus inseparably intertwined for Hegel; his history is philosophized and his philosophy historicized: "in reality we are what we are through history."[76]

Secondly, to take up a point made above, Hegel's argument reflects a reformulation in contractarianism. Hegel is concerned with a theory of the social contract and not a theory of the original contract, hence, his declaration that origins are "philosophically" irrelevant. Hegel's specified opponent in the *Philosophy of Right* when dealing with the idea of the social contract is Rousseau. Though Hegel's interpretation of Rousseau is of doubtful validity, Rousseau's theory can nevertheless be seen as contractarian in the *de jure* sense that it establishes a criterion of legitimacy,[77] namely, what men must continually do or will if they wish to be morally free.[78] Accordingly, it was not a historical or *de facto* thesis. Significantly, Rousseau does without the trappings of the state of nature; indeed the *Second Discourse* is a critique of the specious historicity of that notion. It is because Hegel sees Rousseau's criterion as capricious and implying a faulty bifurcation of man and society that he rejects it. But, in contrast to Hume, he does recognize it as a criterion and not a historical argument. As he says in a different (though closely related context):

---

[70] *PH,* 9, 82.   [71] Cf. *PR,* 11.

[72] *PH,* 75. For a discussion of the relationship of history to philosophy in Hegel: B. T. Wilkins, *Hegel's Philosophy of History* (Ithaca, 1974), 43ff.

[73] *PR,* 279.

[74] *HP,* I, 6.   [75] *PH,* 477, 16; *HP,* III, 546.   [76] *HP,* I, 2.

[77] Cf. P. Riley, "How Coherent is the Social Contract Tradition?" *JHI,* 34 (1973), 543-62, for shift in ideas from the "good" to the "legitimate" state and its relation to social contract theory.

[78] *Du Contrat Social,* Bk. 1, Ch. 1 and Ch. 6.

By dint of obscuring the difference between the historical and philosophical study of law, it becomes possible to shift the point of view and slip over from the problem of the true justification of a thing to a justification by appeal to circumstances . . . when those who try to justify things on historical grounds confound an origin in external circumstances with one in the concept, they unconsciously achieve the very opposite of what they intend. Once the origination of an institution has been shown to be wholly to the purpose and necessary to the circumstances of the time, the demands of history have been fulfilled. But if this is supposed to pass for a general justification of the thing itself, it turns out to be the opposite because, since those circumstances are no longer present, the institution so far from being justified has by their disappearance lost its meaning and its right.[79]

Hegel's rejection of the Rousseauian *theory* of a social contract is thus itself theoretical or philosophical and as this paper has aimed to illustrate Hegel's rejection is closely connected with his espousal of the theory of man as a historical creation.

In conclusion, therefore, it is suggested here that the seventeenth-century use of the social contract became undermined by Hume and others in the eighteenth-century as an historical account, but that its vital ahistorical character, as reformulated and sharpened by Rousseau (and Kant[80]), was itself rejected by Hegel precisely because it was, in virtue of its incorporation of a formal notion of man, ahistorical. Yet this did not mean that Hegel was reproducing Hume, because Hume's own rejection was premised on the very principles that Hegel had rejected in rejecting Rousseau. It is Hegel's theory of the concrete universal, as exemplified in his concept of an individual's ethical life, that is responsible for both this twin rejection and also his supersession of Romanticism.

By seeing Hume and Hegel in conjunction we are able to appreciate that their employment of philosophical and historical arguments in refutation of contractarianism both involve a conception of human nature, a conception which changed in harmony with, but was also fundamental to, a general shift in outlook that occurred between their writings.

University of Glasgow.

---

[79] *PR*, 17; cf. *PH*, 42.

[80] Cf. P. Riley that Kant's reformulation of the Social Contract as an Idea of Reason is "obviously trying to avoid a number of difficulties—above all Hume's 'historical' objection," in "On Kant as the Most Adequate of the Social Contract Theorists," *Political Theory*, I (1973), 451; O. Gierke's work translated as *The Development of Political Theory*, trans. B. Freyd (London, 1939), 111f.

III

JUSTICE AS ARTIFICIAL VIRTUE IN HUME'S *TREATISE*

By Charles E. Cottle

Interpreters of Hume's theory of morals generally assume that all moral judgment, for Hume, falls within the sphere of natural virtue. Consequently, they give little attention to those characteristics of artificial virtue which lead Hume to distinguish artificial from natural virtue. I shall focus on the artificial virtue of justice discussed in Hume's *Treatise of Human Nature,*[1] and point out some of the consequences of Hume's differentiation between natural and artificial kinds of virtue, including differences between moral judgments made from the vantage point of each system. I conclude with some remarks on Hume's contribution to legal theory which are based on the arguments presented by Hume and his interpreters.

Justice, Hume claims, is an artificial virtue.[2] Although Hume labors the better part of three sections in Part Two of Book Three of the *Treatise* defending his claim by explaining the artifice on which justice is based, his distinction between natural and artificial virtue usually receives only perfunctory notice. A generally accepted view holds that the distinction between the two is of little importance. Wolin, for example, asserts, "The essential point was there was no sharp contrast between an 'artificial' rule and a 'natural' one."[3] Plamenatz concurs with Wolin and cites the following statement from Hume:

The only difference betwixt the natural virtues and justice, lies in this, that the good, which results from the former, arises from every single act, and is the object of some natural passion: whereas a single act of justice, consider'd in itself, may often be contrary to the public good; and 'tis only the concurrence of mankind, in a general scheme or system of action, which is advantageous.[4]

Despite the tendency of Hume's interpreters to play down the differences between natural and artificial virtue, I believe Hume's statement implies more than is immediately apparent. A number of characteristics of justice will explicate Hume's comment above for each separates justice from the

---

[1] David Hume, *A Treatise of Human Nature: Being an Attempt to Introduce the Experimental Method of Researching into Moral Subjects,* ed. L. A. Selby-Bigge (Oxford, 1888; rptd., 1968). References to this work contain an abbreviated title, the book, part and section, as well as the page number. For example, THN, III-ii-2, 497 should be read as: *A Treatise of Human Nature,* Book Three, Part Two, 497.

[2] THN, III-ii-1, 477.

[3] Sheldon S. Wolin, "Hume and Conservatism," *The American Political Science Review,* **48** (December 1954), 1006.

[4] THN, III-iii-1, 579 as cited in John Plamenatz, *Man and Society* Vol. I (New York, 1963), 304.

sphere of natural virtue. Indeed, these characteristics are the marks of artificiality on which Hume relies to state his case about justice. Thus, while there may be no "sharp contrast" between the natural and artificial virtues, the distinction is of substantial importance. To show that justice is an artificial, not a natural, virtue, Hume discusses at least five closely associated characteristics of justice which serve as boundary markers between natural and artificial virtue. From his discussion I conclude that:

1) artificial virtue (or at least justice) requires the invention of rules intended as guides to conduct. These rules have certain features in common with the rules of games. The rules of natural virtue, by contrast, are first most appropriately thought of as observable regularities of behavior and only then, as guides to conduct;

2) artificial moral judgment, unlike natural moral judgment, proceeds deductively on the basis of established rules in an attempt to achieve certainty;

3) artificial moral judgment, unlike natural moral judgment, admits no degrees of gradation;

4) artificial moral judgment proceeds by inflexible general rules, whereas the more natural course proceeds by general rules which are flexible; and,

5) the impartiality found in decisions of justice is not the same kind of impartiality found in natural moral judgment.

These five points do not include all the differences between natural and artificial virtue. Other more specific issues, particularly with reference to the dynamics of social approbation, might also be treated with respect to each type of virtue. Such matters, however, go beyond the scope of this paper (cf. Mercer or Roberts), and the following discussion attempts to explicate only the five issues above.

1) Any discussion of Hume's conception of justice should begin with some observations on the manner in which Hume defines justice. While Hume elaborates the topic in the *Treatise,* in about a hundred pages, explicit definitional statements are difficult to find. Generally, writers on Hume's theory of justice have agreed (with some variation) that Hume's justice can be defined as a set of rules which regulate property.[5] Strictly speaking, how-

[5] That finding a definition for justice is a problem for Hume readers is reflected in the diversity of definitions offered by a few of the authors who have written on the subject. C. D. Broad, for example, most closely defines justice as "a set of acknowledged and rigidly enforced rules about the ownership, exchange, and bequest of property." See C. D. Broad, *Five Types of Ethical Theory* (New York, 1930), 103. In close agreement with Broad is D. G. C. MacNabb who defines justice as a "set of rules determining the distribution and transference of property and the keeping of promises." See D. G. C. MacNabb, *David Hume: His Theory of Knowledge and Morality* (Hamden, Ct., 1974), 178. Mercer's important work makes no attempt to define justice. In one section Mercer treats justice as a body of rules. In another, he refers to justice as embodied in the concept of impartiality. See Philip Mercer, *Sympathy and Ethics: A Study of the Relationship Between Sympathy and Morality with Special Reference to Hume's "Treatise"* (Oxford, 1972), 52-53, 124. Similarly, Roberts refers only to the "rules of justice" and never makes a definitional statement. See T. A. Roberts, *The Concept of Benevolence: Aspects of Eighteenth-Century Moral Philosophy* (London, 1973), 98-106. Stewart prefers to talk of the "principles of justice," which he

ever, this definition is incorrect because virtue, artificial or natural, refers to qualities of mind and body, not to actions, nor to rules for action.[6] Thus, as a quality of mind, justice is regarded by Hume as determined by respect for the rules of property which induces one to abstain from using or taking the property of others. My purpose here, however, is not to focus on Hume's view of justice as a quality of mind, which would lead into a discussion of the motives for the performance of just acts and to questions of social approbation. Instead, I wish to look at the nature of the rules themselves, and in so doing, my interpretation of Hume's theory of justice will approximate that given by others who treat his theory of justice as a set of rules which regulate property.

In asserting that justice is an artificial virtue, Hume calls attention to the rules invented for the purpose of guiding and regulating conduct with respect to the possessions of others. In Book Two of the *Treatise*, Hume defines prperty as *"such a relation betwixt a person and an object as permits him, but forbids any other, the free use and possession of it, without violating the laws of justice and moral equity."*[7] It is important to note in this definition that the nature of property depends upon the laws of justice rather than conversely. As those laws vary, so too does property. Perhaps Hume's most explicit statement to this effect is the following in which he is explicating the nature of the relation which we call "property."

Now 'tis evident, this external relation causes nothing in objects, and has only an influence on the mind, by giving us a sense of duty in abstaining from that object, and restoring it to the first possessor. These actions are properly what we call justice; and consequently 'tis on that virtue that the nature of property depends, and not the virtue on the property.[8]

In this passage, the rules of justice not only regulate property, but define it. An immediate consequence of Hume's view is that property does not precede a system of justice. Thus, arguing against earlier views, he contends, for example, that in a state of nature there was no property, and, consequently, no such thing as justice or injustice.[9] Indeed, Hume is so insistent on this point that he asserts, " 'Tis very preposterous, (therefore), to imagine, that we can have any idea of property, without fully comprehending the nature of justice. . . ."[10]

Insofar as property is defined by the rules of justice, it is worth noting that property and possessions are not equated by Hume. If they were equiv-

---

labels the "basic rules of competition." See John Stewart, *The Moral and Political Philosophy of Dåvid Hume* (New York, 1952), 109-19. Plamenatz asserts that justice, for Hume, is a respect for the rules of property. See Plamenatz, *Man and Society,* 303. Sibley defines justice as "the performance of acts out of a sense of duty without regard for the consequences." See Mulford Q. Sibley, *Political Ideas and Ideologies: A History of Political Thought* (New York, 1970), 417. Wolin's important article on Hume makes no attempt to define justice, but treats it as a body of rules securing property rights. See Wolin, "Hume and Conservatism," 1003-06.

[6] See, for example, THN, III-ii-1, 477, and THN, III-iii-1, 575.

[7] THN, II-i-10, 310.   [8] THN, III-ii-6, 527.

[9] THN, III-ii-2, 501.   [10] *Ibid.,* 491.

alent, then he could not maintain that the nature of property depends upon the nature of the rules.[11] Property and possession differ in that while it is often difficult to determine the extent of one's possessions, one's property is determined by reference to legal rules. Property is thus a legal fiction or convention providing for the stability of possessions. Fictions, for Hume, are those ideas for which we do not now have, nor have ever had, any corresponding impression. The fictitious nature of property is shown by Hume's remark:

... this quality, which we call *property,* is like many of the imaginary qualities of the *peripatetic* philosophy, and vanishes upon a more accurate inspection into the subject, when consider'd a-part from our moral sentiments. 'Tis evident property does *not* consist in any of the sensible qualities of the object. For those may continue invariably the same, while the property changes.[12]

The legal fiction of property is, then, both defined and regulated by the rules of justice. These rules are similar to the rules of games in that they are both regulative and constitutive. If one wishes to play a ball game, then he abides by the rules, or it cannot be said that the particular game has been played. The rules prescribe a course of action which must be followed in order to play the game. Such rules exhibit a logical connection between themselves and the activity or objective they define. Flathman suggests that the clearest examples of constitutive rules are laws establishing procedures to be followed to take certain legal actions. "Thus the law of wills and testaments determines what must be done to make a will. The person who does not follow the rules simply does not make a will."[13] In a similar fashion, because Hume's conception of property depends upon the laws which regulate it, one who wishes to hold, acquire, transfer, or even respect property must abide by such rules of justice. For Hume it is definitionally impossible to violate the rules of justice and still respect property rights. Semantically, the rules of justice and property are inseparable.

In the concluding section to a summary of Hume's moral and political philosophy, a noted student of political ideas makes the following observation:

We have noted throughout an ambiguity about whether Hume is saying that men *should* conduct themselves in this way or that, or whether, on the contrary, they do in fact view political right in the way he describes.[14]

These remarks refer in part to Hume's statements, such as: "Property *must* be stable, and *must* be fix'd by general rules" (Emphasis added).[15] A partial solution to the ambiguity in Hume's discussion may be found in noting the

[11] THN, III-ii-3, 506.   [12] THN, III-ii-6, 527.

[13] Richard E. Flathman, "Obligation and Rules," in *Concepts in Social and Political Philosophy,* ed. by Richard E. Flathman (New York, 1973), 75. Flathman's example concerning the law of wills and testaments relates directly to Hume's second "law of nature," the transference of property by consent. See THN, III-ii-4, 514-16.

[14] Sibley, *Political Ideas and Ideologies,* 421.

[15] THN, III-ii-2, 497.

constitutive nature of the rules of justice. The "musts" in the example are imperative in the sense that they render the artificial system of rules internally consistent. They are not necessarily claims about the validity of the system itself except insofar as definitional consistency is such a claim. Artificial systems, whether they be rules of justice or of geometry, are similar in this respect. To assert that parallel lines must never interact is not so much a claim about the nature of parallel lines *per se* as it is about the status of parallel lines in a given system of geometry. A claim that property must be fixed by general inflexible rules holds only if we understand that claim with reference to the laws which define property.

Hume seldom speaks of rules of natural virtue. As part of his analysis, however, he frequently cites regularities which occur in the assessment of virtue. Sometimes, these regularities are labeled "general rules."[16] These general rules of morality differ from the general rules of justice in that the latter are invented guides to conduct, while the former are at first conceptualizations of customary or habitual kinds of behavior, which sometimes become guides to conduct. This distinction is one of origins. For example, it might be deemed a general rule of morality that virtuous qualities are of four types: (1) those useful to others, (2) those useful to the person himself, (3) those agreeable to others, and (4) those agreeable to the person himself.[17] Although Hume does not offer this general rule in any prescriptive sense, it could be, once observed, reformulated grammatically as a series of imperatives (e.g., be useful, be agreeable, etc.) and catalogued among our duties. But Hume argues that these natural rules must operate independently of the notion of duty, or it is unlikely that they could ever become known as such.[18]

To conclude this section, it is pertinent to note that the rules of justice, like the rules of games, are changeable and are subject to as much variation as the passions will allow in a society. The rules (or regularities) of natural virtue are not so easily changed. Hume assumes that they remain the same across time and culture.[19]

2) Another distinction between natural virtue and the artificial virtue of justice resides in noting that when making a moral judgment naturally, every fact and circumstance, as well as the general nature of the question, is pertinent to the decision, whereas this inclusive analysis is not a prerequisite for justice. In the case of natural virtue, the attempt is to determine the intent or character of an individual in a particular situation. As the intent can only be inferred from the actions and passions of those involved, an examination of those actions and passions is necessary before a moral judgment can be made. Stated differently, while the idea of intent remains weak and in doubt, the sympathetic mechanism will not operate, thereby

[16] See, for example, THN, III-ii-6, 531 and THN, III-iii-1, 583. Cf. "general inalterable standards," THN, III-iii-3, 603.
[17] THN, III-iii-1, 591.
[18] THN, III-ii-1, 478.
[19] See, for example, David Hume, "A Dialogue," in David Hume, *An Inquiry Concerning the Principles of Morals,* ed. Charles W. Hendel (New York, 1957), 151-52.

forestalling a moral judgment. Furthermore, it is not unusual to reach a moral judgment only to have the original sensation of pain or pleasure dissipate, or completely change, when confronted with new information which implies a different intent or motive.

The case with justice differs considerably. Justice proceeds according to the strict application of legal rules. In reaching a "just" decision only the essential facts of a case are needed. The facts viewed as essential pertain to the extant laws: Were they, or were they not, violated? Questions of intent and character are irrelevant in a case of justice unless there is a rule to incorporate them. Likewise, much evidence which might be applicable in natural moral judgment is ruled irrelevant in the legal questions of justice. In brief, judgments before a tribunal of law feign a likeness to the deductions of pure mathematics such as geometry. The attempt of justice, in the regulation of property, is to reach a certainty in its decisions not unlike that of other artificial systems. Although pure mathematics is discredited in Book One of the *Treatise* if it claims a certainty beyond "relations of ideas,"[20] the practical results of that certainty are, nevertheless, impressive. The factual questions which appear before courts of law, however, frequently cannot be decided with any degree of certainty. In many cases, precedent, analogy, and other instruments of law are of little value. Where this happens, cases are often in fact determined on the basis of arbitrary and capricious factors.[21]

3) The extent to which legal decisions turn upon arbitrary factors derives in part from that characteristic of justice which allows no degrees of gradation with respect to property rights and obligations. Natural propensities run to the contrary:

Tho' abstract reasoning, and the general maxims of philosophy and law establish this position, *that property, and right, and obligation admit not of degrees,* yet in our common and negligent way of thinking, we find great difficulty to entertain that opinion, and even do *secretly* embrace the contrary principle.[22]

As an example of the significance of this characteristic of justice, Hume considers property disputes settled by arbitration as opposed to those settled according to the strict application of the rules of justice. Because arbitrators find it difficult to believe that rights and obligations rest entirely on one side or the other, they frequently divide the property between the disputants. Civil judges, Hume maintains, do not have such freedom and often "proceed on the most frivolous reasons in the world."[23] Arbitration depends upon the qualities of equity, charity, wisdom, and other virtuous qualities for a "just" decision to be reached. Justice, on the other hand, requires only a respect for the law. If the law is lacking in any respect, then public utility is reached only by accident. The upshot of Hume's dis-

[20] See THN, I-ii-4, 39-53.
[21] THN, III-ii-6, 531; see also, David Hume, *An Inquiry Concerning the Principles of Morals,* ed. by Charles W. Hendel (New York, 1957), 124-25.
[22] THN, III-ii-6, 530.   [23] *Ibid.,* 531.

cussion on this point is that the results of justice are frequently inferior to those reached by more natural principles.

4) Another point considered by Hume concerns inflexible general rules of justice. On most occasions human action proceeds from particular principles. Sometimes people form general rules of conduct, but these are, or should be, flexible and allow of exceptions. The rules of justice, by comparison, are universal and inflexible in application. The rules of justice, therefore, "can never be deriv'd from nature, nor be the immediate offspring of any natural motive or inclination."[24] These inflexible rules cannot be the offspring of any natural motive because all morality depends on the variations of our passions; but since property depends on fixed rules, it should not vary according to the variations of our passions. The rules governing property do not admit of such variation. Hume concludes his train of reasoning:

These rules [the rules of justice], then, are artificially invented for a certain purpose, and are contrary to the common principles of human nature, which accommodate themselves to circumstances, and have no stated invariable method of operation.[25]

The inflexibility of the rules of justice, then, is contrary to the common principles of human nature. Hume reiterates this point by asserting that while property is unintelligible without justice, the latter is unintelligible without motives to just acts which are independent of any abstract sense of justice.[26] Concluding this discussion, he writes:

Let those motives, therefore, be what they will, they must accommodate themselves to circumstances, and must admit of all the variations, which human affairs, in their incessant revolutions, are susceptible of. They are consequently a very improper foundation for such rigid inflexible rules as the laws of justice; and 'tis evident these laws can only be deriv'd from human conventions, when men have perceiv'd the disorders that result from following their natural and variable principles.[27]

Thus, because natural motives are an improper foundation for the inflexible rules of justice, no motives to abide by those rules can be found which are independent of the morality of the rules. Justice, despite its lofty goal of keeping peace in society, remains unintelligible as an abstract moral quality. Hence, unintelligibility punctuates the artificiality of justice. Hume finds none of these difficulties concerning the motives which he associates with the natural virtues.

5) The inflexibility of the rules of justice guarantees the impartiality of their application. As pointed out above, the rules "must extend to the whole society, and be inflexible by spite or favour."[28] The impartiality of

----

[24] *Ibid.*, 532.   [25] Ibid., 532-33.

[26] This point is explained more fully in another section of the *Treatise*. Cf., "In short, it may be established as an undoubted maxim, *that no action can be virtuous, or morally good, unless there be in human nature some motive to produce it, distinct from its sense of morality.*" THN, III-ii-1, 479.

[27] THN, III-ii-6, 533.   [28] THN, III-ii-3, 502.

justice, as is often indicated, should serve to correct the selfishness and partiality which result when persons quarrel from an interested point of view. In fact, the impartiality of justice constitutes an attempt to incorporate the disinterestedness of natural moral judgment into the artificial system.

It is generally recognized that Hume's discussion of moral judgment relies heavily on the observer's "general" or "disinterested" point of view. It is this aspect of his argument which protects his theory of morals from the charge that he argues a morality by the whims of majority decision.[29] Hume's treatment of disinterestedness, however, is not the same as impartiality, for disinterestedness is not entirely devoid of "interest." In making moral judgments, it is true that Hume requires the observer to drop any special reference to his own interests,[30] and in this sense, the observer is impartial. Yet in dropping reference to his particular interests, the observer fixes his view upon the interests of the observed individual or his associates.

Now, in judging of characters, the only interest or pleasure, which appears the same to every spectator, is that of the person himself, whose character is examin'd; or that of persons, who have a connexion with him.[31]

Thus, while the observer is impartial in the sense that he makes no special reference to his own interests, he is partial to the interests of the observed individual or his associates. This "impartial partiality" differs from the impartiality of justice which, in particular decisions, frequently fails to attend to the interests of anyone. Though the rules of justice are ostensibly designed in the public interest, their impartial application often ignores the interest of either party involved and the interest of the public as well.[32]

On the whole, it appears that the distinction between natural and artificial virtue is one of importance, at least where natural virtue is opposed to justice. In attempting to highlight several aspects of the distinction between the two types of virtue, a view of justice has emerged which is at variance with other interpretations of Hume on this issue. Frequently, Hume is portrayed as a champion of legal justice. It is often written that he encourages the strict enforcement of the inflexible general rules of justice.[33] Such views overstate Hume's position. Though justice is adopted by man as a remedy for the discord and contention in society, justice has certain weaknesses which frequently render its application pernicious to society.

---

[29] Cf. Broad, *Five Types of Ethical Theory*, 114, or Sibley, *Political Ideas and Ideologies*, 423.

[30] THN, III-i-2, 472.   [31] THN, III-iii-1, 591.

[32] Mercer's comment on impartiality is appropriate in this context. He notes that while the rule of impartiality instructs that all people be treated equally, impartiality in no way implies "how" people are to be treated. See Mercer, *Sympathy and Ethics*, 124.

[33] See, for example, Broad, *Five Types of Ethical Theory*, 98; F. A. Hayek, "The Legal and Political Philosophy of David Hume," in *Hume*, ed. by V. C. Chappell (Garden City, N.Y., 1966), 170; Mercer, *Sympathy and Ethics*, 112; MacNabb, *David Hume*, 180; Plamenatz, *Man and Society*, 308-10.

Not the least of these weaknesses is the inflexibility of the rules which regulate property.

It is the strict and impartial application of the rules which is supposed to correct the selfishness of man as he finds himself confronted by the scarcity of external goods. Yet, the strict application of these invented "laws of nature" frequently yields fragmentary results which offend man's natural moral sensitivities. As Hume points out, the law is no respecter of persons.[34] The poor man of character may be stripped of all his possessions under the auspices of justice while the rich acquire additional property for which they have no use. Moreover, an appeal to legal justice frequently constitutes an abandonment of reason in favor of decision by caprice. These various concerns lead Hume to comment that

a strict adherence to any general rules, and the rigid loyalty to particular persons and families, on which some people set so high a value, are virtues which hold less of reason, than of bigotry and superstition.[35]

Bigotry and superstition are the major traits of prejudice. Just as men often create prejudice through the "rash" formation of general rules,[36] so may they also institutionalize prejudice by the strict application of the general rules of justice. Despite its weaknesses, however, justice can be useful in settling disputes and preventing discord, even if its only function is to bring the matter to a close. In many conflicts any solution is better than no solution at all. Hume's argument suffices to show, nevertheless, that the utility of justice can be easily undermined if its rules are made to serve situations for which they were not designed. In such cases, the rules of justice fail as the corrective to the natural inclinations of men.

Having surveyed several seldom discussed aspects of Hume's theory of justice, I shall make some concluding remarks about Hume's place in the history of legal theory. It is well known that Hume's analysis of reason undermined traditional theories of "natural law." Reason alone, he argued, cannot give direction to the passions; hence, norms of behavior cannot be merely deduced. Also, it was Hume (or so we are told) who inspired Bentham's utilitarianism. Upon reading Hume the scales fell from Bentham's eyes, but interestingly enough, a reading of Hume does not reveal the greatest happiness principle stated anywhere. Hume, quite simply, was not concerned with counting heads. Undoubtedly, there are several similarities between Hume and Bentham, but it is also true that Bentham moved away from Hume rather quickly toward an emphasis upon codification of the law. Hume, on the other hand, emphasized the nature of the judicial decision itself. The point is that Hume's contribution to legal philosophy extends beyond the destruction of natural law and the inspiration of Bentham.

Hume first argues that a legal system (rules of justice) constitutes a tight logical system, which is an approach to the law sometimes attributed to analytical positivists. But Hume's point is not to support a position which claims that adequate judicial decision can be reached by deduction. Instead, he shows that logical certainty itself is frequently lacking in par-

---

[34] THN, III-ii-3, 502.   [35] THN, III-ii-10, 562.   [36] THN, I-iii-13, 146.

ticular cases and that the system is largely "unintelligible." Although the analytical certainty of justice is shown to be fallacious, Hume suggests that some certainty can be restored with his references to arbitration which allows the referee to consider facts considered irrelevant under the law. Here the logic of deduction is replaced by the logic of causation, the latter being the logic which governs the springs of sympathy and consequently, natural moral judgment. In terms which rely less on his specific theory of morals, Hume is suggesting that judicial decisions will be inadequate when they strive for logical certainty, yet remain divorced from, or ignore, the facts of the social order from which legal norms are derived in the first place. Hume's discussion of justice gives special place to the origins of the law as it arises out of the life of society, and it concerns the effects of the application of the law. These conclusions place Hume's legal theory within the school of sociological jurisprudence.

While Hume's approach to the study of justice shares similarities with a number of theorists interested in the sociology of law, his emphasis on the acquisition of facts for adequate judicial decisions, his arguments showing the fallacies of decision by logical deduction, and his warnings against any strict adherence to fixed principles and general rules in judicial decisions make him a forerunner of American legal "realists" such as Justice Holmes, Jerome N. Frank, and John Dewey. In a summary statement H.L.A. Hart asserts that American "realism" has made students of jurisprudence acutely aware of the "problems of the penumbra" in judicial decisions.

If a penumbra of uncertainty must surround all legal rules, then their application to specific cases in the penumbral area cannot be a matter of logical deduction, and so deductive reasoning, which for generations has been cherished as the very perfection of human reasoning, cannot serve as a model for what judges, or indeed anyone, should do in bringing particular cases under general rules. In this area men cannot live by deduction alone.[37]

If the interpretation of Hume's arguments presented in this article is correct, then Hume anticipated the "realistic" position by some two-hundred years. In his theory of knowledge, he had no profound respect for any conclusions reached by deduction. In morals he displaced knowledge reached by deduction with a knowledge based on an understanding of probability and causality, that is, a knowledge of matters of fact. This transition influenced every aspect of his social and political philosophy. The result was a nominalism which relegated general terms and general rules to conceptual devices for the listing of particulars. Knowledge of particulars, however, could not be logically deduced from general rules. Hence, these rules were to be used as guides in determining the disposition of particular cases. They were not, through deduction, to be used as a substitute for that determination.

University of Wisconsin-Whitewater.

---

[37] H. L. A. Hart, "Positivism and the Separation of Law and Morals," in *Philosophy of Law*, ed. by Joel Feinberg and Hyman Gross (Encino, California, 1975), 46.

IV

HUME AS A POLITICAL PHILOSOPHER

By Robert McRae

Discussing the definition of Logic, Cook Wilson says that although the sciences in general are provided with accepted definitions, " in none of them did scientific reflection begin from a quite general definition of the object of the given science, but with particular problems which the needs or interests of life and experience in one way or another suggested." [1] As the solution of one problem leads on to another there develops a systematic body of knowledge, and the question arises

whether there is any one general conception which covers them all. Now that is a question which does not condition or originate the activity of the science and, accurately speaking, does not belong to that activity at all. On the contrary it presupposes the procedure of the science as already existing and arises from a new kind of thinking, *i.e.* not the thinking which constitutes the method of the science but reflection on that method itself. [2]

He illustrates this with the development of Logic in Greek philosophy, pointing out that it began without any definition of itself. Although by Aristotle it had come to be recognized as comprising a separate subject, it still remained without a definition, and the question of its special sphere was not discussed.

Is it true also of political philosophy that the definition of its object has been entirely *a posteriori?* Classical philosophy undoubtedly developed from questions arising directly out of Greek political life, but the same is not equally true of modern political philosophy. Questions arising out of modern political life have not wholly conditioned or originated modern political philosophy. There were at least two *a priori* factors present; one being certain merely inherited conceptions of that subject, the other the natural science which emerged in the seventeenth century. The new natural science, in transforming the traditional conception of metaphysics, effected, thereby, radical alterations in the classification of the sciences; and, in particular, it determined, in one way or another, the place which political philosophy has in the general scheme of human knowledge, and the sort of inquiry which it ought to be.

This can be seen, for example, in Hume. That Hume is not merely a skeptic in philosophy is shown in his Introduction to the *Treatise of Human Nature.* Here he indicates clearly his constructive plans to put metaphysics on a firm foundation, discusses the nature of philosophy and its divisions, and presents us with a promise which, if fulfilled, would warrant

---

[1] *Statement and Inference,* 24.   [2] *Ibid.,* 26.

the opinion that for system and comprehension Hume comes second only to Hobbes among British philosophers.

In reviewing " the present imperfect condition of the sciences," the clamour and disputes among philosophers, " the weak foundations of their systems," the consequent disrepute into which metaphysical reasoning had fallen and the prejudice of the public against it, Hume determines to effect a rescue by placing the sciences on a new but certain foundation. He perceives that there is one science on which all the others depend, " the capital or centre of these sciences." " There is no question of importance, whose decision is not comprised " in it. " There is none, which can be decided with any certainty, before we become acquainted with that science." In undertaking the inquiry into it, " we in effect propose a complete system of the sciences, built on a foundation almost entirely new, and the only one upon which they can stand with any security." [3]

This capital or centre is the " Science of Man," or, if it be given a name from modern terminology, Psychology. It is in this way that Hume makes one of the natural sciences assume the place which had traditionally been assigned to Metaphysics. We are not left in any doubt by Hume that it is to be conceived as a natural science. The method of inquiry is to be that which has been used with such success by Newton with physical phenomena. It cannot be pursued otherwise than by " careful and exact experiments, and the observation of those particular effects, which result from its different circumstances and situations." [4]

There are two levels among the sciences, which are distinguished as they have a greater or a less dependence upon the Science of Man. Those with the less direct dependence are Mathematics, Natural Philosophy and Natural Religion. (Thus natural theology is dethroned from its place as metaphysics and made a subordinate science.) Those with the more immediate dependence are Logic, Morals, Criticism and Politics (Logic is used in a wide sense to include everything in the *Treatise* under the title " Of the understanding ").

When one of the natural sciences, psychology, assumes the place of First Philosophy, and politics is made subordinate to, and immediately dependent upon it, we have assuredly what is an at least partial predetermination of the nature of political philosophy, and of the sort of questions which it ought to ask. That this is so, is evident from the very first question with which Hume begins his political philosophy. His subject being justice, he asks: why is it that people will act justly from a sense of duty? This for Hume is a psychological phenomenon whose causes must be found. It still remains evident at the end of his political philosophy, where, in his destructive treatment of the contract theory of political allegiance, he argues that an original agreement to submit to government cannot be the reason why

---

[3] *Treatise*, ed. Selby-Bigge, p. xx. [4] *Ibid.*, p. xxi.

men *now* give their allegiance. It cannot be, for the simple reason that most men have never even heard that government was established by an agreement or contract. Other psychological causes must be found, and they are found by Hume.

* * * * *

Traditionally political philosophy had been distinguished from the "theoretical" or "speculative" sciences as a "practical" science. The influence of the natural science of the seventeenth century upon political philosophy raised important questions as to whether political philosophy is a practical science, and, if it is, in what way it is practical. On the one hand there were those who took their lesson from the striking fact that the laws which theoretical natural science elicited could be used in practice as rules for the production of works. Thus political philosophy, if conducted on "scientific" lines, could give rise in practice to rules for the control of men in political life, either in their own interest or in that of the ruler. Thus Hobbes in finding the "causes of commonwealth" (his conception of the search for causes owes much to Galileo), is at the same time discovering the rules for the exercise of sovereignty. "The skill of making, and maintaining commonwealths consisteth in certain rules, as doth Arithmetique and Geometry; not (as Tennis-play) on Practise onely." [5] He hopes for the day when his writings will fall into the hands of a Sovereign, who will " convert this Truth of Speculation, into the Utility of Practice." [6] On this view politics becomes *applied* science, which it never was in the older tradition coming from the Greeks. While for Aristotle the practical sciences are subordinate in dignity to the theoretical, they do not borrow their principles or rules from the theoretical.

On the other hand it was possible to take the position that political philosophy is, and remains, a purely theoretical inquiry. This is the view which Hume shares, and it has a particular interest as developed by him, in that this theoretical science contains within it a *critique* of practical politics; *i.e.*, it enables him to determine the limits of "artifice" in politics, and also to show that the practical principles of politics are not derived from political philosophy in the sense that they would be, if they constituted an applied science.

Among Hume's *Essays* there is one entitled, "That Politics may be reduced to a Science," in which he is concerned with the question whether it is possible to arrive at any general rules for the securing of good government; or whether good government is merely the consequence of the " character and conduct of the governors," "the casual humours and characters of particular men." Hume believes that general principles can be found, and he proceeds to give several examples of such rules. The politics which Hume speaks of here as a "science" is concerned with rules of administra-

[5] *Leviathan*, c. 20.   [6] *Ibid.*, c. 31.

tion. It is a quite different sort of inquiry from his political philosophy, and does not derive its principles from that philosophy. There is, in other words, no need for the legislator to read the political part of the *Treatise of Human Nature* in order to arrive at these rules.

But while the " science of politics " is thus independent of political philosophy, and while the latter remains speculative or theoretical,[7] nevertheless it issues in a critical estimate of the limits to the artifice of politicians, or of how much can be effected by reasoned contrivance.

Here Hume's procedure follows the same general pattern as that which he had employed in his treatment of belief. There he had concluded that in the realm of action certain fundamental beliefs are involved against which speculative reason is impotent; for example, the belief in causal necessity, which can neither be created nor destroyed by reason, or the belief that body exists, which nature has doubtless esteemed " an affair of too great importance to be trusted to our uncertain reasonings and speculations." That body exists is something " which we must take for granted in all our reasonings." [8] Neither of these beliefs is natural in the sense of being original to human nature. They are products of custom (although they are natural in the sense of being found in all men). Custom, Hume concludes, is " the great guide of human life. It is that principle alone which renders our experience useful to us. . . . Without the influence of custom . . . we should never know how to adjust means to ends, or to employ our natural powers in the production of any effect. There would be an end at once of all action, as well as of the chief part of speculation." [9] Against the products of custom reason cannot prevail. " Nature is always too strong for principle." [10]

Similarly in political life there are certain moral attitudes which the rational devices of the politician can neither create nor destroy—though he can *further* them " in order to govern men more easily and preserve peace in human society." " Any artifice of politicians may assist nature," but it cannot produce these attitudes. " The utmost politicians can perform is, to extend the natural sentiments beyond their original bounds; but nature must still furnish the materials." [11] These moral attitudes which are basic to political society are the sense of obligation to act justly (as regards property, transfer by consent, and the keeping of promises) and the obligation of allegiance to government.

Moreover, there are limits to what politicians or abstract reasoning can perform in determining rules for the distinguishing of property or in fixing a title to political allegiance. Public utility may to some extent supply rational grounds for determining these questions, but custom and imagina-

[7] *Treatise*, 621; *Enquiry*, ed. Selby-Bigge, 5f.; Letter to Francis Hutcheson, Sept. 1739.

[8] *Treatise*, 187.   [9] *Enquiry*, 44.   [10] *Ibid.*, 160.   [11] *Treatise*, 500.

tion are also powerful arbiters, and place limits on strict considerations of utility. " Time and custom give authority to all forms of government, and all successions of princes." Vulgar opinion remains the guiding principle for the action of rulers. " It is on opinion only that government is founded; and this maxim extends to the most despotic and most military governments, as well as the most free and most popular." [12] " The opinions of men . . . carry with them a peculiar authority, and are, in a great measure, infallible." [13] Thus we find Hume commending the wisdom of Parliament in choosing William as successor to James II. " As the slightest properties of the imagination have an effect on the judgments of the people, it shews the wisdom of the laws and of the parliament to take advantage of such properties, and to chuse the magistrates either in or out of a line, according as the vulgar will most naturally attribute authority and right to them." [14]

*   *   *   *   *

In his literary career Hume came successively to the subject of politics by two different approaches, through philosophy and through history. The significance of that part of Hume's political philosophy constituting a *critique* of political artifice stands out sharply if it is viewed against the background of his treatment of politics as an historian.

Professor Koyré has said that in the Enlightenment history was not regarded as " something which makes us, but something which we make, which is the entirety of things which man has made, which he is making, and which he is going to—or can—make." [15] Where in the following century history was conceived as in some sense a self-determining process in which man's nature is evolved, the work either of blind material forces or of unhuman spiritual forces, the historian of the eighteenth century thought of history as the record of the results of man's folly (his prejudices, his superstitions or his enthusiasms) or the achievements of his enlightenment (his rationality). Institutions were not the products of growth, but of artifice or human invention (either well or ill contrived).

Hume, as historian, is typical of his period, as is evident from the sort of strictures put upon his history by later historicists, as for example, that he shows an " incapacity to recognize the great forces by which History is moulded, and the continuity which gives it real continuity "; [16] or that he lacks any " conception of institutions as created by the spirit of a people in its historical development." [17] Where Hume detected an attempt to explain civilization by other than human contrivance he repudiated it.

---

[12] *Of the First Principles of Government.*   [13] *Treatise*, 546.   [14] *Ibid.*, 566.

[15] " Condorcet," *Journal of the History of Ideas*, IX (1948), 131ff.

[16] Sir Leslie Stephen, *English Thought*, I, 57.

[17] Collingwood, *The Idea of History*, 78.

" Physical causes," such as geography and climate, in his opinion had almost nothing to do with forming the character of a nation. The real causes are the " moral causes," by which he means " all circumstances which are fitted to work on the mind as motives or reasons. . . . Of this kind are the nature of government, the revolutions of public affairs, the plenty or penury of the people . . . . " [18]   For Hume, the historian, politics remains the politics of artifice, not the politics of growth.   Institutions are products of human invention, not of superhuman or subhuman forces gradually un- folding their effects in history.   Such development as there is in time is the work of man himself, as he overcomes prejudice, superstition or enthusiasm to achieve the enlightened control of human affairs.   While Hume shared the satisfaction of his age in its triumphs of enlightenment over the rude- ness and superstition of the previous centuries, he indulged no great expec- tations of increase in enlightenment.   He was no reformer, though as " spec- tator " of history he was interested in the sort of political conditions most conducive to increase in enlightenment.[19]

It will be seen that the point of view prevailing in Hume's thought as an historian, and in which he shows himself most typical of his time, pro- vides the very material to which Hume the philosopher directs his *critique*. Justice, with all its rules, and government, with all its institutions, are man- made devices, contrived by man to meet the inconveniences of life.   This much is retained by the philosopher and remains fundamental.   But he sees that they are not invented in the way machines are.   Their use develops gradually like language and currency.   There is no deliberate covenant to act justly or to set up government, but an unselfconscious emergence of agreement.   In effect it is no longer man who is the chief agent in politics, but custom.   It is time and custom which build his institutions, determine the objects of his allegiance, and, in sum, produce those opinions or preju- dices which are the final authority in all political life and action.   " It is on opinion only that government is founded."   Man, the creator, the hero of rationalistic politics, is dethroned and custom is king.

University of Toronto.

[18] *Of National Characters.*

[19] *Vide: The Rise and Progress of the Arts and Sciences.*

PART TWO

SOCIETY AND POLITICAL ECONOMY

V

NOTES ON HUME'S PHILOSOPHY OF POLITICAL ECONOMY

By Robert Lyon

Hume's original contributions to specific economic concepts—aside from his general economic philosophy—were chiefly in monetary theory and international trade. In monetary theory he introduced two ideas which did not re-enter the main stream of economic thought until the present age of Keynes. The first is the concept of the importance of the variable of time in economic analysis, the differentiation of the short run from the long run. Had the classical school of economics followed this distinction instead of adhering to the long-run analysis begun by Adam Smith and David Ricardo, the policies followed in the erratic history of capitalism from the early 1800's to the 1930's might have been quite different. The "cultural lag" between thought and policy was immortalized in Keynes' own *General Theory* in which he wrote that "practical men, who believe themselves to be quite exempt from any intellectual influence, are usually the slaves of some defunct economist."[1] The implication is that the debacle of the 1930's might have been averted had the politicians followed the more unorthodox and flexible theories of Malthus rather than those of Smith and Ricardo. To the name of Malthus in support of unorthodoxy in economic policy should be added that of David Hume.

The second contribution of Hume is his emphasis on psychological factors as part of the economic and political data and problems of money and trade. The subject matter of political economy for Hume was man, not a mechanism, a price, or a cost. In an attempt to make economics more "scientific," the classical school gradually eliminated man, and not until the age of Keynes were psychological factors as intervening variables brought back into economics. Indeed, they still are not in the main stream of economic thought, and the works of Katona[2] and Boulding[3] are only the harbingers of what is likely to appear in the future synthesis. In retrospect, the *General Theory* might be considered a pioneer in this area, as it assumes three allegedly universal psychological variables: the propensity to consume, the marginal efficiency of investment, and the liquidity preference.

Hume's contribution to monetary theory bridged the gap between the hard-line mercantilism of his predecessors and the rejection of its truths by his successors of the classical school. He refuted the mercantilist error of identification of wealth and money, but at the same time did not eliminate, as his successors did, the positive or negative role that money might play in the fluctuations of the economy. The modern relevance of Hume's monetary theory is evident in his essay *Of Money*, in which he noted that " ... it is only in this interval or intermediate situation, between the acquisition of

[1] J. M. Keynes, *The General Theory of Employment, Interest, and Money* (New York, 1936), 383.

[2] G. Katona, *The Psychological Analysis of Economic Behavior* (New York, 1951).

[3] K. E. Boulding, *The Image* (University of Michigan, 1956).

35

money and the rise of prices, that the increasing quantity of gold and silver is favourable to industry . . . It is easy to trace the money in its progress through the whole commonwealth; where we shall find, that it must first quicken the diligence of every individual, before it increases the price of labour."[4] The economy thus benefits from an increase in money in the short run, not only because of the possible absorption of temporary unemployment, but also because of the change in the nation's habits of spending and saving.

In this context the relevant supply of money and commodities was that in circulation and exchange. Anticipating Fisher's equation of exchange, Hume stated: "There are only two circumstances of any importance, namely, their gradual increase (of the precious metals) and their thorough concoction and circulation through the state. . . . "[5]

The price of money, interest, was not subject to a process of legal change, but was the natural result of the state of the economy. A low rate of interest reflected a prosperous economy, and emanated from " . . . a small demand for borrowing; great riches to supply that demand; and small profits arising from commerce: and these circumstances are all connected together, and proceed from the increase of industry and commerce, not of gold and silver."[6] The difference between high and low rates of interest " . . . depends not on the quantity of money, but the habits and manners which prevail. By this alone the demand for borrowing is increased or diminished."[7] With the stress on economic activity (the gross national product) and habits, Hume presaged a monetary theory depicting low interest as the resultant of the psychological forces underlying the demand and supply of capital within an expanding economy.

The quantity of money in circulation and the level of profits, when high, constituted economic factors affecting the demand and supply of capital which resulted in a low rate of interest. The quantity of money was subject to governmental regulation, but profits stemmed fundamentally from the frugality of the bourgeoisie. Low profits as well as low interest stemmed from an increase in the gross national product, obviously beneficial to society as a whole.

In the field of international trade Hume showed his ingenuity in exploring several different avenues of economic thought. In crystallizing the theory of the self-regulating mechanism of the distribution of precious metals in the international economy, Hume dismantled what was left of the mercantilist doctrine. He did not confine his analysis, however, to the flow of goods and money among countries, and their adverse effects on the price levels. Following his premises in the *Treatise* and the *Enquiry*, he resorted to a psychological explanation, to the emotive, not the rational, phase of human nature. Hume pointed to the psychological motivation behind the entire mechanism: "We need not have recourse to a physical attraction, in order to explain the necessity of this operation. There is a moral attraction, arising from the interests and passions of men, which is full as potent and infallible."[8] This might be

---

[4]D. Hume, "Of Money," *Writings on Economics*, ed. E. Rotwein (Edinburgh, 1955), 38.

    [5]*Ibid.*, 46.   [6]Hume, "Of Interest," *Ibid.*, 49.   [7]*Ibid.*, 50.
[8]Hume, "Of the Balance of Trade," *ibid.*, 65.

labeled an "achievement motive,"[9] in which "passions" lead "reason," but hardly the "profit motive," which implies calculated rationality.

Hume argued for a self-regulating international economy in the context of changing price levels and trade balances, although his illustrious successor, Adam Smith, ignored it. In pointing out that the international division of labor was the basis of international trade, in contrast to the mercantilist writings, Hume argued that the " ... increase of riches and commerce in any one nation, instead of hurting, commonly promotes the riches and commerce of all its neighbours. . . . where an open communication is preserved among nations, it is impossible but the domestic industry of every one must receive an increase from the improvements of the others."[10] But Hume was no absolute free-trader. One exception, still given some credence today, was his support of the "infant-industry" argument. As he specifically put it: "A tax on German linen encourages home manufactures, and thereby multiplies our people and industry. A tax on brandy increases the sale of rum, and supports our southern colonies."[11]

In economic philosophy, Hume concluded that the only justification of private property was utility. What he called "schemes of community" were given short shrift, since "these ideas of perfect equality. . . . are really, at bottom, impracticable; and were they not so, would be extremely pernicious to human society."[12] In the case of a conflict between private and public interests, the state had not only a right but a duty to intervene to protect the public interest. Indeed as he categorically stated in the *Inquiry*: " . . . public utility is the sole origin of justice. . . . "[13] (i.e., with respect to the law regarding property).

While Hume rejected collectivism and egalitarianism, he recognized that when inequality of income was too marked, undue political power in the hands of the wealthy followed, and even the state of the economy was adversely affected. Further, in hypothesizing a general state of economic equality, Hume anticipated the marginal utility school. He observed that "whenever we depart from this equality, we rob the poor of more satisfaction than we add to the rich."[14] This is reinforced by his general theory of value, in which he claims that "objects have absolutely no worth or value in themselves. They derive their worth merely from the passion."[15]

The notion, often associated in our time with the early New Deal of the 1930's, that any kind of government expenditures, e.g., the proverbial digging and filling up of holes, is as productive as a more beneficent expenditure, such as the building of hospitals, acquired widespread publicity in Hume's time with the publication of Mandeville's *Fable of the Bees*. This poem had

[9]C. McClelland, *The Achieving Society* (Princeton, 1961).

[10]Hume, "Of the Jealousy of Trade," *ibid.*, 78.

[11]Hume, "Of the Balance of Trade," *ibid.*, 76.

[12]"An Inquiry Concerning the Principles of Morals," *The Philosophy of David Hume* ed. V. C. Chappell (New York, 1963), 415.   [13]*Ibid.*, 406.

[14]*Ibid.*, 414–15.

[15]D. Hume, "The Sceptic," *An Enquiry Concerning Human Understanding and Other Essays*, ed. E. C. Mossner (New York, 1963), 165.

satirized the traditional morality of economic prudence and argued for any kind of self-indulgent expenditure so long as it led to employment and wealth.

For Hume, following his principle of utility, there was a valid distinction between useful and useless, or worse than useless, expenditures. In the absence of wasteful expenditures, expenditures beneficial and useful to society might be made. As Hume stated it: "To say, that, without a vicious luxury, the labour would not have been employed at all, is only to say, that there is some other defect in human nature, such as indolence, selfishness, inattention to others, for which luxury, in some measure, provides a remedy; as one poison may be an antidote to another. But virtue, like wholesome food, is better than poisons, however, corrected."[16]

Hume's views on the role of government in economic life were not so doctrinaire as those of Smith, whose views in turn were less extreme than those of subsequent classical economists. The criterion for social and economic policy was not "natural rights" but "utility." And in the early *Treatise* he took a view of government as a vehicle for social progress which would otherwise not be achieved in an economy operating under the "invisible hand." He never changed from this utilitarian position.

Had Hume been living in the 1930's, it seems reasonable to assume that, given his principle of utility in political and economic affairs, he would have been a supporter of the need for the increasing intervention of government in economic life. He would have been a strong advocate of planning on both a national and international level. At a theoretical level there is little question that he would have deplored the solitary course the history of economic thought took in its growing separation from the other social sciences, and would have quickly assented to the need for rewriting economics in light of the insights of what are today called the behavioral sciences, particularly psychology, and what Hume regarded as a kindred discipline, ethics. After all, the avowed goal of the *Treatise*, completed during his young manhood, was none other than to integrate the social sciences, as Isaac Newton had integrated the physical sciences. In this lifelong task he did not succeed, but which economist or political scientist or philosopher to this day has?

Hume's experimentalism and psychologism underlay his religious, political, and economic views. Both the social sciences, i.e., the "moral subjects," and the natural sciences, were capable of offering only probable, not certain, answers. In the political and economic sciences Hume's psychologism reflected itself in his attack on ideas falling under necessary natural laws or principles, for clearly there were none in those sciences. Certainly he was not motivated to uphold old beliefs or establish new ones, but merely to reduce them all to an absolute minimum. It was a lifelong work simply to clear up the debris of centuries of rationalizations and superstitions. And his psychological approach led directly to his stress on custom and utility as the *raison d'être* for the government and the economy.

For Hume the justification of a belief lay not in its origin in experience, but in its consequences. But he never worked out, in any of his writings, how the criterion of true belief was to be established in terms of its consequences, rather

[16]Hume, "Of Refinement in the Arts," *ibid.*, 30.

than its origins, in accordance with the empiricist principle. In any event, his ideas paved the way for the contemporary schools of pragmatism, logical positivism, and analytic philosophy, whose popularity no doubt has had a lot to do with the recent revival of interest in Hume.

With respect to the question of the correlation of "liberal" or "conservative" hues with his philosophic and religious views in Hume's literary spectrum, there is no doubt that he was a "liberal," or even a "radical," by the standards of the middle 1700's. In economics he was clearly a "liberal" for his day, and even more progressive and flexible than his friend, the "founder" of modern economics, Adam Smith. In politics he adhered to such liberal views as freedom of religious and political dissent, and the right of citizens to rebel when they had exhausted all legal avenues of redressing grievances with their rulers[17]; (he supported the colonists, for example, in the Revolutionary War). But he has been labeled by some critics, as a Tory, or a sympathizer with Toryism, because of his attack on the social contract theory, or because of his seeming to give more weight to authority than to freedom, or because of his defense of a monarchical form of government, or because of his defense of private property. But in the context of his day, when the masses were uneducated and illiterate, and any broadening of the electoral base might bring in its wake an oppressive regime, his career *in toto* would seem to refute the conservative charge. The tyranny of the majority—against which J. S. Mill was later to argue in his *On Liberty*—was of serious concern to Hume. But Hume did not take any steps to initiate educational reform; his opinion of the intellectual potential of the human race was not particularly high; in this perhaps there was a trace of "cultural snobbery," which is not the same as "conservatism."

All in all, of Hume it may be said that he was a "liberal" in the four areas of philosophy, religion, political science, and economics. That he was more "liberal" in his philosophic and religious views than in his political and economic views is an observation which fails to consider the difficulty of comparing liberalism and conservatism in such different areas as religion and economics. One can only surmise that he was more liberal in his philosophic and religious views because his denial of or skepticism about such beliefs made no real or significant difference to one's customary habits. But in terms of his own critical premises, skepticism in the areas of politics and economics could make a difference: the rejection of or opposition to certain beliefs in these two areas would affect much of one's practical experience, and would make a significant and practical difference to the collective life, in turn affecting his own. Specifically, belief or disbelief in a deity, for Hume, could make little or no difference in his private life, but belief or disbelief in obedience to the King or Parliament, or in the rightness of private property, might well have logical and practical consequences, in the conduct of men, and of himself in particular.

Temple University

[17]*David Hume's Political Philosophy*, ed. C. W. Hendel (New York, 1953).

VI

THE ACHIEVEMENT MOTIVE IN HUME'S POLITICAL ECONOMY

By E. J. Hundert

In his article on Hume's philosophy of political economy (this *Journal*, **31** [1970], 457–61) Robert Lyon stresses the importance of Hume's analysis of psychological motivation in his economic arguments. Lyon suggests, rightly it seems to me, that Hume posits an "achievement motive"[1] within individuals as the source of their economic activity. This conception is not only central to Hume's general argument, but is of particular significance in his analysis of the behavior of working men. Moreover, the notion of achievement is at the heart of the thinking of Hume's successors, the Classical Economists, particularly Hume's close friend, Adam Smith. As this point is neither treated by Lyon nor in the better known literature on Hume's economics it would seem to deserve further comment.

Hume approached current economic issues from a wider perspective than did his contemporaries.[2] Appreciating that "trade was never esteemed an affair of state till the last century; and there scarcely is any ancient writer on politics who has made mention of it,"[3] he cautioned against the generalizations of economists which were based upon recent experience alone. This historical understanding permitted a long-range questioning of the assumptions of Mercantilist theory and policy developed since Thomas Mun. While borrowing ideas from predecessors,[4] Hume set out to lay bare what he thought to be the unsupportable premises of contemporary thought and action.[5]

Although his analysis of the worker and his motivation ran counter to current opinion, some of Hume's most fundamental assumptions about the working class were identical to those of his contemporaries. He took it as given that men "who are placed among the lower ranks . . . have little opportunity of exerting any other virtue besides those of patience, resignation, industry and integrity,"[6] even under the best circumstances. Indeed, Hume agreed with the renowned Mer-

---

[1]Lyon, 459, refers to the major work on this issue: David C. McClelland, *The Achieving Society* (New York, 1961).

[2]Jacob H. Hollander, "The Dawn of a Science," *Adam Smith, 1776–1926* [1928] (New York, 1966 reprint), 1–21. Unless otherwise noted, citations will be from *Essays: Moral, Political and Literary* (Oxford, 1963). The standard edition of Eugene Rotwein (Edinburgh, 1955) has not been used because it does not contain some important essays, such as "The Stoic," which are referred to in the argument below.

[3]Hume, *Philosophical Works*, eds. T. H. Green and T. H. Grosse (London, 1898), III, 156–57, cited in Rotwein, *op. cit.*, xxx.

[4]This point is stressed by E. A. J. Johnson, *Predecessors of Adam Smith* [1937] (New York, 1960 reprint), ch. IX.

[5]Today Hume is remembered best as an economist for his ideas about bullion and specie flow ("Of Money"). His contributions in this area have no direct relevance to our subject; they are discussed in Rotwein, "Introduction," *op. cit.*, and Marcus Arkin, "The Economic Writings of David Hume—A Reassessment," Joseph J. Spengler and William R. Allen, eds., *Essays in Economic Thought: Aristotle to Marshall* (Chicago, 1960), 141–60.

[6]"Of the Middle Station of Life," 580.

cantilist writer Sir William Temple[7] that the behavior of workers significantly differed from that of other men:

It is always observed in years of scarcity, if it be not extreme, that the poor labour more, and really live better, than in years of great plenty, when they indulge themselves in idleness and riot.[8]

Moreover, his explanation of this behavior put forward the commonly held opinion that the poor were at present incapable of leading a rational existence.[9]

More strongly than most, Hume viewed work as the distinctly creative activity of men and directly related industrious activity to virtue and civilized existence. "Industry, knowledge and humanity," he maintained,

are linked together, by an indissoluable chain, and are found . . . to be peculiar to the more polished, and what are commonly denominated, the more luxurious ages.[10]

Labor is the source of value, "the chief ingredient of the felicity to which thou aspirest,"[11] and idleness a vice to be cured by the medicine of hard work.[12] Hume incorporated much of Puritan social thinking about the nature of work and achievement with a calm assurance; yet his vision was avowedly middle class,[13] exhibiting no trace of urgent concern with the moral corruption of the world. When he maintained that industry promotes the cultivation of the mind, the enlightenment of reason, the moderation of passion, and the development of frugality,[14] Hume confirmed the historical experience of his class, and generalized that experience into an articulated view of social life. With these assumptions Hume approached the condition of laboring men. Rather than deny the seemingly irrational aspects of their behavior or, like contemporaries, take this as proof of their irrational nature, Hume sought to analyze social action in terms of the interaction of man's natural propensities with his material environment.

In the *Treatise of Human Nature* Hume understood men as problem-creating creatures who set tasks for themselves in order to satisfy their natural craving for achievement. In an environment that presents few difficulties, he reasoned, men will not be motivated to exercise their potential.

What is easy and obvious is never valu'd; and even what is in *itself* difficult, if we come to the knowledge of it without difficulty, and without any stretch of thought or judgement, is but little regarded.[15]

Economic activity came under the heading of such self-imposed problems. Men

[7]"Of Taxes," 349–51. [8]*Ibid.*, 351.
[9]"Of the Middle Station of Life," 579. For an analysis of contemporary opinion about the poor: Edgar Furniss, *The Position of the Laborer in a System of Nationalism* (New York, 1920); A. W. Coates, "Economic Thought and Poor Law Policy in the Eighteenth Century," *The Economic History Review*, 2nd ser., **13** (1960), 39–51.
[10]"Of Refinement in the Arts," 278; also, 277.
[11]"The Stoic," 150. For labor as the source of commercial value: "Of Commerce," 288.
[12]*Ibid.*, 151. [13]"Of the Middle Station of Life."
[14]"The Stoic," 150; "Of Interest," 309–10.
[15]Hume, *A Treatise of Human Nature,* ed. Selby-Bigge, (Oxford, 1896), 449.

actively engaged themselves in the pursuit of economic wants in order to satisfy
the passion of avarice, "an universal passion, which operates at all times, in all
places, and upon all persons."[16] Engaged in the pursuit of their own interests,
men better themselves materially and satisfy a desire for work and improvement
common to the race:

There is no craving or demand of the human mind more constant and insatiable
than that for exercise and employment; and this desire seems the foundation of
most of our passions and pursuits. Deprive a man of all business and serious occupation, he runs restless from one amusement to another; and the weight of oppression he feels from the idleness is so great that he forgets the ruin which must
follow from his immoderate expenses.[17]

Hume's view of motivation was not significantly different from the one held
by contemporary economists. He saw society composed of calculating individuals
pursuing their economic interests. Again, like the economists and the Puritans
before them, Hume viewed the world as an arena for human accomplishment,
wherein men worked upon the natural order for their own and society's advantage. Like Locke, he understood the interaction between man and nature as
exhibiting a progress; one which was potentially given in the natural order:

Thy kind parent, Nature, having given thee art and intelligence, has filled the
whole globe with materials to employ these talents . . . ; by art and attention
alone thou canst acquire that ability which will raise thee to thy proper station in
the universe.[18]

The radical nature of Hume's analysis lay in its psychological egalitarianism.
Hume made no distinction between the natural inheritance of different classes of
men. He held that all men first and foremost seek happiness,[19] and that this primarily consisted of action and pleasure.[20] In order to achieve happiness men
worked, for in working toward a certain material reward, pleasure, action, and
avarice were satisfied, while difficulty was overcome. In the world of work and
achievement men confronted their basic desires and thus gained the opportunity
of satisfying them. Indeed, work is initially undertaken to satisfy the passions
common to all men.[21] In this essentially natural and sensuous process men learn
to enjoy the activity itself:

The mind acquires a new vigour; enlarges its powers; and by an assiduity in
honest industry, both satisfies its natural appetites, and prevents the growth of
unnatural ones, which commonly spring up, when nourished by ease and
idleness.[22]

Hume's was the most thoroughgoing commitment to the moral and material

[16]"Of the Rise and Progress of the Arts and Sciences," 114.

[17]"Of Interest," 309; *Treatise,* 451.

[18]"The Stoic," 148.   [19]*Ibid.,* 149.

[20]"Of Refinement in the Arts," 276. Along with action and pleasure Hume included "indolence" as the third component of happiness. Characteristically, he argued for this third
component in a negative manner: "Indolence or repose, indeed, seems not of itself to
contribute much to our enjoyment; but, like sleep, is requisite as an indulgence, to the
weakness of human nature, which cannot support an uninterrupted course of business or
pleasure." *Ibid.,* 276–77.

[21]"Of Commerce," 267.   [22]"Of Refinement in the Arts," 287.

efficacy of work since Locke.[23] His psychological orientation, however, directed his analysis of the working class in a fashion that set him apart from others who otherwise shared this commitment. Hume clearly recognized that the working class, in its current behavior, differed from those belonging to that "middle station of life" which he so admired. At the same time, he thought that contemporary proposals for reform were often harsh and wrongheaded, for they refused to "take mankind as they found them; [one] . . . cannot pretend to introduce any violent change in their principles and ways of thinking."[24] Hume's understanding of motivation made him look *beyond* apparent empirical evidence when discussing the behavior of the working class. His historical perspective included the realization that changes in economic life resulting from the expansion of trade carried with them changed demands on the population,[25] and that, in the case of workers, these demands would be met only if sufficient motivation were present. Workers, like other men, would only undertake their tasks if promised sufficient reward and, Hume reasoned, this reward would tend, as it had with the middle class, to produce increased desire. "If the employment you give him," Hume said of the worker,

be lucrative, especially if the profit be attached to every particular exertion of industry, he has gain so often in his eye, that he acquires by degrees a passion for it, and knows no such pleasure as that of seeing the daily increase of his fortune.[26]

Workers had the avaricious desires of other men: they had a "need for achievement."[27] If their condition prevented them from partaking in the refined pastimes of the middle class, their basic desires were nonetheless the same. Workers would only behave rationally if gratification rather than punishment was held out to them. From experience, Hume held, one could see that "where labourers . . . are accustomed to work for low wages . . . it is difficult for them . . . to better their condition."[28] With the promise of a better livelihood men would exert themselves; only the fulfillment of this promise would create the increased wants necessary for greater effort. The pleasures of luxury and the profits of commerce and industry "raise in them a desire for a more splendid way of life."[29] Sidestepping Mandeville's then infamous association of avarice and progress,[30] Hume nevertheless held that man's avarice had to be satisfied in a progressive social order. If workers were treated as potential rational and acquisitive equals they would be driven by desire to improve their condition, and thus that of society:

The increase and consumption of all the commodities which serve to the

[23]Locke's place in the developing notion of work and achievement is discussed in my "The Making of Homo Faber: John Locke Between Ideology and History," *JHI*, **33** (1972), 3–22.
[24]"Of Commerce," 265.   [25]*Ibid.,* 270.   [26]"Of Interest," 309.
[27]See Norman M. Bradburn and Harold E. Berlow, "Need for Achievement and English Economic Growth," *Economic Development and Cultural Change,* **10** (1963), 8–20 for the use of this category as a tool of historical analysis.
[28]"Of Commerce," 272.   [29]*Ibid.,* 270.
[30]Hume cleverly said of Mandeville, "to talk of a vice, which is in general beneficial to society" is a contradiction in terms ("Of Refinement in the Arts," 287).

ornament and pleasure of life, are advantages to society; because, at the same time they multiply those innocent gratifications to individuals, they are a kind of storehouse of labour, which, in the exigencies of state, may be turned to public service. In a nation where there is no demand for such superfluities, men sink into indolence, lose all enjoyment of life and are useless to the public. . . .[31]

More forcefully than his predecessors,[32] and to a wider audience, Hume attempted to undermine the premises upon which discussion of the working class was based. If he agreed that workers were not social equals, he did so with the recognition that the state had to carefully preserve their opportunities for improvement.[33] In opposition to contemporary opinion, he held the lower orders to be the psychic equals of all men, and posed the radical proposition that the health of society was predicated upon the reasonable satisfaction of the desires of the poor. He attacked the widely held notions about the evils of luxury, suggesting that a progressive society depended upon the material happiness of those who labored. Most significantly, Hume agreed that previous discussion of the behavior of the working class was based upon a grave psychological fallacy. In assuming that the virtues of industrious behavior and achievement orientation resided only with the superior classes, economic writers attacked idleness in a way that, when applied, only served to aggravate the problem. For if the poor were to be treated as rebels against civilized mores, the punishments they received would only further discourage them from industry. In arguing that the poor refused to respond to the demands of the middle class because incentives were not provided, Hume not only opened the way for a reconsideration of their motivation, but for a change in the nature of policy based upon a new view of economic activity and its effect upon working men. In order that such a change be effectively proposed, however, Hume's insights would have to be wedded to a rigorous critique of previous policy and a highly articulated vision of social life in a community of achieving psychic equals.This is precisely what Adam Smith accomplished.[34]

University of British Columbia.

[31]*Ibid.*, 279.

[32]Some of Hume's argument was anticipated in Berkeley's *The Querist, Works* ed. A. A. Luce and T. E. Jessop (London, 1953), VI, 103–92. For an analysis of Berkeley's argument and its influence: T. W. Hutchinson, "Berkeley's *Querist* and its Place in the Economic Thought of the Eighteenth Century," *British Journal for the Philosophy of Science,* **4** (May 1953-Feb. 1954), 52–77; Ian D. S. Ward, "George Berkeley: Precursor of Keynes or Moral Economist on Underdevelopment?" *Journal of Political Economy,* **67** (Feb. 1959), 31–40.

[33]"Of the Balances of Trades," 333.

[34]Joseph Mayer, "Adam Smith's Concept of Man and its Effects," *Social Science,* **28** (June 1953), 131–36; David R. Kamerschen, "Adam Smith's concept of Man and Human Relations," *Journal of Human Relations,* **13** (1965), 446–57.

VII

THE ELEMENTS OF SOCIAL STATUS
IN HUME'S TREATISE

BY STEVEN WALLECH

David Hume in his *Treatise of Human Nature* described the workings of the mind so that a definite image of social order and status clearly emerged. This image reveals a sharp difference between how Hume as an eighteenth-century intellectual envisioned social organization and how social philosophers today view society. Rather than rely on the current vocabulary of "class" and its broad fluid conceptions of social division, Hume used the eighteenth-century terms of "rank, distinction, and character" which connote a rather fixed and stable social order by placing individuals in definite ranks in the social hierarchy with fixed positions within the community.

How did an individual acquire a distinct social status in Hume's social order? What elements of the human mind contributed to the concrete social characteristics that such an order bestowed? How did people in Hume's view fit into the patterns of life he described as social? Hume answered each of these questions in his analysis of the workings of the human mind.

In order to understand Hume's view of social status, one must examine his view of the underlying components of social order by studying first of all Hume's view of the passions as the basic elements that differentiate types of individuals. Once the passions are defined one can understand the positions in the social order that these psychological elements indicate, for the passions imply status by the qualities they communicate and the objects they identify. Finally, in order to grasp the stability and rigidity which Hume depicted as elements of status, one will find that Hume's ideas of passion and social distinction are related to the context of his concepts of the will, property, and justice. Hume's treatment of the passions and social status relative to the will, property, and justice reveals the size, composition, and limits he provided for ranks in society.

Like Jean-Jacques Rousseau in his *Discours sur l'Origine et les Fondements de l'Inégalité parmi les Hommes* (1755), Hume perceived that society is divided on the basis of a wide array of personal characteristics and property. Both authors regarded social distinction as based on individual qualities of merit, such as beauty, strength, and intelligence. Both authors saw that the type and amount of one's possessions divide people into different social ranks and educate them in the manners and values of their status.

Unlike Rousseau, Hume did not see property or civil society as dangerous to human happiness. Whereas Rousseau condemned property as a source of misery and bloodshed, Hume saw property as the basis of human prosperity. For Hume, property divides people into the diverse occupations of civil life which bring peace, order, and wealth to the social setting. For Hume, personal distinction based on property and merit makes human life in its social setting both secure and rewarding.

Hume expressed his vision of society by using a variety of terms popular in the eighteenth-century which placed people into a wide array of "ranks," "posts," "stations," and "orders" of society. Each rank comprised only a small number of people, who possess a particular type of estate, or possess a licence or grant to work at a specific craft or occupation. These rankings are so well established that each carries with it an implicit and definite characterization of the social and moral background of the members of the rank. The social and moral background of each rank, in turn, comprises the degree of personal merit that is associated with estate. Estate and merit combine to make eighteenth-century social division exact. Hume reflects in his writings this precision and clarity of social status, and his vision of it appears clearly in his *Treatise.*[1]

Personal Identity, the Passions, and Distinction

Hume generates a picture of status by describing the relationship between the passions and personal identity. It also establishes a link between the objects of the external world and Hume's concept of the self; the relationship matures under the influence of an individual's emotional responses to the things and people around him. The result of this maturation is a sense of distinction that separates people according to the emotions they feel in response to observations they make about themselves and other people. In order to understand this process, one must look closely at Hume's treatment of the passions in order to see how they shape the individual's self-image.

According to Hume, the issue of the self proposes a complex problem of personal identity which he treats in Book I of the *Treatise.* For the purpose of analyzing Hume's understanding of social distinction, however, the image of the self that appears in Book II serves best. Here Hume describes the self as a ". . . succession of related ideas and impressions, of which we have an intimate memory and consciousness."[2] This conception of self avoids many of the issues raised in Book I, and offers the idea of personal identity as a developing concept which strings to-

[1] For a definition of the word "estate" see the following: J. H. Hexter, *The Vision of Politics on the Eve of the Reformation: More, Machiavelli, and Seyssel* (New York, 1973), 154-55; William Blackstone, *Commentaries of the Law of England* edited and analyzed by Thomas M. Cooley (Chicago, 1884), I, 381; *Oxford Universal Dictionary on Historical Principles* (revised and edited by C. T. Onions (Oxford, 1955), 2005; also see Thomas Dyche and William Pardon, *A New English Dictionary* (1740), (New York, 1972); Samuel Johnson, *A Dictionary of the English Language* (London, 1755); and Thomas Sheridan, *A General Dictionary of the English Language* (Dublin, 1784)—especially for the words "estate," "state," "rank," and "station".

[2] David Hume, *A Treatise of Human Nature* (second edition, analyzed with an analytical index by L. A. Selby-Bigge; text revisions and notes by P. H. Nidditch (Oxford, 1980), 277.

gether a series of reactions to external objects in a ". . . connected succession of perceptions, which we call *self*" (277). This connected succession of perceptions creates an image of self that matures as the individual assimilates bits of information about the world around him and his location within that world.

According to Hume, the kinds of information that help shape an individual's self-image can only come from two sources: the external world and our internal responses. Of all our responses to external objects, those things which excite the passions do the most to shape our personal identity, and from them we can best discern our status. For Hume, the passions provide the central link between the self and the external world. This link allowed his readers to see the mechanics of the formation of personality and to see how different personalities give shape to diversity of status in society.

The passions which most clearly shape personality and define status and distinction are pride and humility, respect and contempt, and envy and malice. They are what Hume called the "indirect passions" derived from the relationship between external objects or persons and internal emotional responses of the self. The self is a developing series of responses to the external world, while the object or other person is that which causes the response, i.e., a passion in the self (277-79, 291).

Of the descriptions of the six indirect passions which most clearly define status in Hume's *Treatise*, his description of pride and humility do most to explain how indirect passions work. External objects, such as property or people, Hume calls the *subjects* that cause pride or humility; these "subjects" are grouped with the personal traits that give each individual the sense of being different from other people. These subjects include:

. . . Every valuable quality of mind . . . imagination, judgment, memory or disposition; wit, good-sense, learning, courage, justice, [and] integrity . . . ; [every valuable quality of body] beauty, strength . . . agility, good mien, address, . . . and dexterity . . . [; and finally, every valuable quality based on external things, such as] our country, family, children, relations, riches, houses, gardens, horses, dogs, clothes, and any [other thing which gives us distinction]. (279)

Each of these "subjects" that cause pride or humility belongs to the individual either as a personal characteristic or as a concomitant of property. Each "subject" that excites pride or humility adds a solid descriptive component to the series of perceptions that make up the self. As these components combine with each other, a complex image of individual personality takes shape. The elements of that image are the fixed units of wealth and estate, the personal qualities of intellectual merit (developed by the leisure that wealth offers), physical strength and dexterity (developed by the habits of occupation), and personal beauty (augmented by the equipage of wealth but frequently an accident of birth). From such a collection of distinctions, a clear, precise, and explicit image of individual merit emerges. Consequently, Hume describes a social order based on a collection of clearly defined individuals. Such a social order lent itself to the eighteenth-century concepts of social division described by the vocabulary of "rank, distinction, and character."

Hume's precise image of individual personality emerges from such passions as pride and humility. According to Hume, the sensations of pleasure or pain which an external object excites within us cause either pride or humility. As the degree of pleasure or pain varies, so does the corresponding degree of pride or humility. Invariably, however, the external object has to be related to the self which experiences the pleasure or pain that generates pride or humility (285):

> . . . *every thing related to us, which produces pleasure or pain, produces likewise pride or humility.* There is not only a relation requir'd, but a close one [which firmly roots the experience of pleasure or pain in the self.] (291)

What produces the pleasure or pain of pride or humility in an individual has to be related explicitly to that particular individual's experience, hence, these sensations of pleasure and pain do not necessarily cause in one person the same response as they cause in someone else. Also, the more people that share the pleasure or pain caused by an external object, the less the bond between that object and any one self. Hume limits the experience of pride or humility to those who relate the object clearly to themselves: "the agreeable or disagreeable object [must] be not only closely related, but also peculiar to ourselves, or at least common to us with a few persons." (291)

The emotions generated by objects that appeal to an individual's person, such as talents of the mind or beauty of the body, lead to distinctions that are peculiar to that individual alone. He or she stands apart as the result of a purely personal characteristic. If, however, pride or humility is a response to the degree of wealth in an individual's estate, the pleasures of these holdings (or the pains of poverty) affect a wide range of people. Not only the individual but also his family and friends are connected to the estate and the powers granted the owner by wealth. Property serves as a powerful device to stimulate pride in the individual owner of the estate, and the power conferred by wealth stimulates pleasure or pain in those associated with him. (315)

Not only does property generate pleasure in the wealthy and pain in the poor but the specific rules that define ownership also affect the degree of pride and distinction associated with possession. These rules convert the passions of pride and humility into explicit social phenomena. Hume states that the nature of these rules and the distinctions of ownership they confer enhance the pleasures of possession. Generally, this increase in pleasure is due to the increased degree of distinction that ownership of larger estates offers. Such distinctions depend absolutely on the universal rules of possession that confer an estate on one person and deny that property to the rest of society. These rules of property guarantee a status that varies with the size of an individual's estate, converting the pleasures of ownership into social distinction:

I may add as . . . [an] enlargement of this system, that *general rules* have a great influence upon pride and humility, as well as on the other passions. Hence we form a notion of different ranks of men, suitable to the powers and riches they are possest of. . . . (293)

Property gains more and more significance in Hume's treatment of the passions as the logic of the *Treatise* unfolds. After he establishes the elements of pride and humility, Hume states that ". . . the relation, which is esteem'd the closest, and which of all produces most commonly the passions of pride is that of property" (309). Property, however, figures not only as the most powerful agent in the passions of pride and humility but is also important in the passions of love and hate. Two variations of love and hate, esteem and contempt, depend almost entirely on the effects of property; these two feelings become the elements of passions which anchor social differences firmly in human emotions: "Nothing has a greater tendency to give us an esteem for any person, than his power and riches, or contempt, than his poverty or meanness. . . ." (357)

Love becomes esteem and hate contempt through the association of ideas. When an individual associates the sensations of one passion with those of another, he transfers his own feelings from one passion to the other. Passion can also be transmitted to other people through the agencies of sympathy and comparison.

Sympathy is that human "agency" that plays the central role in the experience of esteem or contempt. Hume defines sympathy as the human ability ". . . to receive by communication [the] inclinations and sentiments [of others], however different from or contrary to our own" (316). Sympathy is one of three causes for either esteem or contempt; the other two are the pleasures that the elements of property stimulate in our imagination and the pleasures an individual might derive from association with a property owner. These two pleasures, however, are of little consequence when measured against the force of sympathy, for the general pleasures of property are part of the mechanism of sympathy, and agreeable expectations based on association with the rich affect too few people to explain the general esteem everyone feels for the wealthy. (360, 362)

What did sympathy do to create such respect for the wealthy and contempt for the poor? According to Hume, sympathy transfers the sensation of pleasure or pain from an individual's personal experience into a vicarious one; individuals feel what others enjoy (or suffer) (330). Minds function as mirrors of the pains and pleasures of our neighbors, and then reflect these pains and pleasures back to their original source:

. . . the minds of men are mirrors to one another, not only because they respect each other, but also because those rays of passions, sentiments and opinions may be often reverberated, and may decay away by insensible degrees. Thus the pleasure, which a rich man receives from his possessions, being thrown upon the beholder, causes a pleasure and esteem; which, encreases the pleasure of the possessor; and being once more reflected, become a new foundation for pleasure and esteem in the beholder. (365)

When sympathy reflects only the pleasures of wealth, it cannot stimulate envy of the rich. Envy is a passion based on pain due to not having what others possess; sympathy communicates only the joys of sharing possession.

If property generates a vicarious experience of pleasure, then the absence of property stimulates the sensation of pain. The absence of power or the lack of the enjoyment of an estate creates the pains of poverty. Poverty requires the necessity for perpetually currying the favors of the rich so that one can eke out a living. This condition of poverty causes sympathy to communicate pain to others, and this pain encourages a desire to avoid the company of the poor and a tendency to regard their misery with contempt. Finally, for Hume the solitude of the poor as people seek to avoid them is in itself painful, for a ". . . perfect solitude is, perhaps, the greatest punishment we can suffer." (363)

The contrast between the pleasures of wealth and the pains of poverty, compounded by the sympathetic echoes of human response to these two conditions in society, generates basic questions about social existence: How do the rich and the poor feel about the contrast between their circumstances in life? Do the poor feel a constant force of isolation? Are they not alienated in a society based on property rights? Hume addresses these questions when he explores the agency of comparison; here he focuses on the emotional effects of respect and contempt, and reveals one of the major tenets of social division based on distinction.

According to Hume, comparison works on the passions with the same efficacy as sympathy, but the consequences are the opposite: "In all kinds of comparison an object makes us always receive from another, to which it is compar'd, a sensation contrary to what arises from itself in its direct and immediate survey" (594). While sympathy generates a like experience of pain or pleasure, depending on the experience of the individual to whom we are responding, comparison generates the opposite sensations.

These opposite sensations introduce a new agency into the emotions of association—that agency is the consequence of bringing opposites into close proximity to each other. A great estate when set beside a lesser one becomes by contrast, so that the ". . . misery of another gives us a more lively idea of our happiness, and his happiness of our misery" (375). This effect drives a wedge between people, creating an emotional barrier that distances one degree of wealth from another. For Hume, this distance translates itself into the common metaphor that great wealth entails great social elevation, and poverty a low condition in social life. Degrees of wealth entail degrees of social elevation, and the accompanying elevation entails degrees of goodness:

Any great elevation of place communicates . . . a fancy'd superiority over those that lie below, and, *vice versa*, ... Hence it proceeds, that we associate, in a manner, the idea of whatever is good with that of height, and evil with lowness. . . . Kings and princes are suppos'd to be plac'd at the top of human affairs, as peasants and day labourers are said to be in the lowest stations. . . . Virtue, genius, power and riches are for this reason associated with height and sublimity; as poverty, slavery, and folly are conjoin'd with descent and lowness. (343-36)

Comparison, however, also makes those of superior estate uneasy about their social inferiors. Part of this unease is the pain communicated sympathetically from the poor to the rich, but the major part of this discomfort comes from the contrast between the two estates. The rich sense their difference from the poor and seek to create as much real distance between ranks as the metaphor of height suggests:

> This uneasiness . . . must be . . . sensible to the superior; and that because the near approach of the inferior is regarded as a piece of ill-breeding, ... A sense of superiority . . . breeds in all men an inclination to keep themselves at a distance from him, and determines them to redouble the marks of respect and reverence, when they are oblig'd to approach him; where they do not observe that conduct, 'tis proof they are not sensible of his superiority. (393)

The desire for social distance generated by comparison leads to sharp social distinctions demanded by the rich. These signs of superiority ought to stimulate great pain in the poor by creating the basis for the emotions of envy and malice. Hume, however, rejects this simple perception of envy and malice, and instead states that the poor separate themselves emotionally from their social superiors. The greater the differences in rank and estate, the less social proximity exists between the rich and the poor. The less social proximity, the less the poor feel the pains of comparison:

> It may, indeed, be thought, that the greater the disproportion is, the greater must be the uneasiness from the comparison. But we may consider on the other hand, that the great disproportion cuts off the relation, and either keeps us from comparing ourselves with what is remote from us, or diminishes the effect of comparison. (377-78)

If the poor do not always feel envy or malice towards the rich, how do these emotions figure in Hume's social theory? According to Hume, these emotions differentiate people on the basis of comparison and establish the sharp lines of distinction between ranks in society when social distance is slight. The poor can only compare themselves to those in close proximity. This confines their experience of envy or malice to those near their own elevation and helps divide them into discrete ranks (377). The rich are also divided into different ranks, for they experience envy when their immediate inferiors acquire new degrees of status. Unlike the usual definition of envy, where discontent is felt only for a superior, Hume states that as the inferior acquires signs of distinction, he approaches the superior's status and reduces the joys of comparison. This creates envy in the superior who then hopes to resist this loss of social contrast:

> When this distance diminishes, the comparison is less to our advantage; and consequently gives us less pleasure. . . . Hence arises a species of envy, which men feel, when they perceive their inferiors approaching or overtaking them. . . . (377)

This envy then can become malice which ". . . is the unprovok'd desire of producing evil to another, in order to reap a pleasure from comparison." (377) Envy and malice therefore help to create a desire to maintain social differences identified by comparison.

Taken together, the emotions reviewed here reveal a social pattern based on the pleasures and pains that cause them. Pride, respect, envy, and malice affect the rich in such a way as to lead them to associate with each other and deny their company to the poor. Humility, contempt, envy, and malice affect the poor in such a way that they become isolated from their social superiors and insulated against the great distances that separate them from the top of society. Pride, based on property, and humility, based on poverty, absolutely distinguish the rich from the poor as the former experiences pleasure and the latter experiences pain. Respect and contempt are the results of the sympathy that communicates this pleasure or pain. The pleasure of wealth leads to a desire to associate with the rich, while the pain of poverty stimulates a desire, among those with property, to avoid the poor. Comparison create great height and depth in the social structure, and generates the capacity to define rank clearly. Envy and malice establish the barriers between ranks and isolate each rank from the emotional consequences of comparison between widely differing estates. Within each rank, individual merit and property creates local social distinctions. Consequently, even the poor enjoy some of the positive sensations of pride and distinction within their social strata when associating with one another.

The Will, Property, and Justice

According to Hume, the passions and their causes, pleasure and pain, function not only to describe status but also as the source of all our motivations in life. These passions give rise to new motions of our bodies and new perceptions by our minds as we respond to pleasure or pain. Hume excludes the possibility of reason's producing such action, for either reason places us in an abstract world where no action could occur, or reason merely demonstrates the connections between events without associating those connections with us (415). On the other hand, the passions and the social distinctions they define establish connections between ourselves and the external world; these connections provide the impulses to respond to that world in a positive or negative fashion.

Hume reduces reason to the role of handmaiden to the passions when he discusses the issue of free will. Reason cannot provide sufficient force in itself to resist the drives of passion except when reason can demonstrate that a passion is based on a false supposition. Generally, however, passions are original existences in the form of internal impulses that have no equivalent in the world except an equal and opposite passion: "'Tis impossible, therefore, that this passion can be oppos'd by, or be contrary to truth or reason; since this contradiction consists in the disagreement of ideas, consider'd as copies, with those objects, which they represent" [, and not the internal actions of pleasure or pain in our bodies]. (415)

If passions are the causes of all new actions, how do people develop governments and social order to prevent these internal motives from running wild? What, for example, stops envy and malice from reducing the differences of estate and destroying society? Hume answers these questions by explaining the nature of violent and calm passions. When people become accustomed to a prevailing inclination of the will, that motive generally loses its ability to excite or agitate the soul, and merely produces calm action. Agitation occurs when sudden and new passionate feelings are aroused. Stimulated by habits of crime that reduce their motivations to calm and customary passions, some persons select a life of mischief and attack the social order. To prevent their criminal actions, a violent or new passion has to be stimulated within them so that they can resist their customary inclinations:

. . . when we wou'd govern a man, . . . 'twill commonly be better policy to work upon the violent than the calm passions, and . . . take him by his inclination. . . . We ought to place the object in such particular situations as are proper to increase the violence of the passion. For we may observe, that all depends upon the situation of the object, and that a variation in that particular will be able to change the calm and the violent passions into each other, [and that] . . . these kinds of passions [can] pursue good, and avoid evil. (419)

Conversely, once a community has created a standard for normal conduct, the conformity to the calm passions that this standard generates becomes desirable. Hume speaks of the efficacy of custom as a normative force in creating social harmony among the myriad ranks of society. Custom has two original effects upon the mind that in turn establishes standard behavior: facility and inclination. Facility is the easing of excited spirits as an action is repeated; it cuts a path through the surprise and wonderment of a new motivation and its consequent action. Facility leads to the development of habits that make action a more comfortable experience, and inclination is the desire to do what is comfortable. Custom therefore creates, through practice, an accepted pattern of action that becomes pleasurable to the different ranks of the community. (422-24)

That a whole community can conform to custom or will use violent passions to stimulate non-conformists to obey custom reveals Hume's conception of good and evil. Custom is desirable because it removes the pains of new sensation and creates the pleasures of ease through social habits. Violent passions are used to disrupt inclinations that cause mischief and pain in the community. Therefore, good and evil consist of whatever creates social pleasure and reduces social pain:

. . . good and evil, or in other words, pain and pleasure [create the desired actions in men]. Of this kind is the desire of punishment to our enemies, and of happiness to our friends. [The appropriate uses of the] passions, properly speaking, produce good and evil, and [consequently the pleasures and pains that shape our inclinations]. (439)

Once Hume has defined the will in relationship to pain and pleasure, he establishes a connection between his treatment of the passions and the social order they describe. Property provides the foundation for this

social order, and Hume defines property as simply: ". . . a relation
betwixt a person and object as permits him, but forbids any other, the
free use and possession of it, without violating the laws of justice and
moral equity" (310). How could a relationship come about which distinguishes the rights of one individual from another in the use of external
things so that those rights do not violate equity and justice? How can
the establishment of an estate system and its consequent pains and pleasures be fair? How can one individual justly assume a high position in
society and look with contempt on all those below him?

According to Hume, these problems occur as a consequence of the
nature of justice itself, and as a result of the role of property in human
society. Justice and property provide a service to social organization that
validates the distinctions of estate and their corresponding ranks. What
justice does for the social order is to establish the principles of equity
and merit in the customs of society. Property, on the other hand, increases
the ability of each individual to meet the needs of life, by organizing the
habits of labor around the rewards of estate.

Hume states that justice is merely the realization by human beings
that equity and merit can exist among them only if they establish these
principles artificially and maintain them by the force of education and
custom. Hume systematically denies the possibility of justice's being the
result of some natural sense, some form of natural benevolence, or some
form of natural law. For Hume, justice occurs as a result of the circumstances of living and the necessity for a conventional definition of "equity"
(i.e., fairness).[3]

Hume uses the word "artificial" to describe the conventions or customs of justice that appear in society, but "artificial" merely means that
justice is a human construction. Justice is artificial in the sense that
people create customs and habits of fair play among themselves; but
justice is also necessary to the existence of their social groups. These
social groups themselves are necessary to the survival of each of their
members, and therefore justice exists as a means to guarantee the continuation of the human species:

. . . when I deny justice to be a natural virtue, I make use of the word *natural*,
only as oppos'd to *artificial*. In another sense of the word; as no principle of
the human mind is more natural than a sense of virtue; so no virtue is more
natural than justice. Mankind is an inventive species; and where an invention
is obvious and absolutely necessary, it may as properly be said to be natural as
any thing that proceeds immediately from original principles. . . . Tho' the
rules of justice be *artificial* they are not arbitrary. (484)

The necessity of justice depends upon its relation to property. Justice
makes property possible by making estates part of the customs that
maintain the relationships of people. These relationships themselves comprise both the ranks of society and the means for survival in a natural

[3] *Ibid.*, 477-84. For the use of the term "equity" see 483.

environment. Justice and property make possible an ordering of human beings that allows them to withstand the dangers of nature and experience the passions that differentiate them into the distinctions of rank. By themselves, human beings are weak, but in a social order their combinations of labor and mutual dependence enhance their strength. Society based on justice and property makes survival possible:

'Tis by society alone he is able to supply his defects. . . . Society provides a remedy for [human weakness]. . . . By the partition of employment, our ability encreases: and by mutual succour we are less expos'd to fortune and accident. 'Tis by this additional *force, ability*, and *security*, that society becomes advantageous. (485)

Hume states that to form societies, individuals have to become aware of the advantages of social union. Certain advantages become obvious as people discover the reciprocal benefits of mutual support through the family. The affections of family, however, do not extend beyond those linked by familial relationships. Beyond the family, individuals are governed by their tendency towards self-love and selfishness which limits the number of people that the union of family can influence:

. . . in the original frame of our mind, our strongest attention is confin'd to ourselves; our next is extended to our relations and acquaintances; and 'tis only the weakest which reaches to strangers and indifferent people. This partiality, then, and unequal affection [limits the bonds of union beyond the range of the family]. (487-88)

Associations in families, though limited, instruct members of these small groups in the advantages of union. Although the bonds of familial affection are confined to a few people, members of such unions learn that mutual support in a household can provide internal satisfaction of the mind, external advantages of the body, and extended powers of labor. These advantages in turn create a superfluity of wealth that could not originate without the association of the family. (486-87)

Superfluity of wealth, or property, unfortunately can become the target of mischief as rapacious individuals motivated by self-love ravish the newly acquired goods of labor. To remove the danger of this mischief, human beings resort to the use of their reason and judgment to create an artificial system of rewards and punishments to control the will of their neighbors. This artificial system dictates the habits and customs that bestow stability on all possessions. Stability provides security in the ownership of external goods and guarantees peaceful enjoyment of the superfluity of labor. Such a system of custom provides the artificial conventions that define property. (489)

These conventions assuring the stability of property generate the idea of justice. Self-love and selfishness are a threat to external goods, while the conventions to preserve property foster a concept of public interest and public concern. These conventions state: "Property must be stable, and must be fix'd by general rules" (497). The result of these conventions is the establishment of peace and order in society and the extension of the positive rewards of human association. Conversely, these individuals recalling what life had been like prior to the conventions of property can now rejoice in their escape from savagery. Property therefore fosters a general experience of reward in human association, and this sense of reward through association becomes a new convention in itself. This latter convention is called public interest:

> And thus justice established itself by a kind of convention or agreement; that is, by a sense of interest, suppos'd to be common to all, and where every single act is perform'd in expectation that others are to perform the like. Without such a convention, no one wou'd ever have dream'd, that there was such a virtue as justice, or have been induc'd to conform his actions to it. (498)

According to Hume, the establishment of the rule ". . . . concerning the stability of possession, is not only useful, but even absolutely necessary to human society . . ." (501). Property made social organization possible, while at the same time creating those passions that instruct individuals as to their proper location within the social hierarchy. The way Hume defines the necessity for property rights and the emphasis he places on the need for stability of ownership sets the stage for the role of the force behind those passions which establishes the sense of social organization. Therefore, justice, which reinforces the system of estates, in turn reinforces the design of society stimulated by property through the medium of the passions.

Once human conventions establish justice and property, the nature of social order becomes clear. Property is the foundation of all social organization other than that of the family; at the same time, property stimulates those passions which give people the sharp pains and pleasures that define either their sense of superiority or of inferiority to their neighbors. Justice regulates these passions by means of the customs and rules which give felicity and value to their experience. Property establishes the basis of these passions through the organization of the degrees of status that range from the top to the bottom of society. Property and justice taken together create those general rules which maintain the stability and define the status of one's place in the social order. This stability and status make possible a constant stream of internal impressions which result in a personal identity established on the basis of estate and confirmed by law. That personal identity is based on the association of conjoined impressions bringing in their wake pride and humility, esteem and contempt, and envy and malice. In the end, the combination of property, justice, the passions, and personal identity establish for each individual a degree of status in the social hierarchy, and therefore places that individual in a well defined rank.

Pitzer College, Claremont, California.

VIII

HUME ON IDOLATRY AND INCARNATION

By Donald T. Siebert

David Hume's quarrel with religion is well-known.[1] In the *Dialogues concerning Natural Religion* he subjected theological arguments, whether a priori or a posteriori, to a devastating scrutiny and whittled away the basis for any belief in a God who is more substantial than a mere possibility of a First Cause bearing *"some remote Analogy to human Intelligence"* (*D*, 260).[2] As we gather from the stimulating interplay of disputants in that work, Hume enjoyed the challenge of such argumentation; it was a subject that he could pursue with detachment and serenity of mind. Hume's real objection to religion, however, was not that it failed of proof, its conviction relying finally on faith, not reason. That was surely a matter about which he could afford to be indifferent or even amused. Rather, Hume's quarrel with religion stems from his claim that piety is an enemy of morality, and indeed the main enemy. This charge is iconoclastic, for the usual recommendation of religion, even by those who reject it otherwise, is that at least it makes men moral: Cleanthes

[1] Among the better general discussions are James Noxon, "Hume's Concern with Religion," in *David Hume: Many-Sided Genius,* ed. Kenneth R. Merrill and Robert W. Shahan (Norman, Oklahoma, 1976), 59-82; Keith E. Yandell, "Hume on Religious Belief," in *Hume: A Re-Evaluation,* ed. Donald W. Livingston and James T. King (New York, 1976), 109-125; and Norman Kemp Smith, in his edition of the *Dialogues Concerning Natural Religion,* 2nd ed. (New York, 1947), 1-75. Ernest Campbell Mossner's monumental *Life of David Hume* (Oxford, 1954, 1980) should also be consulted along with his article "The Religion of David Hume," *JHI,* **39,** 4 (Oct.-Dec. 1978), 653-64.

[2] The following abbreviations and texts are used throughout this paper:

D   Dialogues concerning Natural Religion, from *The Natural History of Religion,* ed. A. Wayne Colver, and *Dialogues concerning Natural Religion,* ed. John Valdimir Price (Oxford, 1976).

EPM   An Enquiry concerning the Principles of Morals, from *Enquiries Concerning Human Understanding and Concerning the Principles of Morals,* ed. L. A. Selby-Bigge, 3rd. ed. revised by P. H. Nidditch (Oxford, 1975).

History   The History of England. Because there is no standard printing of Hume's *History,* I have simply quoted from my own copy (8 vols; London, 1822) and cited the chapter number, which is the same in the various collected editions. I have compared all of my quotations from the *History* with the wording of the first edition, but I present the corrected edition as reflecting Hume's later judgment. The changes are largely stylistic, there being no significant difference between the first and corrected versions, except as noted below (in note #9).

HL   The Letters of David Hume, ed. J. Y. T. Greig (Oxford, 1932), 2 vols.

NHR   The Natural History of Religion, ed. Colver (cited above).

T   A Treatise of Human Nature, ed. L. A. Selby-Bigge (Oxford, 1888).

Works   The Philosophical Works of David Hume, ed. T. H. Green and T. H. Grose (London, 1875), 4 vols.

advances this defense in the *Dialogues* (*D* 251). Hume attacks even this
last bulwark of religious belief—in the *Dialogues,* and most vigorously
in *The Natural History of Religion.*[3] And on his deathbed he shocked
James Boswell by his contempt for all aspects of religion, including its
vaunted morality. According to Boswell's Journal, "He then said flatly
that the morality of every religion was bad, and, I really thought, was
not jocular when he said that when he heard a man was religious, he
concluded he was a rascal, though he had known some instances of very
good men being religious. This was just an extravagant reverse of the
common remarks as to infidels."[4]

Yet as Hume acknowledged in *The Natural History of Religion* (henceforth *NHR*), religious belief would not disappear once philosophy brings
its light, even in the unlikely event that clergymen should lose interest
in proseletyzing and intimidating helpless men. Religion's "root strikes
deeper into the mind, and springs from the essential and universal properties of human nature" (*NHR,* 92). Hume emphasized in *NHR* that it
is one thing for physico-theologians, deists (Hume referred to them as
genuine theists), and theodicean apologists to point upward to the splen-
dor of Newtonian order, to the reign of universal law and harmony voiced
succinctly by Alexander Pope,

> Nature, and Nature's Laws lay hid in Night.
> God said, *Let Newton be!* and All was Light.[5]

Mankind in fact is more disposed to look downward at the events of life,
shrouded in darkness. Men suffer pain and disappointment, and dread
the future, especially death. They sense mysterious and invisible power
and desperately seek some means of placating it: "No wonder, then, that
mankind, being placed in such an absolute ignorance of causes, and being
at the same time so anxious concerning their future fortunes, should
immediately acknowledge a dependence on invisible powers, possest of
sentiment and intelligence" (*NHR,* 34). This whole disposition of mind
exacerbates their suspicions and fears and leads them to grasp any supposed remedy, however selfish or unworthy of reason, which promises
to protect them. It is not a situation calculated to bring about that
Humean ideal of a civilization marked by open-mindedness, toleration,
cheerfulness, service to others, and an enterprising concern with the things
of this world.

---

[3] In the first *Enquiry* (see the edition of the *Enquiries* listed above, p. 147), Hume
mentioned the possible moral influence of religion, but his own position is somewhat
ambiguous because the speaker for Epicurus does not reply. Later, as we see, Hume
unequivocally rejected the possibility of moral influence.

[4] *The Yale Editions of the Private Papers of James Boswell: Boswell in Extremes, 1776-
1778,* ed. Charles McC. Weis and Frederick A. Pottle (New York, 1970), 11.

[5] *The Poems of Alexander Pope; A One-Volume Edition of the Twickenham Text,* ed.
John Butt (London, 1963), 808.

What can be done? To the privileged few Hume offers the salvation of being like him, enjoying "a manly, steddy virtue, . . . the calm sunshine of the mind," before which "these spectres of false divinity never make their appearance" (*NHR*, 91). But what about "the ignorant multitude" (*NHR*, 27, 33), that is, the "vulgar, indeed, all mankind, a few excepted"? (*NHR*, 57) Philosophy hath neither light nor charms for them, and, as Hume made abundantly clear in *NHR* and in his *History of England*, their delusions born of spiritual mania threaten the stability of a society which the fit, though few, might otherwise enjoy to the fullest. Hume has no programme, as such, no ready answer, but as I hope this paper will show, implicit in *NHR* and other works published later in his career is a growing appreciation of the power of religious rites and images to control or even neutralize the dangerous caprices of pious zeal. And we shall see an important shift in Hume's attitude toward certain forms of Christianity.

Central to the problem of pious zeal is man's attempt to understand the nature of his God, indeed to make his deity concrete. Throughout *NHR* Hume tended to regard this effort to render the incomprehensible familiar to the feeble intellect of man as manifestly absurd. Still, if absurd, it is no less a fact of human nature:

And thus, however strong men's propensity to believe invisible, intelligent power in nature, their propensity is equally strong to rest their attention on sensible, visible objects; and in order to reconcile these opposite inclinations, they are led to unite the invisible power with some visible object. . . . (*NHR*, 46) And as an invisible spiritual intelligence is an object too refined for vulgar apprehension, men naturally affix it to some sensible representation; such as either the more conspicuous parts of nature, or the statues, images, and pictures, which a more refined age forms of its divinities. (*NHR*, 49)

It is important to stress that even though Hume's ridicule of idolatry is more often directed against primitive polytheism, his thesis in *NHR* is that polytheism and the more sophisticated forms of monotheism are not essentially different, except that, for reasons we shall soon explore, polytheism is actually preferable because by promoting sociability and materialism it is less immoral than monotheism. Men are idolaters by nature; the problem for Hume was to ensure that idolatry would be useful and constructive, instead of exerting that malign influence most often observed in human history:[6]

The universal propensity to believe in invisible, intelligent power, if not an original instinct, being at least a general attendant of human nature, may be

[6] Cf. Philo's remark in the *Dialogues:* "If the religious spirit be ever mention'd in any historical Narration, we are sure to meet afterwards with a Detail of the Miseries, which attend it. And no Period of time can be happier or more prosperous, than those in which it is never regarded, or heard of" (*D*, 251).

considered as a kind of mark or stamp, which the divine workman has set upon his work; and nothing surely can more dignify mankind, than to be thus selected from all the other parts of the creation, and to bear the image or impression of the universal Creator. But consult this image, as it commonly appears in the popular religions of the world. How is the deity disfigured in our representations of him! What caprice, absurdity, and immorality are attributed to him! How much is he degraded even below the character which we should naturally, in common life, ascribe to a man of sense and virtue! (*NHR,* 93-94)

In this passage, even allowing for a degree of irony or overstatement, we see Hume ready to countenance the human desire to image the deity— "nothing surely can more dignify mankind"—except of course that men have invariably disgraced themselves in their actual efforts to fashion that image. But here we do see that Hume regards the disfiguring of the deity as the source of religious error. In other words, how man pictures his god and all his ceremonial means of communing with that god will determine the moral nature of his religion, and of course the degree to which he will be a useful or destructive member of his society.

By 1757, the date of *NHR,* the question was not whether man should attempt to make his god concrete, but rather how and to what extent. By contrast, the early Hume regarded the use of icons, vestments, liturgy, and sacred rites of all kinds to be misguided and foolish—but of little consequence to society. In *A Treatise of Human Nature* (Bk. III, 1740) he had dismissed in passing religious ceremonies and symbols. They might be compared to certain legal ceremonies and practices, like those involving promises and contracts, but there is a fundamental difference: such forms do serve a purpose in the law because justice is necessary to society; they serve no purpose in religion except to bedazzle the masses (*T,* 515-16, 523-25). In *An Enquiry concerning the Principles of Morals* (1751) Hume developed this idea more fully.[7] After admitting that "those, who ridicule vulgar superstitions, and expose the folly of particular regards to meats, days, places, postures, apparel, have an easy task . . .," Hume takes up that easy task by ridiculing these superstitions: "A fowl on Thursday is lawful food; on Friday abominable: Eggs in this house and in this diocese, are permitted during Lent; a hundred paces further, to eat them is a damnable sin. This earth or building, yesterday was profane; to-day, by the muttering of certain words, it has become holy and sacred" (*EPM,* 198). Then, after suggesting that legal rites are often just as silly, he makes this striking distinction between legal and religious forms:

---

[7] The first *Enquiry* also reflects Hume's contempt for religious ceremonies, but he never makes them a principal object of concern. Discussing "the effect of resemblance in enlivening . . . ideas," Hume rehearses the reasons which Roman Catholics "usually plead in excuse for the mummeries, with which they are upbraided . . ." (*Enquiries,* 51-52). Hume's reference to these ceremonies is scornful, but his main purpose here is merely to exemplify his argument concerning the power of resemblance.

But there is this material difference between *superstition* and *justice,* that the former is frivolous, useless, and burdensome; the latter is absolutely requisite to the well-being of mankind and existence of society. . . . Were the interests of society nowise concerned, it is as unintelligible why another's articulating certain sounds implying consent, should change the nature of my actions with regard to a particular object, as why the reciting of a liturgy by a priest, in a certain habit and posture, should dedicate a heap of brick and timber, and render it, thenceforth and for ever, sacred. (*EPM,* 199)

Two points stand out that will be of significance later in our discussion: (1) as late as 1751 Hume considered religious forms "nowise concerned" in "the interests of society"; and (2) his language reveals an undisguised contempt for this useless mummery. I shall show how this attitude underwent a marked change.

Another important source of Hume's early opinion of religious forms is a letter written in 1743 to William Mure of Caldwell. In a part of that letter, Hume first divides "every thing we commonly call Religion" into "Devotion & Prayer" and "the Practice of Morality, & the Assent of the Understanding to the Proposition *that God exists*" (*HL,* I, 50). It is a division Hume would characteristically make throughout his writings on religion, and we sense that even that early he was formulating the argument that devotion and prayer could become the bane of the "Practice of Morality." The remainder of the letter concerns the abuses of worship, and it is significant that Hume identifies the conjunction of invisible spirit and concrete object (to which in this paper I am applying the general term "incarnation") as the germ of the problem. Consider Hume's observations:

. . . I assert [the Deity] is not the natural Object of any Passion or Affection. He is no Object either of the Senses or Imagination, & very little of the Understanding, without which it is impossible to excite any Affection. A remote Ancestor, who has left us Estates & Honours, acquir'd with Virtue, is a great Benefactor, & yet 'tis impossible to bear him any Affection, because unknown to us; tho in general we know him to be a Man or a human Creature, which brings him vastly nearer our Comprehension than an invisible infinite Spirit. A man, therefore, may have his Heart perfectly well disposed towards every proper & natural Object of Affection, Friends, Benefactors, Countrey, Children &c, & yet from this Circumstance of the Invisibility & Incomprehensibility of the Deity may feel no affection towards him. And indeed I am afraid, that all Enthusiasts mightily deceive themselves. Hope & Fear perhaps agitate their Breast when they think of the Deity: Or they degrade him into a Resemblance with themselves, & by that means render him more comprehensible. Or they exult with Vanity in esteeming themselves his peculiar Favourites. Or at best they are actuated by a forc'd & strain'd Affection, which moves by Starts & Bounds, & with a very irregular disorderly Pace. Such an Affection can not be requir'd of any Man as his Duty. Please to observe, that I not only exclude the turbulent Passions, but the calm Affections. Neither of them can operate without the Assistance of the Senses, & Imagination, or at least a more compleat Knowledge of the Object than we have of the Deity. (*HL,* I, 51)

Then, after raising several objections to the use of prayer, Hume concludes: "Thus all wise Men have excluded the Use of Images & Pictures in Prayer; tho they certainly enliven Devotion; because 'tis found by Experience, that with the vulgar these visible Representations draw too much towards them, & become the only Objects of Devotion" (*HL,* I, 52). We note in these passages that Hume categorically opposed worship on the grounds that it is impossible even to conceptualize the Deity to any meaningful extent, thus certainly futile to attempt bringing God nearer by means of images or anthropomorphic analogies; worship accordingly degenerates into idolatry, which Hume dismissed with peremptory scorn. At that early stage in his life, Hume found such worship empty and useless.

I am arguing that Hume's attitude toward idolatry and incarnation underwent a change evident by 1757 in *NHR.* The process of this change itself and a reason for the change are to be found in the first volume of the *History of England (1754).* As we observe the process, the reason for the change will begin to suggest itself.

In the early part of the *History,* Hume treated religious ceremonies and forms in that reductive fashion so prominent in the second *Enquiry,* where he said that a priest's muttering a liturgy made "a heap of brick and timber . . . thenceforth and for ever, sacred." An excellent example is Hume's satirical description of (then) Bishop William Laud's consecration of St. Catherine's Church (*History,* Ch. LII). Having emphasized that the Puritans regarded any ceremonial practice even faintly popish with "the greatest horror and detestation," Hume then portrays Laud as imposing such rituals on them almost out of spite, as if determined to rub their noses in abominations. That aspect of Laud's excesses must have amused Hume, for he pretends that Laud's main intention was to offend the humorless Puritans, who "considered not, that the very insignificancy of these ceremonies recommended them to the superstitious prelate, and made them appear the more peculiarly sacred and religious, as they could serve to no other purpose." It is surely not fair to Laud, but it does underline Hume's complete inability at this point to see any value in these empty forms other than that of vexing Roundheads. Hume then describes the consecration at great length, indeed in sufficient detail to serve as a guidebook for priests. Laud went about the consecration with exaggerated formality, bowing and kneeling, pronouncing blessings and imprecations with punctilious regularity and strained solemnity. Hume presents every symbolic nuance:[8]

---

[8] I am omitting more than a page of detailed description. It is significant to note that the whole passage is a fairly close paraphrase of Hume's source—John Rushworth, *Historical Collections* (London, 1721), II, 76-77—*except* that Hume tends to dramatize

As he approached the communion-table, he made many low reverences: and coming up to that part of the table where the bread and wine lay, he bowed seven times. After the reading of many prayers, he approached the sacramental elements, and gently lifted up the corner of the napkin in which the bread was placed. When he beheld the bread, he suddenly let fall the napkin, flew back a step or two, bowed three several times towards the bread; then he drew nigh again, opened the napkin, and bowed as before.

Next, he laid his hand on the cup, which had a cover upon it, and was filled with wine. He let go the cup, fell back, and bowed thrice towards it. He approached again; and lifting up the cover, peeped into the cup. Seeing the wine, he let fall the cover, started back, and bowed as before. Then he received the sacrament, and gave it to others. And many prayers being said, the solemnity of the consecration ended. The walls and floor and roof of the fabric were then supposed to be sufficiently holy. (*History,* Ch. LII)

The whole description, particularly the final comment (which is not in Hume's source but is rather all his own), exemplifies the ideas of the second *Enquiry.* Clearly in this passage Hume regarded such forms as nothing but mummery. Their only function, as far as he was concerned, was to scandalize the Puritans, a bit of torment they apparently deserved.

The general comments about Laud's innovations also reveal Hume's scorn for this pointless ceremony, consonant with his remarks in the letter to Mure:

All kinds of ornament, especially pictures, were necessary for supporting that mechanical devotion, which was purposed to be raised in this model of religion: but as these had been so much employed by the church of Rome, and had given rise to so much superstition, or what the Puritans called idolatry; it was impossible to introduce them into English churches, without exciting general murmurs and complaints. . . . The crucifix too, that eternal consolation of all pious Catholics, and terror to all sound Protestants, was not forgotten on this occasion.

Hume reminds us that ceremonial worship depends upon pictures or icons, and I suspect that at least in one respect Hume agreed with the Puritans that such worship might well be called idolatry. Once again Hume was simply contemptuous of this "mechanical devotion."

This gleeful debunking of sacred rites is characteristic of Hume, and yet in the *History* we also notice a somewhat less derisive attitude toward these ceremonies beginning to develop. Hume enjoyed mocking super-

---

the episode and exaggerate a few details. For example, whereas in Rushworth, Laud on two occasions bows "several" times, in Hume he bows "frequently" or makes "many low reverences." Other dramatic touches such as the clause "he suddenly let fall the napkin" are Hume's interpolation. And in addition to the final sarcastic remark, the tone of the passage reflects Hume's lack of sympathy with the entire affair. Thus Rushworth wrote, "When the Curses were ended, he pronounced a number of Blessings . . ."; Hume wrote, "The imprecations being all so piously finished, there were poured out a number of blessings. . . ."

stitious practice, without doubt, but he had to consider the implications
of the other extreme, the amorphous simplicity of Puritan religion. What
was the capacity of man for a spiritual communion liberated from the
dross of material ornaments and liturgy? What would happen when these
apparently meaningless forms were discarded? Writing of James I's efforts
to introduce traditional ceremonies into the Kirk, Hume speculated on
these problems in a passage which deserves complete quotation:

The fire of devotion, excited by novelty and inflamed by opposition, had so
possessed the minds of the Scottish reformers, that all rites and ornaments, and
even order of worship, were disdainfully rejected as useless burdens; retarding
the imagination in its rapturous ecstasies, and cramping the operations of that
divine spirit, by which they supposed themselves to be animated. A mode of
worship was established, the most naked and most simple imaginable; one that
borrowed nothing from the senses; but reposed itself entirely on the contemplation of that divine essence, which discovers itself to the understanding only.
This species of devotion so worthy of the Supreme Being, but so little suitable
to human frailty, was observed to occasion great disturbances in the breast, and
in many respects to confound all rational principles of conduct and behavior.
The mind, straining for these extraordinary raptures, reaching them by short
glances, sinking again under its own weakness, rejecting all exterior aid of pomp
and ceremony, was so occupied in this inward life, that it fled from every
intercourse of society, and from every cheerful amusement, which could soften
or humanize the character. It was obvious to all discerning eyes, and had not
escaped the king's, that, by the prevalence of fanaticism, a gloomy and sullen
disposition established itself among the people; a spirit, obstinate and dangerous;
independent and disorderly; animated equally with a contempt of authority, and
a hatred to every other mode of religion, particularly to the Catholic. In order
to mellow these humours, James endeavoured to infuse a small tincture of
ceremony into the national worship, and to introduce such rites as might, in
some degree, occupy the mind, and please the senses, without departing too far
from that simplicity, by which the reformation was distinguished. The finer arts,
too, though still rude in these northern kingdoms, were employed to adorn the
churches; and the king's chapel, in which an organ was erected, and some
pictures and statues displayed, was proposed as a model to the rest of the nation.
But music was grating to the prejudiced ears of the Scottish clergy; sculpture
and painting appeared instruments of idolatry; the surplice was a rag of popery;
and every motion or gesture, prescribed by the liturgy, was a step towards that
spiritual Babylon, so much the object of their horror and aversion. Every thing
was deemed impious, but their own mystical comments on the Scriptures, which
they idolized, and whose eastern prophetic style they employed in every common
occurrence. (*History,* Ch. XLVII)

Here we see a rather different treatment of sacred rites. Faced with
the other extreme—worship stripped of any ceremony at all—Hume
was no longer as inclined simply to dismiss "mechanical devotion" as
idolatry or superstition, pointless and absurd. He did not advocate these
ceremonies, of course, though he seems quite sympathetic to James's

efforts toward reform. In any case, writing the history of this troubled age made him sensitive to a new problem, one much more far-reaching in its implications than the mere nonsense of idolatry. He still maintained that a mode of worship dependent on a rational contemplation of the Supreme Being is perhaps the most appropriate to a spiritual idea, but such a rarefied conception is far beyond the capacity of most worshipers. And what happens to these worshipers instead? They withdraw from the world of the senses, from an awareness of this life, and retreat into a state of uncontollable, self-deceiving rapture. This passage reveals Hume's essential objection to religion, as he expounded it later in *NHR*, particularly to the religion of the enthusiastic Puritans. In its peak of fervor, enthusiasm is the least tolerant form of religion, and, of even greater but related significance, it is the most destructive of civilization. Rational behavior, sociability and politeness, concern for one's fellow creatures, and an enterprising, courageous spirit, are all displaced by the whimsies of solitary man; a chaos of inner passions, and those the most sullen and bitter, threatens to tear apart the outward fabric of society, established by centuries of tradition and gradual progress. A final irony is that their rage against idolatry notwithstanding, these extremists were themselves idolaters—bibliolaters—worshiping in the Old Testament a literature in style and subject least likely, in Hume's eyes, to make them rational or humane. The religion of the fanatics posed a threat to all that Hume regarded as sacred, to use a word which in any other Humean context would be unthinkable.

So large did this threat bulk that later in the *History* Hume moved from ridicule of liturgy to an endorsement of ritual as a means of insulating worshipers from the consequences of unchecked spiritual zeal. Hume had earlier made Laud's liturgical excesses into an example of that prelate's own zeal and of the patent folly of superstition itself. When he came to evaluate Laud's place in history, Hume had changed his mind. It is surprising to learn that however sectarian were his motives or misguided his means, it is regrettable that Laud did not succeed in his liturgical reforms. Indeed, quite plainly Hume's first sentence reflects his own changing view:

Whatever ridicule, to a philosophic mind, may be thrown on pious ceremonies, it must be confessed, that, during a very religious age, no institutions can be more advantageous to the rude multitude, and tend more to mollify that fierce and gloomy spirit of devotion, to which they are subject. Even the English church, though it had retained a share of popish ceremonies,[9] may justly be thought too naked and unadorned, and still to approach too near the abstract

[9] Although nearly all of Hume's corrections are stylistic, the wording of the first edition, compared at this point with the corrected version, may suggest a continuing shift in Hume's attitude toward sacred rites from one of antagonism to toleration: the first version's "popish superstition" is mollified into "popish ceremonies," a change consistent with Hume's desire here to recommend rather than condemn these practices.

and spiritual religion of the Puritans. Laud and his associates, by reviving a few primitive institutions of this nature, corrected the error of the first reformers, and presented to the affrightened and astonished mind, some sensible exterior observances, which might occupy it during its religious exercises, and abate the violence of its disappointed efforts. The thought, no longer bent on that divine and mysterious essence, so superior to the narrow capacities of mankind, was able, by means of the new model of devotion, to relax itself in the contemplation of pictures, postures, vestments, buildings; and all the fine arts, which minister to religion, thereby received additional encouragement. The primate, it is true, conducted this scheme, not with the enlarged sentiments and cool reflection of a legislator, but with the intemperate zeal of a sectary; and by overlooking the circumstances of the times, served rather to inflame that religious fury which he meant to repress. But this blemish is more to be regarded as a general imputation on the whole age, than any particular failing of Laud's; and it is sufficient for his vindication to observe, that his errors were the most excusable of all those which prevailed during that zealous period. (*History*, Ch. LVII)

Admittedly, Hume is not recommending "pious ceremonies" without qualification, nor championing the Church of England and its primate. Nonetheless, this final assessment of Laud reflects a considerable degree of new sympathy with practices formerly regarded as useless idolatry. For Hume it is a matter of accommodation, of making the best of human weaknesses. As long as mankind is religious — and that seems a disposition well-nigh universal — anything serving as an antidote to the poison of fanaticism is to be promoted. Such an antidote is found in religious ceremony and images, which have the additional advantage of readily engrafting themselves on the high culture of a society. Anything drawing man out of himself and into contact with his fellows or with the objects of this world is beneficial, and curiously for Hume sacred rites came to have that function.

This new-found toleration of idolatry seems to have grown out of Hume's experience in writing the history of this peculiar age, one in which the religious principle was at the bottom of so much that went on: "Religion can never be deemed a point of small consequence in civil government: but during this period, it may be regarded as the great spring of men's actions and determinations" (*History*, Ch. LXI). We see Hume moving from amusement and incredulity at the antics of the Puritans, to genuine concern about the threat to a stable society which such fervor posed. It is this concern, once again, which explains his embracing any exigency, even idolatry, which might oppose this tide of delusion and hypocrisy. And it is well to remind ourselves that to Hume the ultimate consequence of unrestrained enthusiasm is immorality, a refrain heard frequently in the *History:*

Among the generality of men, educated in regular, civilized societies, the sentiments of shame, duty, honour, have considerable authority, and serve to counterbalance and direct the motives derived from private advantage: but, by the predominancy of enthusiasm among the parliamentary forces, these salutary principles lost their credit, and were regarded as mere human inventions, yea moral institutions, fitter for Heathens than for Christians. The saint, resigned over to superior guidance, was at full liberty to gratify all his appetites, disguised under the appearance of pious zeal. And, besides the strange corruptions engendered by this spirit, it eluded and loosened all the ties of morality, and gave entire scope, and even sanction, to the selfishness and ambition which naturally adhere to the human mind. (*History*, Ch. LIX)

The mockery of the biblical idiom—"mere human inventions, yea moral institutions"—reveals how much Hume had come to detest the canting Puritans, whose values gave the lie to everything he held dear.

So much so, that we likewise see a shift in Hume's attitude toward the extremes of enthusiasm and superstition—that is, formless Protestant fundamentalism and form-bound, tradition-centered Roman Catholicism. Before writing his *History*, Hume had treated this dichotomy of Christian practice in his essay "Of Enthusiasm and Superstition," part of *Essays, Moral and Political* (1741). There Hume severely blames both extremes, but not to the same degree. He condemns Roman Catholicism without qualification because it ultimately enslaves mankind. And it is significant that among the causes of Catholic timorousness and melancholy, Hume lists "ceremonies, observances, mortifications, sacrifices, presents, or . . . any practice, however absurd or frivolous, which either folly or knavery recommends to a blind and terrified credulity" (*Works*, III, 145). On the other hand, Hume at least accords the enthusiasts or independent Protestants a kind of backhand praise: being marked by a spirit of liberty, their zeal finally levels out into an attitude of moderation and toleration, once the fury of enthusiasm has spent itself; because their religion is formless and independent, they soon cool off and become indifferent to anything save the common affairs of life (*Works*, III, 148-50). Hume repeats this characterization in the *History*, when he contrasts the more tolerant Independents with the more inflexible Presbyterians, who retain more forms and dogma and are thus less capricious, willy-nilly zealots than their Puritan brethren the Independents (*History*, Ch. LVII). By the time he had taken his account up to the Restoration, however, Hume had had ample opportunity to see how tolerating and moderate the Independents were, and by then he was in no mood to damn them with even the faintest of praise. If, according to his theory, they would finally subside into toleration, indifference, and worldliness, history showed no evidence thus far; on the contrary, it showed what pernicious mischief they could work in the meantime. Thus the neat antithesis "Of Enthusiasm and Superstition," which implicitly favors enthusiasm, had disappeared by the end of the Commonwealth years in Hume's *History*. It is no longer weak, fearful, melancholy, and *ignorant* devotees of superstition versus hopeful, proud, presumptuous, warmly imaginative, and *ignorant* fanatics (*Works*, III, 145). Both extremes are absurd, oftentimes

dangerous, and those qualities like hope and pride which favor the enthusiasts in any Humean catalogue of virtues are now given only the
most unflattering interpretation. Likewise, the superstitious are no longer
much blamed for their ceremonies. By this point in the *History*, and later
in *NHR*, superstition is less objectionable than enthusiasm.

We note that this remarkable shift in Hume's views is from the
theoretical formulation which derives mainly from the *Treatise* to judgments elicited by the facts of history. The theoretical Hume makes little
allowance for religious worship of any kind, but least of all for the
"mechanical devotion" manufactured out of ceremonies and icons, out
of superstition and idolatry. Those who practice it most, like the Roman
Catholics, are most blamed. As Hume pronounces bluntly in the *Treatise*,
"The *Roman Catholicks* are certainly the most zealous of any sect in the
christian world . . ." (*T*, 115). The historical Hume, on the other hand,
perceives the dangers to civilization proceeding from a warm, unstable,
uncontrolled imagination—the solipsistic zeal of fanatical Protestantism—and he shifts his ground. Enthusiasts are now most blamed, and
those who observe superstitious forms are perhaps less to be feared.
Formerly, idolatrous worship was absurd, distracting, and therefore *useless*; now idolatrous worship is *merely* absurd, *but* distracting and therefore *useful*. It is a change of some moment. The implications of this
change in *NHR* need to be explored next.

It is first necessary to consider where Hume's thesis leads. I have
indicated above that his essential objection to religion is a moral one:
piety is in far too many cases no high recommendation of a person's
character; indeed from an appearance of piety we may infer hypocrisy
or self-deception at least, and perhaps some form of cruelty or knavery.
No radical cure for man's religious bent is available. The moral philosopher instead attempts to treat religious mania by encouraging a certain
temper of mind. If this mania thrives on introspection, fear, and gloom,
then the opposite state of mind should prove resistant to the mania.
Perhaps the most important constructive passage in *NHR* occurs at the
end of Section XIV: "Whatever weakens or disorders the internal frame
promotes the interests of superstition [by this point in Hume's thought,
"superstition" denotes all of the more zealous commitments to religious
principles, including "enthusiasm"]: And nothing is more destructive to
them than a manly steddy [*sic*] virtue, which either preserves us from
disastrous, melancholy accidents, or teaches us to bear them. During
such calm sunshine of the mind, these spectres of false divinity never
make their appearance" (*NHR*, 91).

Some may object that Hume's observation is valid enough on its own
terms, but beside the point. One cannot will the "calm sunshine of the
mind" any more than one can decide to be happy and thereby let the
sunshine in. And, as I remarked earlier, such salvation appears designed
for men who are already like Hume, in any case. However, is it possible

to cultivate those dispositions in *all* people which tend toward equanimity, a state of mind in which the world is accepted as it is?

Hume saw that people have a natural tendency to believe in a spiritual order; they also have a tendency to connect or unite invisible power with visible object, to seek an incarnation of the spiritual order as it might be termed. The hold of the spiritual thus becomes much stronger, for it is now part of the world of fact and experience. The two are conjoined; indeed with many people, the two are one. The problem that emerges is an interesting one.

For Hume there are two conflicting considerations. (1) Religious belief may be, probably will be, reinforced by this incarnation, and Hume certainly insists that even the highest forms of theism draw strength from the constant reference to an imaged or incarnate deity: Men "fluctuate betwixt these opposite sentiments. The same infirmity still drags them downwards, from an omnipotent and spiritual deity to a limited and corporeal one, and from a corporeal and limited to a statue or visible representation. The same endeavour at elevation still pushes them upwards, from the statue or material image to the invisible power; and from the invisible power to an infinitely perfect deity, the creator and sovereign of the universe" (*NHR*, 58). (2) On the other hand, in the *History* when Hume appeared to commend Laud's return to ceremony, visible signs did draw people like the mad enthusiasts out of their theogenic reveries. Hume's remark in *NHR* that the Jews and Mahometans have banished "all the arts of statuary and painting . . . lest the common infirmity of mankind should thence produce idolatry" (*NHR*, 58) may lead us to infer his approval, but he cannot have favored what was for him the fanatical spirit of those religions nor finally have opposed idolatry, within certain limits. Hume's implicit endorsement of pagan idolatry is based, I shall argue below, on the light hold which that religion had on the lives of the ancients, and on the energy and hope which grew out of Greek mythology, the offspring of a polyphiloprogenitive Zeus.

How so? Hume claimed that men do not really believe in the absurdities of religious fables and dogma. They may try, but "nature is too hard for all their endeavours, and suffers not the obscure, glimmering light, afforded in those shadowy regions, to equal the strong impressions, made by common sense and by experience" (*NHR*, 74). But therein lies the difference between the two theisms, between the casually evolved, unsystematic, mythological religions and the scriptural, systematic, scholastic modern forms. The latter place the believer in an awkward position, straitjacketed by codified dogma, which happens to be even more absurd (said Hume) than the pagan, and thus tormented by doubt and guilt (*NHR*, sections XII-XIII). The monotheist cannot enjoy confident serenity, that quality *sine qua non* to Humean virtue. His primitive cousin the pagan, on the other hand, wears a much looser, more comfortably fitting religious mantle. Hume in fact repeatedly uses such a metaphor:

pagan religion "hung loose upon the minds of men" (*NHR*, 80).[10] It follows that the ancient is happier, for the many fables of his religion, being at least plausible and certainly entertaining, do not make many demands on him or oppress him with guilt; he is freer to make the most of *this* life.

One concludes that Hume does not object to the spirit becoming flesh, as long as it is the flesh of a worldly Jupiter and not of an unworldly Jesus. For that matter, whether frolicking on earth or disporting himself on Olympus, Jove remains very human, quite in contrast to Jehovah, who is often very mysterious and unapproachable. And what are the consequences of taking either conception of the Deity seriously? The entire history of persecution, including the seventeenth century in England, shows unmistakably what happens when a somewhat more sophisticated type of incarnation *is* taken seriously, when the spirit is believed to illuminate the individual will. By contrast, the other sort of incarnation has a strikingly different complexion. The ancient mythology, to Hume, is inherently comical and absurd, and yet it makes for pleasant stories and even great art. It is vivifying and occasionally exemplary. We are hardly apt to give it much credence, but if we did, our mood would be happy and our behavior hedonistic at worst:

> ... the fables of the pagan religion were, of themselves, light, easy, and familiar; without devils or seas of brimstone, or any objects, that could much terrify the imagination. Who could forbear smiling, when he thought of the loves of *Mars* and *Venus*, or the amorous frolics of *Jupiter* and *Pan*? In this respect, it was a true poetical religion; if it had not rather too much levity for the graver kinds of poetry. We find that it has been adopted by modern bards; nor have these talked with greater freedom and irreverence of the gods, whom they regarded as fictions, than the antients did of the real objects of their devotion. (*NHR*, 75)

Hume laughs at the reason why the *Amphitrion* of Aristophanes was staged at Rome: "The *Romans* supposed, that, like all old letchers, [Jupiter] would be highly pleased with the rehearsal of his former feats of activity and vigour, and that no topic was so proper, upon which to flatter his pride and his vanity" (*NHR*, 41). But how pleasant a representation, and how little calculated to excite superstitious forebodings! Hume keeps the "pious *Alexander*" in his place by mordant irony: "One great incitement to the pious *Alexander* in his warlike expeditions was his rivalship of *Hercules* and *Bacchus*, whom he justly pretended to have excelled" (*NHR*, 63). But the point, notwithstanding Hume's superior vantage, is that this "pious" emulation did contribute to human enterprise

---

[10] Two paragraphs earlier Hume wrote, "... superstition sate so easy and light upon them" (*NHR*, 78), and at the very end of this section he used the same figure: mythology "sits also so easy and light on men's minds ..." (*NHR*, 81).

(as well as to drunkenness, but what of that?) Hume's title for this section is [A comparison of polytheism and theism] "With regard to courage or abasement,"[11] and there is no mistaking his celebration of the courage engendered by polytheism—that is, pagan idolatry.

Despite his claim that men never in fact believe in a spiritual reality, so powerful are the "impressions, made by common sense and by experience" (*NHR*, 74), Hume seemed to fear the possibility that religious preoccupations *could* supplant the reality of nature, unless men were constantly succored by contact with the external world. He did not mind the worship of an idol, as long as the idol remained more of a thing or object than an incarnation. If, to use Hume's phrasing, "profane reason" were to have any chance of defeating "sacred mystery" (*NHR*, 66), it would have to employ the weapon implied by the epithet "profane": it would have to commit sacrilege upon the sacred object, divesting the icon of its mysterious association and reaffirming instead its material reality. This is the intention behind much of Hume's rather crude raillery. The Egyptians worship cats—but only grown cats: they "drown the holy spawn or little sucking gods, without any scruple or remorse" because common sense dictates that "a couple of cats, in fifty years, would stock a whole kingdom" and "entirely starve the men" (*NHR*, 72). So much for feline incarnation. Even the more specious doctrine of transubstantiation, supported by all the learning of the Church of Rome, receives a similar jolt from everyday reality. In one of the "pleasant stories" mocking the real presence, Hume tells of a counter falling by accident among the holy wafers. The unfortunate communicant receiving this hard object exclaims at last to the priest: "*I wish . . . you have not committed some mistake: I wish you have not given me God the Father: He is so hard and tough there is no swallowing him*" (*NHR*, 67).[12] Confronted with such a real presence, there is indeed no swallowing any religious doctrine. Such is the effect of the numerous anecdotes interwoven into Hume's text.

Thus subtly Hume fights religion on its own ground. His treatment of holy objects tends to reverse the sacramental precedence of invisible and spiritual over visible and material. Sensation is first, and the order of reality it suggests displaces the nebulous witchings of imagination. Is the image just an object or an incarnation of the spirit? With Hume the spiritual dimension was a threat, and it can never gain an ascendent over the imagination when one focuses on the physical properties of the object:

---

[11] The section-titles do not appear in the first edition (*Four Dissertations*, 1757). Hume added them to "help the Reader to see the Scope of the Discourse," hoping to answer an objection to *NHR* "that it wants order" (*HL*, I, 250-51).

[12] Hume next relates another blasphemous story concerning a converted Turk who so confuses his catechism that he concludes there is no God because yesterday he ate him during the Eucharist (*NHR*, 67-68).

it is a shape fashioned from oak; it is made of cold, white, heavy marble.[13]
Hume tolerated paganism because its gods were so palpably real, *objects*
of human contrivance first and foremost, incapable of suggesting any
large and mysterious spirit; and when they represented anything beyond
themselves, it was usually something familiar—the sun or the moon, or
deities with enough human frailty and passion to make them our distant
relatives. To be sure, Hume found the ethics of paganism congenial, but
that happy influence on man was, after all, a result of mythology's
palpable incarnations.

Though *NHR* is more pessimistic than the second *Enquiry*, Hume
still believed that men can be basically moral *if* religion does not assume
too much importance in their lives, and it never can when men are not
seduced from believing in the primacy of mundane fact and experience.
Hume seemed to recognize that man needs to invest objects with significance, that he is a contriver of symbols, a Vates or Maker. The recognition of this fact in *NHR*, as it probably is in most of Hume's philosophy,
is grudging and somewhat disapproving. But it exists nonetheless. Hume's
many references to the poets—Homer, Hesiod, Sophocles, Euripides,
Milton, to name only the more sublime—confirm this impression. The
poets tell idle stories, it is true, but in so doing they *can* also demonstrate
the extent of human capacity *in this life*, the resilience and resourcefulness
of man the civilized animal.[14] The subject of art is not unrelated to the
subject of religious images. It is not incidental that along with *NHR*, the

---

[13] Kemp Smith regards this insistence on the literalness or concreteness of images in
the thought process as one of the "chief defects in Hume's teaching in Book I of the
Treatise," namely, "his professed denial of abstract ideas, and his consequent not infre-
quent assumption that all intellectual processes have to be carried on in terms of images
which are in all respects as specific and detailed as the happenings they recall." See
Kemp Smith's *The Philosophy of David Hume* (London, 1949), 427-48. Whether or not
it is a defect, this tendency in Hume's thought does support the argument that Hume
considered concrete referents as essential to ratiocination and conceivably, then, as an-
tidotes to theogenic fantasy. Thus consider, for example, this confident assertion in the
Treatise: "A person, who desires us to consider the figure of a globe of white marble
without thinking on its colour desires an impossibility . . ." (*T*, 25); or this statement in
the first *Enquiry*: "An extension, that is neither tangible nor visible, cannot possibly be
conceived; and a tangible or visible extension, which is neither hard nor soft, black nor
white, is equally beyond the reach of human conception" (*Enquiries*, 154-55).

[14] No philosopher ready to banish the poets from the republic would remark in a
footnote (and by the way, in Hume the footnotes often contain his most intriguing
material): "The following lines of *Euripides* are so much to the present purpose that I
cannot forbear quoting them: . . . [and I cannot forbear quoting his translation, though
Hume also gives the Greek first] *There is nothing secure in the world; no glory, no*
prosperity. The gods toss all life into confusion; mix every thing with its reverse; that all
of us, from our ignorance and uncertainty, may pay them the more worship and reverence"
(*NHR*, 35n). The citation supports Hume's attack on religion, but it also underlines that
sense of human frailty and helplessness which Hume actually pitied—what we might
call the "poetical" dimension of *NHR*.

leading work in the *Four Dissertations* of 1757, two of the others, *Of Tragedy* and *Of the Standard of Taste*, concern art and its religious uses.

Of Tragedy seeks to explain how a representation of human suffering can please. We need not follow the details of Hume's explanation here,[15] but we should note that underlying Hume's reasoning is an assumption about art perfectly consonant with Hume's ideas about images. Tragic art pleases because it demonstrates man's ability to shape his suffering and thereby control it; he emerges a victor, not a victim. The emphasis is always to be on *this* life, not on an afterlife. For Hume tragic art must display man in an active role, wresting a kind of triumph from defeat, exhibiting "a noble courageous despair." The most pernicious art, on the other hand, panders to gloom and weakness, to *otherworldly* values, by showing only "passive suffering" in "such horrible subjects as crucifixions and martyrdoms" (*Works*, III, 265). That religion should foster this corrupting art comes as no surprise to a reader of *NHR*.

The last dissertation is *Of the Standard of Taste*. For Hume taste was not just a metaphor. We taste art or we taste morality just as we taste food. It is interesting and significant that Hume would place so much emphasis on the objective reality of what taste discovers. In other words, this esthetic *and* moral faculty does not rely on inspiration from without—or from within, as in the case of a fanatical imagination—but detects only the secondary qualities of objects. Hume tells the story of Sancho's two kinsmen in *Don Quixote* who respectively tasted leather and iron in their wine; though ridiculed by their companions, they had their good taste confirmed by the discovery of a key attached to a leather thong in the hogshead (*Works*, III, 272-73). It is a real presence, we are tempted to think, but the wine's essence is altered by a very sensible and ordinary phenomenon. (I would suggest that Hume may be implying that *taste* would always belie the miracle of the consecrated wine.) Taste depends upon a clear understanding, experience, freedom from prejudice, but all these advantages derive from an accurate sensation of external reality. Few will have good taste, but those few will be capable of judging correctly, whether of wine, art, or morality. Hume simply left no room for the vagaries of a superstitious imagination.[16]

To an important extent, then, *The Natural History of Religion* and much of Hume's later work concern the nature of incarnate symbols. What are the implications of fusing outward and visible signs with invisible, spiritual power? How strong is our belief in such incarnation,

[15] A superb analysis is that of Ralph Cohen, "The Transformation of Passion: A Study of Hume's Theories of Tragedy," *Philological Quarterly*, 41 (1962), 450-64; and "The Rationale of Hume's Literary Inquiries," a contribution to *David Hume: Many-Sided Genius*, 97-115.

[16] As with *Of Tragedy*, *Of the Standard of Taste* ends with a warning about how a corrupt taste, nurtured by religious zeal, can vitiate and disfigure art (*Works*, III, 283-84).

and what is its power for good or ill? How are the images of religion and art intertwined? I have argued that Hume came to appreciate how extensive and deep-seated is man's belief in this incarnation, and Hume concluded that such belief is not necessarily pernicious, if tempered and restrained by the precedence of object over spirit—rather more of the outward and visible sign than of the inward and spiritual grace. He may have begun with a skeptical rejection of any spiritual order and especially of the foolish idolatry, indeed the abject superstition, which faith in such an order often breeds. Hume saw, however, that skepticism is not for most men, and that even arrant idolatry, object-centered and buttressed by the world of sensation, is far more productive of happiness and stability in human civilization than the idle fantasies of a solitary imagination.[17]

University of South Carolina.

---

[17] In Hume's later Tudor (1759) and medieval (1762) volumes of the *History*, one will find no strong condemnation of idolatry per se. Certainly the enlightened Hume had little sympathy with anything medieval, most of all, the medieval Church; but he blamed the Church mainly for priestcraft and the reliance on terrifying mystery. Indeed, at one point he came close to defending the Catholics against Protestant ridicule: "Protestant historians mention . . . with great triumph [various absurd relics]. But such fooleries, as they are to be found in all ages and nations, and even took place during the most refined periods of antiquity, form no particular or violent reproach to the Catholic religion" (*History*, Ch. XXXI).

PART THREE

HUME AS HISTORIAN

IX

HUME, HISTORY, AND HUMAN NATURE

By S. K. Wertz

I. David Hume has been frequently accused by his critics of having grossly misunderstood the nature of historical judgment, and consequently, of failing to grasp the elements constituting the historical enterprise. General consensus has it that his idea of history is inadequate for a reason not unique to Hume but shared by all eighteenth-century historians and perhaps the most predominant (if not the most remembered) characteristic of eighteenth-century historiography. The major flaw in Hume's understanding, as the critics see it, is in his conception of human nature. The statement from Hume most frequently quoted in this regard comes from the first *Inquiry:* "Mankind are so much the same, in all times and places, that history informs us of nothing new or strange in this particular. Its chief use is only to discover the constant and universal principles of human nature."[1] In the course of this paper, I shall examine the interpretation and argument which critics have based on these two sentences, and then reexamine Hume's writings in the light of the accusations. I shall show that the critics' view is simply mistaken or unfounded, and that Hume's idea of history is far more sophisticated and individual than the critics' view of it.

David H. Fischer is one of the most recent historians to single Hume out in this regard, and has gone so far as to say that this type of reasoning employed in history constitutes a fallacy. Fischer dubs this as "the fallacy of the universal man."[2] This fallacy is allegedly committed when an historian makes inferences on the assumption that a people or individuals are intellectually and psychologically the same in all times, places, and circumstances. But such an assumption does not rest on historical premises; an historical judgment or conclusion should be based on historical statements—not on nonhistorical assumptions like the above. Human nature is assumed to remain constant, and from this nonhistorical premise we are supposed to infer historical particulars (continuities). Fischer cites an American Civil War historian, Kenneth Stampp, as an example: "I have assumed that the slaves were merely

[1] David Hume, *An Inquiry Concerning Human Understanding,* ed. C. W. Hendel (Indianapolis, 1955), 93.

[2] David H. Fischer, *Historians' Fallacies: Toward a Logic of Historical Thought* (New York, 1970), 203–06. Fischer's reference to Hume's work is misleading: the passage quoted above is from the first *Inquiry* and not what we now call the *Essays,* which is the *Moral and Political Essays.* (The *Philosophical Essays* was an earlier work on the human understanding, and not to be confused with the former essays.)

ordinary human beings, that innately Negroes *are,* after all, only white men with black skins, nothing more, nothing less."[3] The fallacy which occurs here is that it is assumed as self-evident that Stampp himself would have responded in much the same way an African Negro slave would have in his predicament, and hence, an African Negro slave *did* respond in the same way as a white liberal professor of history who worked in twentieth-century Berkeley, California, would if he were shackled, put on a block, and then sold to a nineteenth-century plantation owner in Bibb County, Alabama. Such armchair reasoning is no substitute for empirical investigation when the latter is called for. Needless to say, African Negroes—much less nineteenth-century ones—do not fit into this white liberal stereotype. This sort of reasoning ignores important cultural differences and certain institutional changes at that time which did affect the Black consciousness and behavior, and these changes and differences need to be listed as among the characteristics of the African Negro—they should be reflected in the historian's judgment or reasoning. The conclusion does not follow from the premise supplied; hence the argument is a *non sequitur,* and more precisely, a fallacy of *a priori* motivation.

A passage from Hume's *History of England* which is suggestive of this sort of fallacious reasoning occurs in his discussion of the scandals in the political parties of late seventeenth-century England, where Hume adds that:

Charles I was a tyrant, a Papist, and a contriver of the Irish massacre: the church of England was relapsing fast into idolatry: puritanism was the only true religion, and the covenant the favourite object of heavenly regard. Through these delusions the party proceeded, and what may seem wonderful, still to the increase of law and liberty, till they reached the imposture of the popish plot, a fiction which exceeds the ordinary bounds of vulgar credulity. *But however singular these events may appear, there is really nothing altogether new in any period of modern history:* and it is remarkable, that tribunitian arts, though sometimes useful in a free constitution, have usually been such as men of probity and honour could not bring themselves either to practise or approve.[4]

"Man-in-general" or mankind does not change from one time, place, or circumstance to another; this is the reason behind Hume's (italicized) remark. So when we find Hume opening his narrative as follows, what

[3]Kenneth Stampp, *The Peculiar Institution: Slavery in the Ante-Bellum South* (New York, 1965), vii. My discussion of Stampp as an example of the fallacy of the universal man varies from Fischer's: mine is couched more in argumentative terms and in the context of inference, where Fischer's is concerned with assumptions. For a criticism of Fischer's general conception of fallacies, see Louis O. Mink's review essay in *History and Theory,* 10 (1971), 107–22, esp. 109f.

[4]David Hume, *History of England,* 6 vols. (New York, 1880), VI, 319; italics mine.

we shall expect to find in the *History of England* when he makes historical comparisons is similarities and continuities: "The only certain means by which nations can indulge their curiosity in researches concerning their remote origin, is to consider the language, manners, and customs of their ancestors, and to compare them with those of the neighbouring nations."[5] Another historiographer, J. B. Black, would also support Fischer's interpretation. Black argues that "Hume sees only similarity."[6] These conceptions form a commonplace view of Hume which may be seen most clearly in Black's account, and for convenience, may be labeled as "the standard interpretation."[7]

Black, on behalf of the standard interpretation, maintains that: "Hume did not grasp the elements of the problem [of historical explanation], because he was dominated, as indeed were all the eighteenth-century *philosophes,* by the belief that human nature was uniformly the same at all times and places" (86). Nor is Black alone on this point. Alfred Stern also holds that "Hume maintained the thesis of an invarible human nature."[8] And R. G. Collingwood likewise held that Hume, like other men of the Enlightenment, was barred "from scientific history by a substantialistic view of human nature which was really inconsistent with his philosophical principles [his skepticism]," and that "Human nature was conceived substantialistically as something static and permanent, an unvarying substratum underlying the course of historical changes and all human activities. History never repeated itself but human nature remained eternally unaltered."[9]

So critics agree that the concept of human nature is central to Hume's idea of history, and in this connection he is often grouped with his contemporaries, Montesquieu and Voltaire. However, this interpretation has been pushed so far that when one carefully looks at Hume and then at the standard interpretation, one becomes suspicious, for there exists a marked difference between his words and their in-

[5] Hume, *History,* I, 1. Reprinted in *David Hume: Philosophical Historian,* eds. D. H. Norton and R. H. Popkin (Indianapolis, 1965), 111.

[6] J. B. Black, *The Art of History: A Study of Four Great Historians of the Eighteenth Century* (New York, 1965), 86.

[7] Black, "Hume," *ibid.,* 77–116. The following historians also adopt the standard interpretation: H. E. Barnes, *A History of Historical Writing* (2nd ed., New York, 1963), 148, 155–59, 167; S. B. Barnes, "The Age of Enlightenment," *The Development of Historiography,* eds. M. A. Fitzsimmons and A. G. Pundt (Harrisburg, 1954), 155–57; Duncan Forbes, "Introduction," in his edition of Hume's *History of Great Britain* (Baltimore, 1970), 16; T. P. Peardon, *The Transition in English Historical Writing, 1760–1830* (New York, 1966), 9–23; and J. W. Thompson, *History of Historical Writing,* 2 vols. (New York, 1942), II, 69–72.

[8] Alfred Stern, *Philosophy of History and the Problem of Values* (S'Gravenhage, 1962), 147. Stern cites the same passage from the *Inquiry* that Fischer does.

[9] R. G. Collingwood, *The Idea of History* (London and New York, 1946), 76 and 82 respectively.

terpretation. Indeed, one begins to understand why an historian like Laurence L. Bongie makes the methodological remark: "He [the historian] should consult Hume and Montesquieu, not the reason of the Age of Reason."[10] Much of Hume's argument and reasons are missed by the standard interpretation. In fact, much of this view, I shall argue, is not representative of Hume's idea of history at all. Collingwood goes so far as to suggest that the historical outlook (the Enlightenment's and Hume's) was not genuinely historical (77). So, a portrait of Hume as a philosophical historian struggling with problems and attempting to find historical solutions is absent.

In the remainder of this paper, I shall construct a competing interpretation which is truer to the spirit of Hume's letter than the standard interpretation. I shall also attempt to show that the statements singled out in the standard interpretation which leads Fischer and others to conclude that Hume was a victim of the fallacy of universal human nature in his historical procedure suggest a different meaning and implications than what has been attributed to them.

II. Let us first make some concessions. As an historian Hume was very much concerned with continuities and similarities in making historical comparisons. A glance at any of the six volumes of the *History* testifies to that; for example, his comparison between the government of England in the reign of Elizabeth and that of Turkey (IV, 207). A preoccupation with similarities and continuities is part of the historian's disease. But as Fischer says, "Significant elements of continuity cannot be understood without a sense of the discontinuities, too" (204). This is obviously a large part of what constitutes historical understanding; the location of some happening or phenomenon into its period (or some equivalent concept) with the sort of observations and judgments which reflect a delicate balance between periodization and individualization— between continuity and discontinuity—is one of the marks of the historian's activity. Now the question is, Does Hume possess any such balance—a sense for discontinuities, too? To answer this question, let us look at Hume's narrative.

In his discussion of Charles I, Hume makes the following judgment:

But as these [strict legal] limitations were not regularly fixed during the age of Charles, nor at any time before; so was this liberty totally unknown, and was generally deemed, as well as religious toleration, incompatible with all good government. No age or nation, among the moderns, had ever set an example of such an indulgence: and it seems unreasonable to judge of the measures embraced during one period, by the maxims which prevail in another (IV, 469).

This passage suggests that Hume was aware that the historian must be

[10]Laurence L. Bongie, *David Hume: Prophet of the Counter-Revolution* (London and New York, 1965), 71.

careful not to fall into the error of reading one's own concepts and values back into those of other periods. In a passage from the *Treatise*, which offers some explanation as to why one is tempted to reason this way, Hume states:

To this principle [sympathy] we ought to ascribe the great uniformity we may observe in the humours and turn of thinking of those of the same nation; and 'tis much more probable, that this resemblance arises from sympathy, than from any influence of the soil and climate, which, tho' they continue invariably the same, are not able to preserve the character of a nation the same for a century together.[11]

So what similarity the historian observes within a given period or nation is to be sought for in (and attributed to) *sympathy*. And furthermore, similarities observed between periods and nations in historical comparisons have the same origin, on Hume's account.[12] So the historian's observed similarities are based on the principle of the uniformity of human nature. But it is here where the critics of Hume have done less than justice to his historical epistemology.

Hume identifies the uniformity of "the humours and turn of thinking" with "the character of a nation." This is given content by Hume's argument concerning liberty and necessity in the first *Inquiry:*

The mutual dependence of men is so great in all societies that scarce any human action is entirely complete in itself or is performed without some reference to the actions of others, which are requisite to make it answer fully the intention of the agent. . . . In proportion as men extend their dealings and render their intercourse with others more complicated, they always comprehend in their schemes of life a greater variety of voluntary actions which they expect, from the proper motives, to co-operate with their own. In all these conclusions they take their measures from past experiences (98).

When Hume adds that "men . . . are to continue in their operations the same that they have ever found them," he has in mind something like the following example from the first *Inquiry:* "He [an artisan] also expects that when he carries his goods to market and offers them at a reasonable price, he shall find purchasers and shall be able, by the money he acquires, to engage others to supply him with those commodities which are requisite for his subsistence" (98-99). Hume does not have in mind, as many have suggested, the specific actions of the artisan in this economic-socio-political framework as part of the uni-

[11]David Hume, *A Treatise of Human Nature*, ed. L. A. Selby-Bigge (Oxford, 1888), 316–17.
[12]The basis for this can be seen, for example, in the *Treatise* (316) where Hume says that our ability to sympathize with others and "to receive by communication their inclinations and sentiments" extends to those whose sentiments are "different from, or even contrary to our own." How this applies to the past I show below.

formity, such as what the artisan was thinking about along the way, why he must sell on this particular day, that he chose this market rather than another because his relatives were there, and so on. Hume makes this perfectly clear in the following statement on method from the *Inquiry:* "The philosopher, if he be consistent, must apply the same reasonings to the actions and volitions of intelligent agents. The most irregular and unexpected resolutions of men may frequently be accounted for by those [i.e., historian and/or biographer] who know every particular circumstance of their character and situation" (97). In the contemporary idiom of philosophy of history, the latter type of explanation seems to be accomplished for Hume by detailed description, an idea similar to one argued for by Collingwood and William Dray.[13] And, of course, explanation through narrative description is quite a different concept from the idea of explanation according to the principle of uniformity or regularity, which is the one generally attributed to Hume.

The appearance of scientific rigor must not be overlooked when evaluating Hume's contribution to philosophical historiography and the philosophy of history. The Newtonian influence and Hume's success in employing the conceptual achievements of the "new science" in a study of man separates him from previous British historians. The uniformity Hume sought was one which would make of a study of man, including history, a discipline comparable to the new science. His early work, the *Treatise,* marks a step towards laying a theoretical foundation which would make history a respectable, scientific pursuit for modern man, a "moral science." This foundation was due in part to the science of man having to utilize concepts and techniques which are essentially historical in character. Uniformity was one such idea; it can perhaps be better understood in the context of the Introduction to the *Treatise* in which Hume argues that a science of man is not only superior to the other sciences but is also the basis for the others (xix). There is a dependence of the sciences on the science of man because the connection with human nature is "more close and intimate"; and this connection is, of course, sympathy. As he states in Book Two: "Every human creature resembles ourselves, and by that means has an advantage above any other object, in operating on the imagination" (359). Because of this "fact," inquiries that have as their objects human action and human nature are the only ones in which we can expect assurance and conviction. (This assurance and conviction is reflected in Hume's manner of exposition in the *History.*)

Hume's expectations would be viewed today as an oversimplifica-

[13]William Dray, "Explanatory Narrative in History," *Philosophical Quarterly,* **4** (1954), 15–27, and *Laws and Explanation in History* (London and New York, 1957).

tion of man's psychology, if not actually premised on a number of false-hoods. Nonetheless, his expectations are also premised on the discovery he thought he had made in finding sympathy and sensitivity as the keys to understanding man's behavior in the past as well as in the present.[14] Before leaving the *Treatise,* the claims of the standard interpretation need special attention, especially to the extent that Hume held to the uniformity of human nature. I have already given some indication as to what kind of uniformity was sought and what was presupposed by the view. However, to exhibit the variety of meanings of the word "uniformity," one may observe the reasoning in the following theory from the *Treatise.* It is also an excellent statement of the philosophy of history that is reflected in Hume's other writings:

The skin, pores, muscles, and nerves of a day-labourer are different from those of a man of quality: So are his sentiments, actions and manners. The different stations of life influence the whole fabric, external and internal; and these different stations arise necessarily, because uniformly, from the necessary and uniform principles of human nature. Men cannot live without society, and cannot be associated without government. Government makes a distinction of property, and establishes the different ranks of men. This produces industry, traffic, manufactures, lawsuits, war, leagues, alliances, voyages, travels, cities, fleets, ports, and all those other actions and objects, which cause such a diversity, and at the same time maintain such an uniformity in human life (402).

A careful reading of the above passages indicates that Hume makes allowance for diversity, and hence has a probabilistic account of uniformity on this level.[15] From a contemporary point of view, this is what is minimally required of explanations in history. As Karl Lambert and Gordon Brittan have pointed out: "The laws that the 'Humean' account requires can be either deterministic or statistical."[16] And both kinds of laws are found in Hume. Moreover, it is the statistical or probabilistic account that we find to be the case with his historical explanations of

[14]No doubt there is an unnoticed parallel between Collingwood and Hume on this point of historical epistemology. See note 16.

[15]For Hume's discussion of probability, see the *Treatise,* e.g., 403-04.

[16]Karl Lambert and Gordon G. Brittan, Jr., *An Introduction to the Philosophy of Science* (Englewood Cliffs, 1970), 96. Let me digress a moment. These gentlemen would not completely agree with my interpretation, for they (like many others) see the "Humean" account of explanation solely in terms of Hume's famous and overworked analysis of causality. My argument is that Hume's own explanations in the *History* and their foundations we have seen thus far from the *Treatise,* suggest an alternative view of history and explanation in Hume than the one traditionally painted by those who wish to put Hume in the positivist's camp. I am arguing here that one finds considerable evidence to see the definite beginnings of Bradley's, Collingwood's, and Dray's theories of history and historical explanation in Hume's thought. See 27ff. of Lambert and Brittan for their account of Hume's view.

specific actions. (Evidence for this will be presented below.) The stronger sense of *uniformity* (which Black mistakenly regarded as the only sense for Hume) is *Hume's belief in the uniformity of "the whole fabric" of human life.* This belief is in terms of the very conditions of likelihood, the limits of explanation; it is the limits that are deterministic. The distinction between these two levels, the deterministic and the statistical, in Hume's theory of explanation has not been fully appreciated. On the basis of such a distinction, we are able to answer the question: How does Hume think it is possible for "actions and objects . . . [to] cause such a diversity, and at the same time maintain such a uniformity in human life?" Hume's best reasoning in support of this assertion is in the following argument taken from the first *Inquiry:*

I grant it possible to find some actions which seem to have no regular connection with any known motives and are exceptions to all the measures of conduct which have ever been established for the government of men. But if we could willingly know what judgment should be formed of such irregular and extraordinary actions, we may consider the sentiments commonly entertained with regard to those irregular events which appear in the course of nature and the operations of external objects. *All causes are not conjoined to their usual effects with like uniformity.* An artificer who handles only dead matter may be disappointed of his aim, as well as the politician who directs the conduct of sensible and intelligent agents (96; italics mine).

This is the context of the question that Hume raises in the first *Inquiry:* "What would become of *history* had we not a dependence on the varacity of the historian according to the experience which we have had of mankind?" (99). To this potent rhetorical question, Hume succinctly adds: "It seems almost impossible, therefore, to engage either in science or action of any kind without acknowledging the doctrine of necessity, and this [includes] *inference* from motives to voluntary action, from characters to conduct" (99).

This statement is one which leads Hume to affirm uniformity, and a uniformity, at that, mainly of statements and limits. But his concept is markedly different from that of previous thinkers on this point, in that the inferences he speaks of in the above passage are based upon an appeal to analogical reasoning from probabilities. Here the inference is from human action. The statement, of course, never has the certainty of an a priori statement or a limiting principle, so that sort of uniformity is ruled out. Words in Hume's writings like "necessity," "contradiction," and "certainty" are highly misleading (if they are read in a literal, formal way) and probably have increased misunderstanding. An example of this is: "This possibility is converted into certainty by further observation . . ." (96). Probabilities are confirmed by observations, but possibilities are obviously not, since these are modal considerations of logic. Furthermore, Hume almost always adds qualifications to his statements in the *Inquiry*. These qualifications, like the following one, are left out in the standard interpretation: "This [the manners of men different in different ages and countries] *affords room for many general observations concerning the gradual change of our sentiments and inclinations,* and the different maxims which prevail in the different ages of human creatures" (95; italics mine).

So from the *Inquiry* passage above we can expect significant change in the details of nations or national characters. Hume's reasoning seems to confirm, as historians today would agree, that it would be a fallacy for an historian to attribute a characteristic of one national character to another without proper observance of the above maxim.

III. Let us now turn to the *History* to see if our reconstruction of Hume's idea of history and its foundations adequately portrays his account of human nature and action in the narrative. The question concerning the uniformity of human nature in the *History* is a complex one, and cannot be answered straightforwardly as in the *Inquiry*. There are passages which suggest that what Hume meant by "uniformly" does not exclude contingency in human affairs. A possible counter-example of this from Hume is "We may change the names of things; but their nature and their operation on the understanding never change."[17] But the kind of uniformity to which Hume is referring here is physical (rather than moral) necessity; e.g., a chain of events which are necessary but not sufficient conditions for the existence or the occurrence of an event. Hume's example makes this clear: ". . . if he throw himself out of the window and meet with no obstruction, he will not remain a moment suspended in the air." However, in the first *Inquiry*, Hume thinks an analogous type of necessity is present in moral subjects too: "Were a man whom I know to be honest and opulent, and . . . with whom I lived in intimate friendship, to come into my house, where I am surrounded with my servants, I rest assured that he is not to stab me before he leaves it in order to rob me of my silver standish." Hume adds, unless he be seized with a frenzy, but this is to "change the suppositions" (100). The presumption here is in the idea that morals change gradually (95).

Hume attributes "moral necessity" to much of human behavior. It is here that Hume allows for contingency. For example, when an historian reads in a document about the execution of a prisoner who resists it, the historian, through an imaginative effort of what Hume referred to as "physical necessity" (deterministic laws), can consider what that event was like for that particular individual. Thus, the uniformity Hume speaks of is inferred from the principles of sympathy and resemblance to statements about the uniformity of human nature. No understanding of the past would be possible without these presup-

[17] Hume, *Treatise,* 407; *Inquiry,* 100.

positions. Hume's example clarifies this:

The same prisoner, when conducted to the scaffold, forsees his death as certainly from the constancy and fidelity of his guards as from the operation of the wax or wheel. His mind runs along a certain train of ideas: The refusal of the soldiers to consent to his escape, the action of the executioner: the separation of the head and body; bleeding, convulsive motions, and death.[18]

According to Hume, the historian can imagine this train of ideas and use them in his narrative as "fact" (soft data). The events are molded together by their physical (and moral) necessity. On this basis, Hume allows the notion of fact to include imagination, but only insofar as it follows a chain such as is evidenced by nature. It is from this basis and its implications that we find Hume writing the *History* as he does and the many passages which suggest the interpretative approach. An example is the execution of Queen Anne, in which Hume uses only one secondary source (Burnet), and in which the narrative follows the above pattern of reasoning and interpretation of the event:

The queen now prepared for suffering the death to which she was sentenced. She sent her last message to the king, and acknowledged the obligations which she owed him in thus uniformly continuing his endeavour for her advancement. From a private gentlewoman, she said, he had first made her a marchioness, then queen, and now, since he could raise her no higher in this world, he was sending her to be a saint in heaven. She then renewed the protestations of her innocence, and recommended her daughter to his care. Before the lieutenant of the Tower, and all who approached her, she made the like declarations; and continued to behave herself with her usual serenity, and even with cheerfulness. "The executioner," she said to the lieutenant, "is, I hear, very expert, and my neck is very slender:" upon which she softened her tone a little with regard to her protestations of innocence. She probably reflected that the obstinacy of Queen Catherine, and her opposition to the King's will, had much alienated him from the Lady Mary. Her own maternal concern, therefore, for Elizabeth, prevailed, in these last remarks, over that indignation which the unjust sentence, by which she suffered, naturally excited in her. She said that she has come to die, as she was sentenced by the law: She would accuse none, nor say anything of the ground upon which she was judged. She prayed heartily for the king, called him a most merciful and gentle prince, and acknowledged that he had always been to her a good and gracious sovereign; and if any one should think proper to canvass for cause, she desired him to judge the best. She was beheaded by the executioner of Calais, who was sent for as more expert than any in England. Her body was negligently thrown into a common chest of elm-tree, made to hold arrows, and was buried in the Tower (III, 133–34).

In this passage, statements like "When brought, however, to the scaffold, she softened her tone . . ." and "She probably reflected that

[18] Hume, *Treatise,* 406; *Inquiry,* 100.

the obstinacy of Queen Catherine . . ." and "Her own maternal concern
. . ." are difficult to explain in terms of hard data (documents and
monuments). However, according to what Hume means by physical
necessity and moral evidence (and necessity) in the *Treatise,* there is a
basis or justification for the above psychological assertions about
Queen Anne. Also, there is a pragmatic element in statements like
these; they make the narrative interesting and supply connections
among the hard data. Character analysis of historical figures is indicative of the historian's understanding of human nature; and in
Hume, the above statements and ones like ". . . the unjust sentence, by
which she suffered, *naturally* excited in her" utilize his notions of sympathy and resemblance in historical understanding. The statement
"She *probably reflected* that the obstinancy of Queen Catherine . . ."
ending with the "conclusion," "Her own maternal concern, therefore,
for Elizabeth, prevailed, in these last moments . . ." is based upon two
interrelated principles. One is the analogy Hume draws between Queen
Anne and Elizabeth in their behavior. The second is the principle of resemblance: there is the "similar station in life" between the two women.
Hume utilizes this principle to such an extent that he will premise
character analyses on statements like "The method in which we find
they [the nobility] treated the king's favourites and ministers is proof of
their usual way of dealing with each other."[19]

From the context one may say that this statement is a general law
or methodological principle and that the particulars are subsumed
under it or "covered" by it. But these passages and others do not show
that Hume believed, implicitly or explicitly, in a constancy of human
nature which entails that ". . . history is simply a repeating decimal."[20]
*Constancy of human nature, for Hume, is a methodological principle
which makes history possible; that is, possible for there to be any consistency and credibility in what the historian says.* Apparently Black in-
correctly identifies constancy of human nature with historical events,
but this identification is not suggested by Hume. This error is probably
due to Black's failure to draw the distinction between methodological
and substantial uniformity. For instance, "No people could undergo a
change more sudden and entire in their manners, than did the English
nation during this period."[21] Hume makes other statements in the *History* which answer Black's "repeating decimal" charge:

It is needless to be particular in enumerating all the cruelties practised in England during the course of three years that these persecutions lasted: the
savage barbarity on the one hand, and the patient constancy on the other, are
so similar in all those martyrdoms, that the narrative, little agreeable in itself,

[19] Hume, *History,* II, 113.
[20] Black, *The Art of History,* 98.
[21] Hume, *History,* V, 426.

would never be relieved by any variety. Human nature appears not, on any occasion, so detestable, and at the same time so absurd, as in these religious persecutions, which sink men below infernal spirits in wickedness, and below the beasts in folly (III, 341).

This passage illustrates an important idea. The emphasis Hume puts on the narrative relieved by variety shows that dissimilarity was considered important to Hume not only in the structure of an historical narrative, but also in the presentation of an adequate, well-rounded picture of the past.[22] Also, Hume's historical thoughts on individuals and periods are reflected by his use of the notion of human nature in his narrative. His discussion of Queen Elizabeth, which illustrates the myth of absolute constancy of human nature in history, perhaps better exhibits this point: ". . . she knew the inconstant nature of the people. . ." (III, 416). Novelty in history, Hume recognized, arises from individual human actions.

With regard to passion and reason in human nature, Hume remarks about Mary, Queen of Scots:

In order to form a just idea of her character, we must set aside one part of her conduct, while she abandoned herself to the guidance of a profligate man; and must consider these faults, whether we admit them to be imprudences or crimes, as the result of an inexplicable, though not uncommon, inconstancy in the human mind, of the frailty of our nature, of the violence of passion, and of the influence which situations, and sometimes momentary incidents, have on persons whose principles are not thoroughly confirmed by experience and reflection.[23]

Noteworthy here is the reference to persons and their principles which is a methodological technique for evaluating the historical figures within Hume's narrative. It appears from this passage that Hume would assert that what seems to be an inconstancy in human nature for one person or group may not be so for another. This is because the question of the constancy or inconstancy of human nature is couched in the light of principles which are premised on the historian's understanding, or in this case, on Hume's understanding. Also, Hume's idea of historical explanation includes the inconstancy of human nature (in the relative sense) and the exceptional. The individual events are not sacrificed; rather, as the *History* testifies:

We must here, as in many other instances, lament the inconstancy of human nature, that a person endowed with so many noble virtues, generosity, sincerity, friendship, valour, eloquence, and industry, should, in the latter period

[22]The idea of "relief by variety" reminds one of Aristotle's *Poetics* (1459a35), in which he says of the historian that some "episodes . . . relieve the uniformity of his narrative," *The Basic Works of Aristotle,* ed. Richard McKeon (New York, 1941), 1480.
[23]Hume, *History,* IV, 75.

of his life, have given reins to his ungovernable passions, and involved not only himself but many of his friends in utter ruin (IV, 167).

This reflective remark by Hume plays a central role in his concept of history. If there are many instances, or memorable events and characters, that demonstrate the lamentable inconstancy of human nature, and if man is subject to ungovernable passions which affect his life and others, then there are instances which fall outside the uniformity which Newtonian science and philosophy demand. So Collingwood is right in claiming that Hume is not scientific in the Newtonian sense. For example: "[Charles's] attachment to France, after all the pains which we have taken, by inquiry and conjecture, to fathom it, contains still something, it must be confessed, mysterious and inexplicable" (VI, 229). Because there are instances like these (ones where not all the particulars are known), and because they are memorable to man, history is of the utmost importance to Hume. Accordingly, historians should be challenged to provide an explanation of such instances. According to Humean thought, the significant contribution of history is that it discloses the consequences of irregular changes that affect human history. This can be seen in the following passage from the *History:* "This event [the rise and eventual political power of Sir John Savile] is memorable, as being the first instance, perhaps, in the history of England, and any king's advancing a man on account of Parliamentary interest, and of opposition to his measures. However irregular this practice, it will be regarded by political reasoners as one of the most early and most infallible symptoms of a regular established liberty" (IV, 312–13). This typifies a common explanatory model: the irregular shown to be regular.

If all these passages exemplify the subject matter of history, then the principle of sympathy may be seen as the cornerstone of Hume's *History.* For sympathy, and what Hume refers to as "conjecture" (viz. supplying the missing particulars), are the only means to an understanding of the data of history. The consulting of common experience creates the standard or criterion. Hume's slogan in the *Treatise,* "Consult common experience" (487), operates as a disciplinary guide for the historian's imaginative or conjectural use of his data. In detail:

By means of this *guide* [the principles of human nature] we mount up to the knowledge of men's inclinations and motives from their actions, expressions, and even gestures, and again descend to the interpretation of their actions from our knowledge of their motives and inclinations. The general observations, treasured up by a course of experience, give us the *clue* of human nature and teach us to unravel all its intricacies.[24]

This important passage cannot be overemphasized. It gives us a

[24]Hume, *Inquiry,* 94; italics mine.

reasonable account of the activity of a critical historian who is in the process of assessing evidence.

IV. Since we have reconstructed the general lines of Hume's idea of history, we are now in a better position to conclude our earlier discussion on inconstancy or diversity in human action by observing some important ideas which may be seen in several interesting passages from the *History* within their philosophical framework. At times Hume uses the phrase "human nature" to refer both to man's nature and to the actions which proceed from his nature, but he applies it as well to actions that are atypical. Constancy and inconstancy of human behavior on a socio-political level form a tacit criterion for Hume's historical judgments concerning importance and merit for narration. This can be seen in detail by the following passages from the *History*:

[Elizabeth] had established her credit on such a footing, that no sovereign in Europe could more readily command any sum, which the public exigencies might at any time require. During this peaceable and uniform government, England furnishes few materials for history; and except the small part which Elizabeth took in foreign transactions, there scarcely passed any occurrence which requires a particular detail (III, 554).

The great popularity which she [Elizabeth] enjoyed proves that she did not infringe any established liberties of the people: there remains evidence sufficient to ascertain the most noted acts of her administration; and though that evidence must be drawn from a source wide of the ordinary historians, it becomes only the more authentic on that account, and serves as a stronger proof that her particular exertions of power were conceived to be nothing but the ordinary course of administration, since they were not thought remarkable enough to be recorded even by contemporary writers. If there was any difference in this particular, the people in former reigns seem rather to have been more submissive than even during the age of Elizabeth (IV, 185).

Such passages indicate that what is most central to Hume's concept of history is not the similarity among events or persons in different periods; rather, the novel, the extraordinary, and the remarkable which is characteristic of change and important consequences are the data of history. Obviously there are rhetorical reasons for stressing extraordinary events; it makes the narrative more interesting and represents a more complete picture of that period of the past which is under investigation, for it approximates how we experience and comprehend the present. Once the novelty of some event has been recorded and interpreted, historical interest diminishes. In other words, it is the *appearance* (origin) of some new turn in the drama of mankind that is of central concern to history and the historian.

The last of the above quotations illustrates a technique which Hume uses throughout the *History*. Whenever Hume feels that documentation is necessary to substantiate a particular fact in his narrative, he will cite as many primary and/or secondary sources as agree on that point. Hume decides on the authenticity of the evidence from this consensus.[25] Hume's slogan, "consult common experience," means in the *History* "consult the consensus in reports." Hume's procedure here concerning the actions of men, which is derived from a consideration of their motives, temper, and situation, depends on the assumption or notion that people involved in documenting events do not purposefully try to falsify their material. The most obvious counterexample to this (one to which Hume himself fell victim) comes from the Elizabethan period in which personalities and records were distorted and falsified to please the ruling family.

A declaration that the historian employs other means, such as reasoning in the absence of consensus, is suggested in the following synoptic remark:

At this era, it may be proper to stop a moment and take a general survey of the age, so far as regards manners, finances, arms, commerce, arts, and sciences. The chief use of history is, that it affords materials for disquisitions of this nature; and it seems the duty of an historian to point out the proper inferences and conclusions.[26]

So besides the use of history as discovering the principles of human nature, which Black and other historians are fond of quoting, there is this other use—one Hume labels also as a chief use.

The foregoing analysis of Hume on history and human nature has suggested conclusions which are contrary to Black's. The result of this

---

[25] Hume, *History,* e.g., II, 416. Hume's procedure in documentation is perhaps best seen in Vol. I in a note at the beginning in which he discusses the difficulty of writing a history of remote ages. He uses the similarities and dissimilarities of language as a means of historical dating and of inferring what happened among the ancient Britons. Guided by the inferences of earlier historians, Hume says: "We may infer from two passages in Claudian, and from one in Orosius and another in Isidore, that the chief seat of these Scots was in Ireland." (Quoted from *David Hume: Philosophical Historian,* 116n.) The common consensus criterion also explains why Hume's treatment of the ancient and medieval periods is weak; for known facts, source material, and techniques for handling data were of small measure during his time, in addition to there being a certain lack of interest on Hume's part. But even this is not wholly true, for he does give an excellent, unprecedented account of the plight of the Jews in Medieval England. However, as we progress in time historically, Hume relies less and less on this criterion.

[26] Hume, *History,* V, 426. An example of a proper inference for an historian to make would be in determining the origin of an event which had significant consequences; e.g., *History,* III, 369: "This [ca. 1558] seems to have been the first intercourse which that empire [Russia] had with any of the western potentates of Europe." However, Hume probably had more in mind than this. He would also have included political and moral judgments, or at least judgments that are not capable of being true or false by the facts alone, e.g., "the best form of government is. . . ." So on the issue of moral judgments in history, Hume would have sided with those who argue for their inclusion.

is that Hume's view of human nature and its use in historical inquiry is
more diversified and complex than the commonplace conceptions have
made it out to be. Any failure on Hume's part to provide an adequate
conception of history and theory of historical explanation will not be
found in an inadequate static conception of human nature. That concept in Hume's philosophical thought and historical practice is not as
impoverished as some critics have led us to believe.[27]

Texas Christian University.

[27] For further discussion of the relationship between history and human nature in
Hume, see my dissertation, *Humean Models of Historical Discourse* (Ann Arbor,
1970), ch. II. I have explored another issue in Hume's philosophy of history that is important to the topic discussed here in an essay, "Kant and Hume on Conjectures in History," *Aquinas and Kant: Proceedings of the 1974 Lewis and Clark Philosophy
Conference,* ed. T. P. M. Solon (Godfrey, 1974), 79-100.

I wish to thank the Research Foundation of Texas Christian University for a research grant which provided financial support in the writing of the present essay.

X

HUME AND JOHNSON ON PROPHECY AND MIRACLES: HISTORICAL CONTEXT

By James E. Force

In a discussion in this journal, Donald T. Siebert attempts to revise our picture of the relationship between Dr. Samuel Johnson and David Hume. Siebert questions Mossner's contention that Johnson is an implacable enemy of Hume's thought by showing how often Johnson utilizes Humean philosophy. Siebert states that "By focusing on Johnson's treatment of Hume's well-known essay 'Of Miracles' . . . , I wish to argue that regardless of his antagonism to Hume, Johnson by no means blindly rejected Hume's reasoning."[1] Siebert specifies that he wishes to show "that Johnson must have found much of Hume's inquiry stimulating and useful—a kind of thinking to be reckoned with, certainly not rejected out of hand."[2]

To show that "nowhere does Johnson simply brush away Hume's arguments," Siebert especially emphasizes Boswell's report that Hume's argument is right. Siebert quotes Boswell's account:

Talking of Dr. Johnson's unwillingness to believe extraordinary things, I ventured to say, "Sir, you come near Hume's argument against miracles, 'That it is more probable witnesses should lie, or be mistaken, than that they should happen.'" JOHNSON. "Why, Sir, Hume, taking the proposition simply, is right. But the Christian revelation is not proved by the miracles alone, but as connected with prophecies, and with the doctrine in confirmation of which the miracles were wrought" (*Life*, III, 188).[3]

Siebert is right in his assumption that the hard-headed Johnson often sounds remarkably like Hume when, for example, he refuses to believe the miraculous reports of the vulgar and of travelers.[4] Both men detest "enthusiasm." However, Siebert is mistaken in his assertion that Johnson never rejects Humean reasoning "blindly" or "out of hand." In the lengthy citation above from Boswell's biography where Johnson proclaims Hume's argument against the possibility of believing in a miraculous event on the basis of historical testimony, there is ample evidence against Siebert that Johnson is in fact blindly ignoring the essential element of Hume's essay. Indeed, Johnson's statement that "the Christian revelation is not proved by the miracles alone, but as connected with prophecies" indicates that quite possibly Johnson had not even read Hume's essay and only knew of its line of argument in the most general terms, probably via Boswell. If Johnson

---

[1] Donald T. Siebert, Jr., "Johnson and Hume on Miracles," *Journal of the History of Ideas*, **36** (July-Sept. 1975), 543. [2] *Ibid.*, 544. [3] *Ibid.* [4] *Ibid.*

had read Hume's essay "Of Miracles" he would have noticed (given his explicitly stated reliance on prophecy as the chief apologetic argument for Christianity) the concluding paragraph of Hume's discussion "Of Miracles":

What we have said of miracles may be applied, without any variation, to prophecies; and indeed, all prophecies are real miracles, and as such only, can be admitted as proofs of any revelation. If it did not exceed the capacity of human nature to foretell future events, it would be absurd to employ any prophecy as an argument for a divine mission or authority from heaven.[5]

To see how crucial this paragraph is, I will trace the development of the argument from prophecy in the first half of the eighteenth century. Once this historical context is presented, I will show how Hume endeavors to link the argument from prophecy with the argument from miracles only to be able to destroy both. Thus, Hume's attack on prophecies is not accomplished *en passant* but is integral to Hume's skeptical criticism of establishment theism.

I. *The Argument from Prophecy: The Citadel of Orthodoxy*

The argument from prophecy depends on the definition of prophecy prevalent in the first half of the eighteenth century. Johnson's famous dictionary (1755) defines the noun "prophecy" as "a declaration of something to come; prediction" and defines the verb "to prophesy" as "to predict; to foretell; to prognosticate."[6] A prophecy is a prediction and to prophesy is to predict.

In the argument from prophecy, prophetic predictions connect the Old Testament with the figure of Jesus, the anticipated messiah, and thus gives the argument a distinctly historical complexion. With the passage of time, the prediction can be either confirmed, refuted, or reinterpreted.

The argument from prophecy has a long history in Christian philosophizing; it begins with Justin Martyr who is cited, by the deist Anthony Collins, as believing that "predictions fulfilled are the strongest demonstration of the truth."[7] Nearer to Hume's time, Ralph Cudworth makes much of fulfilled prophetic predictions as a test of truth regarding Jesus' messiahship. Unlike the reports of miracles,

---

[5] David Hume, *Enquiries Concerning Human Understanding and Concerning the Principles of Morals*, reprinted from the posthumous edition of 1777 and edited by L.A. Selby-Bigge; Third Edition, with text revised and noted by P.H. Nidditch (Oxford, 1975), 130-31.

[6] Samuel Johnson, *A Dictionary of English Language: in which the Words are deduced from their originals, and illustrated in their different significations by examples from the Lost writers* (London, 1755), s.v. "prophecy" and "prophesy."

[7] Anthony Collins, *The Scheme of Literal Prophecy* (London, 1727), 343.

predictions which are fulfilled with the passage of time cannot "possibly be imputed by Atheists, as other things, to mean *Fear* and *Fancy*, nor yet to the *Fiction of Politicians*."[8] For Cudworth as for Justin Martyr, Christianity is the true religion and its deniers false because the Bible "contained in it so many unquestionable Predictions of Events to follow a long time after . . ."[9] which in fact did follow.

The argument from prophecy, as shaped just prior to the opening of the eighteenth century by John Locke, guarantees the reasonableness of Christianity because of the way Jesus fulfills the Old Testament prophecies of a miracle-worker. Miracles and prophecies here stand in a mutually supporting synthesis, the latter predicting the former and the former confirming the latter. For Locke, the miracles of Jesus are only significant becaue they were prophesied.[10]

The other major intellect dominating the intellectual gateway to the eighteenth century, Isaac Newton, also regards prophecy as the foundation of Christianity. In such prophecies as the seventy weeks of Daniel, which Newton, the Biblical chronologist,[11] understands as a sure proof that Jesus is the messiah because He fulfills the prediction, Newton finds a guarantee of the reasonableness of Christianity.[12]

---

[8] Ralph Cudworth, *The True Intellectual System of the Universe wherein All the Reason and Philosophy of Atheism is Confuted, and its Impossibility Demonstrated* (London, 1678), 714.   [9] *Ibid.*, 713.

[10] John Locke, *The Reasonableness of Christianity as Delivered in the Scriptures* (London, 1695), 55. See also Edward Stillingfleet, *Origines Sacrae, or a Rational Account of Christian Faith, as the Truth and Divine Authority of the Scriptures, and the matters therein contained* (London, 1662), 262, and George Stanhope, *The Truth and Excellence of the Christian Religion Asserted Against Jews, Infidels, and Hereticks, in sixteen sermons Preached at the Lecture Founded by the Honourable Robert Boyle, Esq; For the Years 1701, 1702* (London, 1702), 26. The eight sermons for 1701 are separately titled *The Christian Interpretation of Prophecies Vindicated.*

[11] Newton, as Manuel has shown, regards himself as an historian, as well as a scientist. He considers the prophecies of Daniel and the Book of Revelations which refer to events already fulfilled in history, i.e., the historical prophecies which include those predicting the messiah, as useful sources for historians, if properly interpreted. The problem, of course, is that the greater part of these works is written in language which does not refer immediately to the historical world although Newton, following Joseph Mede, is convinced that the Book of Daniel and the Book of Revelations is nothing less than the panorama of history "from the beginning of the Captivity of Israel, until the Mystery of God should be finished." See Joseph Mede, *The Apostasy of Latter Times*, in *The Works of Joseph Mede*, ed. J. Worthington (London, 1672), 654. Newton fully accepts this view of the sweep and range of these prophecies and works out a lengthy method which is basically a table of conversion. In his unique hermeneutic method, Newton assumes that an event mentioned figuratively in a historical prophecy in Daniel as occurring in the "world natural" refers to an historical event in the "world politic." See Isaac Newton, *Observations Upon the Prophecies of Daniel and the Apocalypse of St. John* (London, 1733), 16.

[12] Newton, *Observations Upon the Prophecies*, 252.

As a youth Newton conjectures about the actual date of the fulfillment of Christ's second coming by incautiously choosing the year
1680.[13] Later he becomes more reticent about interpreting the exact
date of the fulfillment of apocalyptic prophecies.[14]

Unlike Locke (who appropriates miracles into his version of the
argument from prophecy as one of the prophetic predictions fulfilled
by Jesus), Newton relies almost exclusively on other predictions fulfilled by Jesus and ignores miracles as a rational argument for the truth
of Christianity. Newton rarely discusses miracles and when he does
he indicates that they are not really disturbances or violations in
nature's laws but are simply unusual events which excite wonder in
the mind of the vulgar. Newton says, "For miracles are not so called
because they are the works of God, but because they happen seldom
and for that reason excite wonder."[15] As the debate concerning
prophecies develops, this tendency to ignore miracles and concen-
trate on grounding Christian apologetics solely in the argument from
prophecy continues until, under pressure from such deists as Anthony
Collins, miracles are once again pressed into service as a completely
independent rational argument.

By 1713 Anthony Collins had become a leader of the "new sect"
of freethinkers whose members regularly convened at the Grecian
Coffee House in the Strand near Temple Bar.[16] In his first major
rationalistic assault on traditional religion in his *A Discourse on Freethinking* (1713), Collins argues that freethinking is based on the foun-
dational rights of a man freely and rationally to ascertain and weigh
the evidence for his beliefs and to stick to what his reason reveals to
him even when such beliefs are contrary to religious authority.[17] Applying his freethinking to the Bible Collins notes the vast number of
widely differing textual interpretations regarding, for example, the
canon of Scripture, the Trinity, the eternity of Hell's torments, and
the text of Scripture itself. Variant readings on these and other points
necessitate free-thought and the supremacy of reason over religion.
For Collins reason inevitably leads rational men to the abandonment
of revealed religion.

The great classicist, Master of Trinity College, Cambridge, and
former Boyle Lecturer, Richard Bentley, replies to Collins' book by
claiming, first, that the most genuine freethinkers and rationalists
such as the Newtonians and the members of the Royal Society utilize

[13] Frank E. Manuel, *The Religion of Isaac Newton* (Oxford, 1974), 99-100. Manuel
cites evidence discovered in Newton's manuscripts in Jerusalem.

[14] Newton, *Observations Upon the Prophecies*, 252.

[15] Newton, *Theological Manuscripts*, ed. H. McLachlan (Liverpool, 1950), 17.

[16] J. H. Monk, *The Life of Richard Bentley* (London, 1830), 268.

[17] A. Collins, *A Discourse on Freethinking* (2nd ed., London, 1713), 171-76.

the canon of scientific reason to support religion. The scientists who have cast so much light on the workings of nature have all been "hearty professors and practisers of religion, and among them several priests."[18] Second, Bentley, a genuine expert in textual exegesis (which Collins was clearly not) shows that merely because there are many differing interpretations of a particular passages does not render the text utterly unreliable and open to doubt. The critical apparatus of sound scholarship still serves to elicit both the true text and a sound exegesis but, as Bentley shows in detail, these are jobs for real experts and not for amateurs such as Collins.

Bentley triumphs. He shows clearly that Collins does not show any real contradictions in Holy Writ and that Collins lacks the scholarship to pursue such historical criticism. But in applying the critical tools of the classical philologist to a defense of scripture, the Bible is reduced to the level of any other historical document. As Leslie Stephen points out, such a defense is as damaging as the assault itself.[19] Thoroughly routed by Bentley and by the savage burlesque of Jonathan Swift and the counter-attacks of others,[20] Collins departs for Holland. He reappears on the scene in 1724 with a frontal assault on the argument from prophecy in a work which the strident apologist, William Warburton, declared one of the most plausible arguments against Christianity ever written[21]: *A Discourse Concerning the Grounds and Reasons of the Christian Religion.*

It is an indication of the importance of prophecy as a proof of Christianity in the first half of the eighteenth century that Collins chooses to attack Christianity by attacking the proofs from prophecy and the claims of interpreters of prophecy. He ignores miracles as inconclusive proofs that Jesus is the messiah even if they did happen. Like his mentor Locke, Collins firmly believes that the importance of miracles in demonstrating the central tenet of Christianity, i.e., that Jesus is the expected messiah, is that they were predicted in prophecy:

Those miracles were prophesy'd of in the Old Testament, like other Matters of the Gospel; and therefore they are no otherwise to be consider'd as Proofs

---

[18] Bentley writes the following work under the pseudonym of Phileleutherus Lipsiensis. *Remarks upon a Late Discourse* (6th ed., London, 1725), I, 24.

[19] Leslie Stephen, *History of English Thought in the Eighteenth Century*, 2 vols. (New York, 1962), I, 172.

[20] See Swift, *Mr. Collins' Discourse of Freethinking, put into plain English, by way of abstract, for the use of the Poor* (London, 1713). Other replies in the storm of protest to Collins' work come from divines such as William Whiston, Benjamin Hoadly, Daniel Williams, Benjamin Ibbot (who directs his Boyle Lectures of 1713 and 1714 against Collins), the Whig Richard Steele, and the philosopher and future Bishop of Cloyne, George Berkeley.

[21] Leslie Stephen, *History of English Thought, I*, 179.

of those Points, than as fulfilling the Sayings in the Old Testament, other
Gospel-matters and Events or (as a Boylean Lecturer well expresses it) as
comprehended in, and exactly consonant to the Prophesies concerning the
Messias. In that Sense they are good Proofs, and in that Sense only. For, as
I have before observed, if Jesus is not the Person prophesy'd of as Messias
in the Old Testament, his Miracles will not prove him to be so, nor prove his
divine Mission.[22]

   Collins perceives that the core of Christianity is that Jesus is the
messiah, but also that the only "proof" which can establish this core
tenet is the argument from prophecy. If this argument is valid,
"Christianity is invincibly establish'd on its true Foundation."[23] If, on
the other hand, the argument is invalid, "then is Christianity false."[24]
The good deist Collins attempts to show that the argument from
prophecy is invalid by casting doubt on any exegetical attempt by
Biblical scholars to connect the Old and New Testaments. Relying on
the Biblical scholarship of Richard Simon, Collins attacks the *literal*
version of the argument, which holds that Jesus directly and literally
fulfills Old Testament prophecies, maintaining that the very text of the
Bible is so corrupt that a reconstruction of the original text is simply
not possible.[25]

   Collins' immediate opponent in this assault on the argument from
prophecy is his old antagonist, William Whiston.[26] In 1722 Whiston
published his long projected response to the deist criticism of the
"Ancient Knots and difficulties" involved in the *literal* argument
from prophecy entitled *An Essay Towards Restoring the True Text of
the Old for Testament And for Vindicating the Citations made thence
in the New Testament*. Whiston treats the deist attack on the literal
connection between New Testament references to Old Testament
prophecies as a problem engendered by corruptions and mistakes in
our copies of the Old Testament. Whiston's method of correcting the
text is to use the most ancient and uncorrupt versions to correct the
text, which is more or less the way Biblical scholars proceed today.

[22] Anthony Collins, *A Discourse Concerning the Grounds and Reasons of the
Christian Religion* (London, 1737), 33. The "Boylean Lecturer" cited in this text by
Collins is George Stanhope, *The Truth and Excellence of the Christian Religion
Asserted Against Jews, Infidels, and Hereticks...* (London, 1702), Sermon 8, p. 19.
    [23] Collins, *Discourse Concerning the Grounds and Reasons of the Christian Reli-
gion*, 24.   [24] *Ibid.*, 28.
    [25] *Ibid.*, 193.
    [26] Collins, the leader of a group of freethinkers who met regularly at the Grecian
Coffee House in the Strand near Temple Bar, mentions that Whiston "frequents the
most publick Coffee-Houses, where most are prone to show him respect, and none
dare show him any Disrespect; the Clergy either flying before him, or making a feeble
Opposition to him." *Ibid.*, 244. From Whiston's *Memoirs* (London, 1753), 158, we
know that "he and Collins often dined at Lady Caverly's house in Soho Square, and
to have frequent, but friendly debates, about the truth of the bible and the Christian
religion."

In one innovative recommendation Whiston proposes a "Great Search" for the most ancient Hebrew copies "in all Parts of the World," anticipating the discovery of the complete text of *Isaiah* from the second century B.C.[27]

For Collins, however, reconstructing the true text of the Bible is impossible in principle because all prophetic texts are mere fables. Besides, Collins argues "that a *Bible restored,* according to Mr. W.'s *Theory,* will be a mere WHISTONIAN BIBLE, a BIBLE confounding and not containing the *True Text* of the Old Testament."[28]

Collins also flays the argument from prophecy in its *allegorical* form which holds that Jesus fulfills Old Testament prophecy "typically" or allegorically, not literally. The butt of this part of his polemic is the "learned Surenhusius," a Dutch writer who claimed to have rediscovered the ancient Jewish method of deriving a prophecy's "hidden," typical meaning. Surenhusius' rules of interpreting prophetic language include such cryptographic embellishments as "changing the order of words, adding words, and retrenching words, which is a method often used by St. Paul."[29] Collins' point is clear: according to Surenhusius' absurd method, prophecies are made meaningless when they are rearranged to suit the requirements of the particular interpreter.

Collins' all out attack on both forms of the argument from prophecy indicates that he (as well as Locke, Newton, and Whiston) assumes Christianity to be founded mainly on that argument. The avalanche of protests shows how sensitive religious writers were to this line of attack. By Collins' own count there had appeared by 1727 thirty-two intensely hostile replies which sought to defend the argument from prophecy.[30]

One of the most interesting replies to Collins, especially in the light of Hume's "Of Miracles," is Whiston's own counter-counter-attack in which he explicitly attempts to apply the constructive criticisms of the Royal Society to the interpretation of prophecy. Whiston argues that feigned hypotheses have no place in scriptural interpretation in which the experimental method should reign supreme as it does in the physical sciences. For Whiston, as well as for some of his philosophic contemporaries, prophecies are predictions which may be verified to a degree of probability ("moral certainty") by examining the testi-

[27] Whiston, *An Essay Towards Restoring the True Text of the Old Testament And for Vindicating the Citations made thence in the New Testament* (London, 1722), 333. Whiston does make some glaring errors, most notably in his incorrect dating of the so-called *Apostolic Constitutions*. But his general method is sound and also corresponds on many particular points with modern textual scholarship.

[28] Collins, *Discourse* (London, 1724), 196.

[29] *Ibid.*, 60.

[30] Collins, *Scheme of Literal Prophecy Considered* (London, 1727), Preface.

mony of the most ancient historical testimony. Such a procedure is analogous to a scientific experiment because ultimately these testimonies are based on the sense experience, memory, and documents of the reporters. The following text shows how Whiston clearly believes that he is extending the experimental philosophy of the Royal Society, the College of Physicians, and the law courts into the realms of natural and revealed religion.

Nor do I find that Mankind are usually influenc'd to change their Opinions by any Thing so much, as by Matters of Fact and Experiment; either appealing to their own Senses now; or by the faithful Histories of such Facts and Experiments that appealed to the Senses of former Ages. And if once the Learned come to be as wise in Religious Matters, as they are now generally become in those that are Philosophical and Medical, and Judicial; if they will imitate the Royal Society, the College of Physicians, or the Judges in Courts of Justice; (which last I take to be the most satisfactory Determiners of Right and Wrong, the most impartial and successful *Judges of Controversy* now in the World:) If they will lay no other Preliminaries down but our natural Notions, or the concurrent Sentiments of sober Persons in all Ages and Countries; which we justly call the Law or *Religion of Nature*. . . . And if they will then proceed in their Enquiries about Reveal'd Religion, by real Evidence and Ancient Records, I verily believe, and that upon much examination and Experience of my own, that the Variety of Opinions about those Matters now in the World, will gradually diminish; the Objections against the Bible will greatly wear off; and genuine Christianity, without either *Priestcraft* or *Laycraft*, will more and more take Place among Mankind.[31]

Whiston utilizes the constructive critical methodology proposed by John Wilkins (and, with minor changes in terminology, by Tillotson, Chillingworth, Boyle, Glanville, Locke, and Newton) to argue that the evidence that Old Testament prophecies are literally fulfilled by Jesus yields not absolutely certain knowledge but only morally certain knowledge.[32]

Of the thirty-two adverse replies to Collins' *Discourse,* the most common approach (exemplified by Whiston's own response above), is to defend the argument from prophecy. Collins ignores miracles and most of his respondents do, too, in the mad scramble of 1725 to salvage the argument from prophecy. However a second, minority mode of defense shifts the ground of debate by denying Collins' explicitly proclaimed premise that fulfilled prophecy is the only "reasonable" foundation and attempts to vindicate religion on the

[31] William Whiston, *A Supplement to the Literal Accomplishment of Scripture Prophecies Containing Observations on Dr. Clarke's and Bishop Chandler's late Discourses on the Prophecies of the Old Testament* (London, 1725), 5-6. This text is one of the most direct statements of the relationship between religion and science among the Newtonians on this subject. See James E. Force, "Linking History and Rationale Science in the Enlightenment: William Whiston's *Astronomical Principles of Religion, Natural and Reveal'd* (1717)" in the facsimile edition of that work forthcoming from the Georg Olms Verlag in Hildesheim, West Germany.
[32] Whiston, *A Supplement*, 8.

basis of the reported miracles of Jesus. The few thinkers who fall in this category tend to consider the argument from prophecy as a sort of ravelin, a mere outwork, and, conceding its conquest, fall back to what they consider the main line of defense of the Christian religion against the deists, the argument from miracles.

The argument from miracles, considered as separate and independent of that of prophecy, does not, of course, originate in these responses to Collins' attack on the argument from prophecy. If anything, they only breathe new life into an argument which dates back to the early Christian centuries.[33] In the fifty years preceding the writing of Hume's essay there is a steady stream of apologists, from Grotius through Stillingfleet and Charles Leslie, who argue that the miracles which Jesus performed are sufficient to prove the truth of revealed scripture.[34] Nevertheless, the argument from prophecy continued for two decades to be the most important single rational argument for the truth of the Christian revelation. Even Bishop Sherlock, whose famous work, *The Trial of the Witnesses* is one of best defenses of the credibility of such miracles as the Resurrection,[35] accepts

[33] R. M. Grant, *Miracle and Natural Law in the Graeco-Roman and Early Christian Thought* (Amsterdam, 1952).

[34] Hugo Grotius, *The Truth of the Christian Religion*, trans. Simon Patrick (London, 1680), 21. Interestingly enough, even Grotius ultimately understands miracles to confirm Jesus as the Messiah because he performs them as predicted in prophecy. *Ibid.*, 58: Bishop Stillingfleet emphasizes that miracles are the best rational evidence which tends to confirm the truth of a Divine testimony but he also discusses "The Tryal of Prophetical Predictions and Miracles." See his *Origines Sacrae: Or a Rational Account of the Christian Faith, as to the Truth and Divine Authority of the Scriptures, and the Matters Therein contain'd* (London, 1662), 177-78, 184; Charles Leslie, *A Short and Easie Method with the Deists* (London, 1698), 4. Another very important statement of the argument from miracles is one which is independent of and contemporary with the Collins-Whiston controversy over prophecies. This is John Conybeare's sermon, *The Nature, Possibility and Certainty of Miracles Set Forth: and the Truth of the Christian Religion Prov'd from Thence: A Sermon Preach'd before the University of Oxford, at St. Mary's, on Sunday, December 24th 1721* (London, 1722). See also John Green, *Letters to the Author of the Discourse of the Grounds and Reasons of the Christian Religion* (London, 1726) and Theophilus Lobb, *A Brief Defense of the Christian Religion* (London, 1726).

[35] Sherlock's book is written in answer to six essays by Thomas Woolston. In the last line of *The Scheme of Literal Prophecy Considered* (London, 1727), Anthony Collins promises soon to publish "a discourse upon the miracles recorded in the Old and New Testaments" (439). Woolston attempts to carry out this deist enterprise in a work entitled *Six Discourses on Miracles* (London, 1727-1729). Sherlock then answers Woolston by attempting to demonstrate the credibility of the Apostles, who are charged (in a mock trial at one of the Inns of Court) with giving false evidence. Sherlock argues in legal style that their testimony is believable because many men forsake their old beliefs and embrace Christianity because the Apostles are willing to face death rather than renounce their testimony and because there is no *a priori* assumption against miracles. See Thomas Sherlock, *The Trial of the Witnesses*, in *Works* (London, 1830), V, 170 and 182. Like Whiston, Bishop Sherlock puts great stock in the common sense methodology of the law courts.

102

JAMES E. FORCE

prophecy as the most fundamental argument for revealed religion. Whether or not Jesus is the Messiah still "must be try'd by the Words of Prophesy."[36]

By the middle of the eighteenth century, the argument from prophecy was still the dominant argument for the truth of revealed religion. Its formulation grew largely out of a controversy between the Newtonian, William Whiston, and the deist, Anthony Collins. Such is the historical context of Johnson's remark that while Hume's argument in "On Miracles" may be telling against (the possibility of believing) miracles, ". . . the Christian revelation is not proved by the miracles alone, but as connected with prophecies, and with the doctrine in confirmation of which the miracles were wrought."[37]

II. *Hume's Quarrel with the Argument from Prophecy*

It is difficult to believe that Hume could have been unaware of this controversy. Perhaps the real mystery is that his essay is not entitled "Of Prophecy." "Of Miracles" appeared in the *Enquiry* of 1748 (it was excised from the *Treatise* published in 1739). It begins with a section designed to show what the proper method of reasoning is in deciding whether to believe a miracle happened. As in the inference from effect to cause, so too in this case, "A wise man proportions his belief to the evidence."[38] The evidence for miracles derives from human testimony and our own experience and is regarded "as a *proof* or a *probability* according to the conjunction between any particular kind of report and any of argument has been found to be constant or variable."[39]

In the first section, Hume concentrates on the conflict between each individual's experience of the operation of natural law and a miracle. Although Hume considers the idea of necessity in causation indemonstrable, he does recognize a regularity of succession in practical human experience because of a generally observed constant

---

[36] Thomas Sherlock, *The Use and Intent of Prophecy* (London, 1732), 49.

[37] In the phrase ". . . and with the doctrine in confirmation of which the miracles were wrought," Johnson reiterates one of the basic anti-Catholic principles standard since it was first stated by the Bishop of Norwich, Joseph Hall, in the seventeenth century: "Miracles must be judged by the doctrine which they confirme; not the doctrine by the miracles." *The Oxford English Dictionary*, s.v. "Miracles." For the good Anglican Bishop, "Biblical" miracles are true while "Catholic" miracles are false. This polemical point is reiterated in 1752 by John Douglas, later Bishop of Salisbury, in his answer to Hume's essay, *The Criterion: or, Miracles Examined.* Hume's interest in miracles probably begins with the miracles reportedly performed at the tomb of the Abbé Pâris. Mossner conjectures that while on the scene in Paris (Hume stayed in France from 1734 to 1737) Hume's interest in the "problem" of miracles was stirred. See Ernest Campbell Mossner, *The Life of David Hume* (London and Edinburgh, 1954), 95.

[38] David Hume, "Of Miracles," 110.　　　　[39] *Ibid.*, 111.

conjunction of successive events in experience. Laws of nature, for
Hume, are established because of universally firm and unalterable
human experience of such a succession of events. A miracle, however, is by definition "the violation of laws of nature."[40] Because a
miracle is a violation of that for which we have a "firm and unalterable"[41] experience, the evidence for a miraculous event must be of a
degree of strength which is impossible to obtain. The more miraculous
an event appears to be, the more contrary to our daily experience of
the operation of the laws of nature and, consequently, the less believable it is.

Hume acknowledges the possibility of apparent exceptions to
natural law but argues, with the example of the native Indian's ignorance of the freezing of water in Northern climates, that such exceptions are due to limited experience. They are not really violations of
the law of nature but result from a lack of experience, in this case a
lack of experience of the ineluctable regularity with which water
freezes below a certain temperature.

To believe in a miracle requires evidence that is impossible to
obtain because it runs counter to our unalterable experience to the
contrary. And when one considers how susceptible to deception and
error are the historical testimonies of such prodigies, the "plain consequence" is the "general maxim":

That no testimony is sufficient to establish a miracle, unless the testimony be
of such a kind, that its falsehood would be more miraculous than the fact
which it endeavours to establish; and even in that case there is a mutual
destruction of arguments, and the superior only gives us an assurance suitable to that degree of force, which remains, after deducting the inferior.
When anyone tells me, that he saw a dead man restored to life, I immediately
consider with myself, whether it be more probable, that this person should
either deceive or be deceived, or that the fact, which he relates, should really
have happened. I weigh the one miracle against the other; and according to
the superiority, which I discover, I pronounce my decision, and always reject
the greater miracle.[42]

The second section of this essay examines the sorts of testimony
upon which the credibility of miracles is founded to see if there are any
which satisfies the criterion that their falsehood would be a greater
miracle than the miracles which it purports to establish in the first
place. Hume finds no examples where falsehood of such testimony
would be more miraculous than the event it is used to confirm. Hume
first indicts the credibility of enthusiasts who rush to affirm the mirac-

[40] *Ibid.*, 114.   [41] *Ibid.*
[42] *Ibid.*, 115-16. Hume here neatly uses the same standards recommended in
Whiston's mitigated skeptical methodology for the establishment of the plausibility of
"Reveal'd Religion, by real Evidence and Ancient Records" to establish their im-
plausibility. See Note 31.

ulous tales of travellers.[43] Johnson echoes this point in places indicated by Siebert, but the agreement is more one of similar temperaments than a sign that Johnson "must have found much of Hume's inquiry stimulating and useful—a kind of thinking to be reckoned with, certainly not rejected out of hand."[44]

Human fascination with miraculous tales is not the only factor which reduces their credibility. According to Hume, there are three others. First, no miracle has ever been testified to by a sufficient number of hard-headed, enlightened Scotsmen, i.e., "men of such unquestioned good-sense, education, and learning, as to secure us against all delusion in themselves."[45] Second, it is only the ignorant and barbaric who believe in miracles and this "forms a strong presumption against them"—to the rational man it is obvious that enlightenment banishes superstition and hence such reports "grow thinner as we advance nearer the enlightened ages."[46] Finally, no testimony for a particular miracle is entirely univocal; there is always counter-testimony.[47]

Johnson tacitly accedes to these points when he states that "taking the proposition [of the possibility of believing in miracles] Hume is right." Nevertheless, Johnson insists that though Hume is right about miracles, the truth of the Christian religion rests on the argument from prophecy. With this opinion, Johnson joins the ranks of most other apologists in the first half of the eighteenth century.

Believing as he did in the primacy of prophecy, it seems highly probable that, if he had been aware of Hume's argument in detail, Johnson would have addressed himself to Hume's final paragraph. There Hume argues that the canons of credibility which subvert belief in miracles likewise subvert belief in prophecy. Prophecy, properly considered, is miraculous because by his own exertions no prophet could foreknow future events.[48] If prophecy is properly understood,

---

[43] *Ibid.*, 129-30.
[44] Siebert, "Johnson and Hume on Miracles," 544. Siebert cites two examples of Johnson's refusal to credit wild tales about miracles which show Johnson "sifting through empirical evidence in a manner which Hume could have found only commendable."
[45] Hume, "Of Miracles," 218.   [46] *Ibid.*, 131-32.   [47] *Ibid.*, 134.
[48] Hume clearly has to interpret prophecy as beyond human power in order to define them as a sub-class of miracles. They thus require proof in their character as miracles, which is impossible both on the grounds of Pt. II which shows why testimony about the occurrence of miracles is too implausible to be believed and on the grounds of Pt. I as contrary to the laws of nature. But it might be asked why a prophetic prediction which comes true *necessarily* violates a law of nature. There is a sense of prophecy which holds that its fulfillment is just a concurrence between the prophet's prediction and the often quite natural events which come to pass as predicted. But neither Hume nor his opponents use "prophecy" in this sense. For them, prophecies are supernatural, miraculous communications between man and God utterly beyond human power. They are thus violations of natural law and require proof in their character as a miracle.

as Locke understood it, for example, then it is a miraculous violation
of natural law as established in the course of human experience and,
consequently, prophecy is too implausible to be believed. With a
single super-Deistic stroke, Hume does away with Biblical criticism.
The "true text" really does not matter. As long as the Bible contains
miracle stories founded on human testimony and as long as it contains
stories of fulfilled prophetic predictions, which it presumably always
will, no matter how the text is revised by textual critics, it will be in
principle unbelievable. Miracles *and* fulfilled prophecies are violations of the laws of nature and there is nothing which can constitute
adequate evidence for such a violation. The ironic tone of Hume's
remark at the beginning of the essay that he hopes his one argument
will "be an everlasting check to *all* kinds of superstitious delusion"[49]
becomes clear.

Johnson avers that "taking the proposition simply" he finds Hume
is right in his argument. However, when he also adds "the Christian
revelation is not proved by the miracles alone, but as connected with
prophecies," Johnson, for whatever reason, blindly rejects Hume's
reasoning. In falling back from the argument from miracles to the
argument from prophecy, Johnson brushes aside the fact that Hume's
essay is explicitly directed against both.[50]

University of Kentucky.

---

[49] Hume, "Of Miracles," 110. Emphasis added. For a recent catalog of specimens
of Hume's irony in his assaults on our rational abilities to know if God exists, or what
he is like, as well as for an account of Hume's own personal "religion of man" see
Ernest Campbell Mossner, "The Religion of David Hume," *Journal of the History
of Ideas,* **39,** no. 4 (Oct.-Dec., 1978), 653-63.

[50] Very few interpreters of Hume have seen this point. One of the best critics of
Hume's argument, C. S. Peirce, sees the importance for Hume's argument of defining
"laws of nature" in such a way as to emphasize their prophetic or predictive nature
and presents a cogent criticism of Hume's use of the calculus of probabilities in
proportioning his belief or non-belief in historical testimony regarding miracles as the
result of our expectations. But even the astute Peirce dismisses Hume's ironic concluding paragraph asserting that its only purpose is to "fling a gratuitous insult to
Christians, in order to give *éclat* to the chapter and to provoke angry replies." See
Philip P. Wiener, "The Peirce-Langley Correspondence and Peirce's Manuscript on
Hume and the Laws of Nature," *Proceedings of the American Philosophical Society,*
91, no. 2 (1947), esp. 214-28.

XI

WAS HUME A TORY HISTORIAN?

FACTS AND RECONSIDERATIONS

By Ernest Campbell Mossner

When Hume wrote in *My Own Life* a few months before his death, "that in above a hundred Alterations, which farther Study, Reading, or Reflection engaged me to make in the Reigns of the two first Stuarts, I have made all of them invariably to the Tory Side," he was, in effect, deliberately inviting posterity to label him a Tory historian. And posterity has not failed to do so. With Hume and posterity in apparent agreement, there might seem to be no problem at all. Nevertheless, when the entire body of Hume's thought is taken into consideration, a problem appears. For this singular dogmatism over the Stuarts is to be reconciled with the deeply rooted skepticism of the *Treatise of Human Nature* and the *Enquiry Concerning Human Understanding,* with the refreshingly creative skepticism of the *Political Discourses,* and with Hume's persistent claim to impartiality in the *History of England* itself.

The paradox, biographical and philosophical, of this dual Hume who drops his philosophy when he picks up his history is so egregious as to warrant reconsideration. For although perplexing all students of Hume, it has never been faced, fairly and squarely. Only recently an able writer on "The Permanent Significance of Hume's Philosophy" has been forced into the seeming equivocation: "Hume himself was a Tory in politics, chiefly because he disliked the humbug of the Whig historians. But I think he was a Liberal in my large [non-party] sense, like most of the great eighteenth-century thinkers."[2] The present paper, it is hoped,

---

[1] Hume, *My Own Life,* in *Letters,* ed. J. Y. T. Greig, (Oxford, 1932), I, 5.

[2] H. H. Price, "The Permanent Significance of Hume's Philosophy," *Philosophy* (Jan., 1940), p. 8, *n.* 1.

may shed some rays of light in clarification of this Hume of Professor Price, a Hume who is at once a Tory and a Liberal.

But before approaching that central problem, three preliminary questions must be answered: First, precisely what did Hume mean by the statement quoted from *My Own Life*? Second, how did he employ the terms *Whig* and *Tory*? And third, what changes did he actually make during the more than twenty years of correcting the first Stuart volume?

I

1. To be fully comprehensible, the autobiographical passage on the Stuart revisions must be read in its context. Hume is explaining how he came to write the *History of England:*

> In 1752, the Faculty of Advocates chose me their Librarian, an Office from which I received little or no Emolument, but which gave me the Command of a large Library. I then formed the Plan of writing the History of England; but being frightened with the Notion of continuing a Narrative, through a Period of 1700 years, I commenced with the Accession of the House of Stuart; an Epoch, when, I thought, the Misrepresentations of Faction began chiefly to take place. I was, I own, sanguine in my Expectations of the Success of this work. I thought, that, I was the only Historian, that had at once neglected present Power, Interest, and Authority, and the Cry of popular Prejudices; and as the Subject was suited to every Capacity, I expected proportional Applause: But miserable was my Disappointment: I was assailed by one Cry of Reproach, Disapprobation, and even Detestation: English, Scotch, and Irish; Whig and Tory; Churchman and Sectary, Free-thinker and Religionist; Patriot and Courtier united in their Rage against the Man, who had presumed to shed a generous Tear for the Fate of Charles I, and the Earl of Strafford: And after the first Ebullitions of this Fury were over, what was still more mortifying, the Book seemed to sink into Oblivion. Mr Millar told me, that in a twelve-month he sold only forty five Copies of it. I scarcely indeed heard of one Man in the three Kingdoms, considerable for Rank or Letters, that cou'd endure the Book. I must only except the Primate of England, Dr. Herring, and the Primate of Ireland, Dr Stone; which seem two odd Exceptions. These dignifyed Prelates separately sent me Messages not to be discouraged. . . .

But though I had been taught by Experience, that the Whig Party were in possession of bestowing all places, both in the State and in Literature, I was so little inclined to yield to their senseless Clamour, *that in above a*

*hundred Alterations, which farther Study, Reading, or Reflection engaged
me to make in the Reigns of the two first Stuarts, I have made all of them
invariably to the Tory Side.* It is ridiculous to consider the English Constitution before that Period as a regular Plan of Liberty.[3]

Regarding the inception of the *History of England,* this recital
of Hume's is downright misleading. At least as early as 1739
when he published the *Treatise of Human Nature,* he had indicated
an intention of writing history indefinitely in the future; and
again, at least as early as 1745, he had actually begun composition
of certain sections of the English history.[4] What he meant by the
statement, *"I then formed the Plan of writing the History of
England,"* can only be, that in 1752 for the first time, he found the
opportunity in the unexpected Librarianship of carrying through
to a conclusion his still somewhat disjointed historical projects.

Regarding the Stuart volume in particular, several points need
to be stressed. Hume maintains: (1) that he was impartial; (2)
that he was independent; (3) that his work, therefore, was rendered obnoxious to both parties; (4) that his independence is
especially observable in his not turning to the Whigs when it was
to his obvious interest to do so. What Hume does not say in this
somewhat belligerent expression of his independence of the Whigs
is that he wrote as a Tory. The customary inference that independence of the one party necessitates adherence to the other is an
easy one, but should always be regarded with some suspicion. This
initial suspicion must be greatly augmented in the case of a professed skeptic who has publicly committed himself to the proposition that "nothing can be more unphilosophical than to be positive
or dogmatical on any subject."[5] Certainly final judgment ought
to be suspended until after weighing the evidence of the revisions
in the light of eighteenth-century party history.

2. *Whig* and *Tory* are badges covering a multitude of sins.
Party names seldom change, although parties do. Whig and Tory

[3] Hume, *loc. cit.,* I, 4–5.

[4] The manuscript evidence in proof of this statement is presented in the writer's
"An Apology for David Hume, Historian," forthcoming in *PMLA.*

[5] Hume, *Enquiry Concerning the Principles of Morals,* in *Works,* ed. T. H. Green
and T. H. Grose, (London, 1874–75), IV, 253.

of 1750 are not the same as Whig and Tory of the Restoration Era, nor Whig and Tory of the Napoleonic Era. Hume was eminently conscious of the necessity for the historical as well as for the philosophical evaluation of labels.[6] His analysis of *party* draws the distinction between *Real* and *Personal*. A *Real* party represents real differences of political principles; a *Personal* party, mere differences of prejudice concerning persons. *Real* differences include those of *interest, principle,* and *affection.*

In the seventeenth century Hume recognizes real political differences involving both *interest* and *principle,* and also *affection,* between country-party and court-party, Whig and Tory. By the middle of the eighteenth century the first two, though still surviving in essence, have become greatly confused in practice, and Whig and Tory popularly have become factional distinctions without important real differences other than that of *affection.* Their essential real differences begin to become clarified again before the end of the century with the re-birth of a vital Toryism resulting in the final conversion of Old Whigs into New Tories. Not until the Napoleonic Era, however, did Tory become synonymous with Conservative and Whig with Liberal.

In 1750 the clearest real difference between the parties was that of *affection.* A friend to the Stuarts was a Tory, no matter how liberal his political principles, nor how unique his ideas.[7] On his death-bed some weeks after composing *My Own Life,* Hume candidly confessed to the inquisitive James Boswell that he had become friendlier to the Stuart family as he progressed in his historical studies and, further, expressed the hope that he had vindicated the first two of them for good from the aspersions of the Whig historians. Unquestionably it was this personal feeling for the Stuarts that, despite deep religious scruples, inspired the messages of encouragement from those "two odd Exceptions," the primates of England and of Ireland. On an earlier occasion, Hume had told Boswell[8] the delightful anecdote of how the Archbishop of

[6] *Cf.* "Of Parties in General," *Works*, III, 129–30.

[7] *Cf.* "Of the Parties of Great Britain," *Works*, III, 139 and *n.* 2 for the party definitions.

[8] *Cf. Private Papers of James Boswell from Malahide Castle* (privately printed, 1928 ff.), 12: 232; 11: 41–42.

Canterbury had sent him a gift of ten guineas and an offer of an apartment in the episcopal palace at Lambeth whenever he visited London. But however friendly to the Stuarts, it must be emphasized, Hume was never even remotely inclined to Jacobitism, a political lost cause that he heartily detested and publicly repudiated in the essay "Of the Protestant Succession," the conclusion of which, he admits, "shows me a Whig, but a very sceptical one."[9] A philosopher does not confuse feelings for persons with political principles.

The distinction between persons and principles Hume elucidated in a letter of 1756, not long after the first appearance of the Stuart volume: "My views of *things* are more comformable to Whig principles; my representations of *persons* to Tory prejudices. Nothing can so much prove that men commonly regard more persons than things, as to find that I am commonly numbered among the Tories."[10] Nor is there any contradiction between that statement and the published remark of 1742 concerning the Tory party: "There are few men of knowledge or learning, at least, few philosophers, since Mr. Locke has wrote, who would not be ashamed to be thought of that party."[11] For, in the latter case, he was referring to the then political principles of the Tories, involving, as they did, *indefeasible right* and *passive obedience*. It is significant that in the 1770 edition, the passage is omitted as no longer applicable to changing political conditions.

3. The evidence of the revisions of the Stuart volume has never been viewed in its entirety. In 1846 John Hill Burton, presenting a short list of typical revisions in his *Life and Correspondence of David Hume*, concludes that Hume "has not exaggerated the extent or character of his alterations; for an inspection of the various editions of his History which came under his own revision, shows him, by turns of expression, structure of narrative, and other gentle alterations, approaching closer and closer to despotic principles."[12] And although Burton goes on to admit of "a very few

[9] Hume, *Letters*, I, 111.
[10] *Ibid.*, I, 237.
[11] Hume, *Works*, III, 143.
[12] Burton, *Life and Correspondence of David Hume* (Edinburgh, 1846), II, 74-75.

alterations in an opposite spirit,'' his apparent general confirmation of the isolated sentence from *My Own Life* has precluded further and fuller investigations. Yet two considerations invalidate Burton's judgment: in the first place, he has not systematically examined all of the revisions; and, in the second place, he is clearly not giving party names their mid-eighteenth-century connotations.

The following *Table of Revisions*[13] is the result of a systematic collation of four different editions of the apposite volumes of the *History of England*, representing the early, the middle, and the late stages of revision. 148 variants have been noted and classified as *Whig, Tory,* or *Neutral.* By *Whig* is indicated sympathy for the Parliamentarians or antipathy toward the Stuarts. By *Tory* is indicated sympathy for the Stuarts or antipathy toward the Parliamentarians. By *Neutral* is indicated no expression of feeling for either Stuarts or Parliamentarians. The category of *Neutral* is not to be confused with purely stylistic changes, of which there are a great many, nor yet with Hume's general policy of toning-down. For the last, there is the express authority of Gibbon: ''Mr. Hume told me that in correcting his history he always laboured to reduce superlatives and soften positives.''[14]

The classification[15] employed in the *Table of Revisions* is in

[13] The actual editions collated were those of 1754, 1759, 1767, and 1792. But as the 1767 edition represents changes that appeared first in 1762, and as the 1792 edition represents changes that appeared first in 1778, the dates 1762 and 1778 have been substituted in the *Table of Revisions.*

For generous and able assistance in the preparation of the collation, the writer wishes to express sincere thanks to the following members of the English Department and graduate students at Syracuse University: the Misses Bentley, Crum, Drew, and Murray; and Messrs. Carr, Elmer, Grover, Kirchofer, Korstad, Kreinheder, Roach, Shafer, and Waite.

[14] Note in Gibbon's hand in the first volume of the *Decline and Fall* in the British Museum. *Cf.* D. M. Low, *Edward Gibbon, 1737-1794* (London, 1937), p. 20.

[15] A few examples under each heading will be given by way of illustration, those previously cited by Burton being avoided.

Whig

(1) [change favoring Parliamentarians]

(1754), p. 328: "That the same violence by which he had so long been oppressed, might not still reach him, and extort his consent to the dishonorable and pernicious ordinance of the militia, Charles had resolved to remove farther from London."

complete consonance with the opinions of Hume already outlined. Though admittedly not definitive, nor—because of the necessarily subjective element—partaking of the force of factual statistics, the resultant figures are yet suggestive.

Table of Revisions to the "Reigns of the two first Stuarts" (1754)

	Date	Whig	Tory	Neutral	Total	Percent
	1759	11	32	40	83	56.1 [56]
	1762	4	15	7	26	17.6 [18]
	1778	9	18	12	39	26.3 [26]
Total		24	65	59		
Percent		16.3	43.9	39.8		
		[16]	[44]	[40]		

(1759 and later) : "That the same violence by which he had so long been oppressed, might not still reach him, and extort his consent to the militia bill, Charles had resolved to remove farther from London."

(2) [change opposing Stuarts]

(1754), p. 309: "Never sovereign [Charles I] was blessed with more moderation of temper, with more justice, more humanity, more honor, or a more magnanimous disposition."

(1778) : "Never was sovereign blessed with more moderation of temper, with more justice, more humanity, more honour, or a more gentle disposition."

(3) [omission of anti-Parliamentarian passage]

(1754), p. 432: "The sacred character, which gives the priesthood such authority over mankind, becoming more venerable from the sufferings endured for the sake of principle by these distressed royalists, aggravated the general indignation against their prosecutors, *who had robbed them of possessions, secured to them by every law, human and divine, with which the nation had hitherto been acquainted.*" [Clause in italics later omitted.]

Tory

(1) [change favoring Stuarts]

(1754), p. 156: "But he [Charles I] was too apt, in imitation of his father, to consider these promises as temporary expedients, which, after the dissolution of the parliament, he was not any farther to regard."

(1759 and later) : "But he was apt, in imitation of his father, to imagine, that the parliament, when they failed of supplying his necessities, had, on their part, freed him from the obligation of a strict performance."

(2) [change opposing Parliamentarians]

(addition in 1778) : "Charles, naturally disgusted with parliaments, who, he found, were determined to proceed against him with unmitigated rigour, both in invading his prerogative, and refusing him all supply, resolved not to call any more, till he should see greater indications of a compliant disposition in the nation."

A study of this *Table of Revisions* suggests three inferences:
(1) From the biographical viewpoint, the majority of the alterations were made early: some 56 percent during the first period; 18
percent during the middle period; and 26 percent during the latest.
And not only were they made early, but half of the Tory changes
were made in the first revision of 1759.

This conclusion is in specific contradiction of the insinuation of
Burton that Hume progressed steadily in the direction of "despotic
principles." The preponderance of early changes was the necessary consequence of writing the *History of England* backwards.

---

(3) [omission of passage favoring Parliamentarians]
(1754), p. 30: "most of their [the parliament's] measures, during this session, were
sufficiently respectful and obliging; though they still discover a vigilant spirit, and
a careful attention towards public good and national liberty."
[1778 omits *public good and* in the last clause.]

The above Tory changes may be compared with Hume's own list of revisions
"from the plaguy Prejudices of Whiggism." *Cf.* letter of March 12, 1763, in Hume,
Letters, I, 379.

Neutral

(1) [changes necessitated after appearance of Tudor volume]
(additional note in 1759 and later): "This history of the house of Stuart was written
and published by the author before the history of the house of Tudor: Hence it
happens that some passages, particularly in the present Appendix, may seem to be
repetitious of what was formerly delivered in the reign of Elizabeth. The author,
in order to obviate this objection, has cancelled some few passages in the foregoing
chapters."

(2) [omission of philosophical passages; *cf. n.* 18 below]
(1754), p. 315: "Such propensity have mankind to discord and civil disorder, that
names alone, without any opposition of interest or principles, will often be sufficient
to excite them, at the hazard of their own lives, to seek the slaughter and destruction
of their fellow-citizens."
[omitted in 1759 and later]

(3) [additional explanation] ,
(added in 1759 and later): "The truth is, after the commencement of war, it was
very difficult, if not impossible, to find security for both parties, especially for that
of the parliament. Amidst such violent animosities, power alone could ensure safety;
and the power of one side was necessarily attended with danger to the other. Few
or no instances occur in history of an equal, peaceful, and durable accommodation,
that has been concluded between two factions which had been inflamed into civil war."

The period immediately following the original publication was also
the period of severest criticism, to which Hume, as will have been
observed, was peculiarly sensitive. Considerable toning-down,
especially of comments on religion, was a matter of prudence.
Finally, it is abundantly evident, Hume revised throughout the
course of his life, indicating a willingness to correct which is the
attitude of the skeptic and the opposite of the dogmatist. It is
decidedly not the attitude of the party historian whose mind is
made up at the outset once and for all.

(2) Hume was deliberately prevaricating in stating that all of
the revisions were made invariably to the Tory side, when actually
some 40 percent are neutral and 16 percent Whig.

The simplest explanation of this distortion of the facts is that,
at the moment of writing *My Own Life,* Hume was seeking to emphasize how completely independent of the Whig party he had been
during a period when a Whig history would have been handsomely
rewarded. This scrupulous avoidance of the venal taints of Whig
association Hume unfortunately overstressed to the detriment of
his own reputation as historian.

(3) In reality, Hume far more closely approximated the ideal
of philosophical indifference or historical impartiality than he
seemed to give himself credit for in the notorious passage of *My
Own Life.*

Like all men, Hume was subject to passions and prejudices;
but unlike most men, he was customarily able to view himself coolly
and fairly. A notable example of his endeavor to maintain a philosophical indifference in the face of distrust of mob violence is
afforded in a letter of 1772 to his publisher, William Strahan:

> If the Press has not got further than the 160th page of the sixth Volume,
> Line penult., there is a Passage which I should desire to have restord. It is
> this: *The full prosecution of this noble Principle into all its natural Conse-
> quences has, at last, through many contests, produced that singular and
> happy Government which we enjoy at present.*
>
> I own that I was so disgusted with the Licentiousness of our odious
> Patriots, that I have struck out the words *and happy,* in this new Edition;
> but as the English Government is certainly happy, though probably not
> calculated for Duration, by reason of its excessive Liberty, I believe it will
> be as well to restore them: But if that Sheet be already printed, it is not

worth while to attend to the matter. I am as well pleas'd that this Instance
of Spleen and Indignation shoud remain.[16]

II

Historical impartiality does not require that history be written
without bias: every historian must have initial assumptions by
which to make interpretations, and such assumptions properly
constitute his bias. Hume's *History of England* reflects, naturally
enough, his political theory which, itself, is the product of his basic
philosophy of human nature. The interpretations of the *History
of England,* therefore, are conscious rather than sub-conscious,
reasoned rather than emotional, explicit rather than tacit. And
Hume is always aware of the broader aspects of history:[17]

The philosophy of government, accompanying a narration of its revolutions, may render history more intelligible as well as instructive. And
nothing will tend more to abate the acrimony of party-disputes, than to
show men, that those events, which they impute to their adversaries as the
deepest crimes, were the natural, if not the necessary result of the situation,
in which the nation was placed, during any period.[18]

One of Hume's best short statements of the utilitarian political
principles guiding his interpretations of seventeenth-century
English history appears in a letter of 1764 to Mrs. Catherine
Macaulay, the Whig historian:

For as I look upon all kinds of subdivision of power, from the monarchy
of France to the freest democracy of some Swiss Cantons, to be equally
legal, if established by custom and authority; I cannot but think, that the
mixed monarchy of England, such as it was left by Queen Elizabeth, was a
lawful form of government, and carried obligations to obedience and allegiance; at least it must be acknowledged, that the princes and ministers who
supported that form, tho' somewhat arbitrarily, could not incur much blame

[16] Hume, *Letters,* II, 260–61. The passage was restored.
[17] The wider aspects of Hume's ideas of history are discussed in the writer's
above-mentioned "An Apology for David Hume, Historian." That paper also presents the general features—as the present does the specific—of Hume and party.
[18] This passage is from the original Stuart volume of 1754, pp. 245–46. It was
later cancelled when Hume decided to omit or to relegate to the foot-notes most of
the strictly non-narrative sections.

on that account; and that there is more reason to make an apology for their antagonists than for them. I grant, that the cause of liberty, which you, Madam, with the Pyms and Hampdens have adopted, is noble and generous; but most of the partizans of that cause, in the last century, disgraced it, by their violence, and also by their cant, hypocrisy, and bigotry, which, more than the principles of civil liberty, seem to have been the motive of all their actions. Had those principles always appeared in the amiable light which they receive both from your person and writings, it would have been impossible to resist them; and however much inclined to indulgence towards the first James and Charles, I should have been the first to condemn those monarchs for not yielding to them.[19]

Hume's political theory belongs to that large, non-party, Liberal tradition indicated by Professor Price. But the practical lessons of history that he teaches are colored by a cautionary skepticism concerning the likelihood of continuous human progress that belongs to what may with equal justice be called the large, non-party, Conservative tradition. Both of these traditions are timeless; but in so far as the one becomes identified with Whiggism and the other with Toryism, then, to that extent, Hume is in both camps. Such identifications, however, were developments of the nineteenth century.

If, then, a specific answer is to be offered to the original question posed by this paper, *Was Hume a Tory historian?*, that answer must take a plural form. For the problem is a problem of semasiology. With some confidence now, in light of the facts and reconsiderations already presented, it may be said: (1) That Hume's *History of England* was deemed Tory by his contemporaries chiefly because it was "inclined to indulgence towards the first James and Charles"; (2) that Hume as a skeptic repudiating the dogmas of both parties is a Liberal in the large, non-party (and, historically speaking, nineteenth-century) sense; (3) that Hume as a skeptic chary of planned progress is a Conservative

[19] *Cf. European Magazine and London Review* (November, 1783), p. 331. This letter does not appear in Greig's edition, but will be included in the supplement to be brought out by Drs. R. B. Klibansky and W. G. Maclagan of Oriel College, Oxford. The letter to Mrs. Macaulay is to be compared with Hume's statement in an essay of 1758, "Of the Coalition of Parties," on the function of his *History of England. Cf. Works,* III, 469, paragraph 3.

in the large, non-party (and, historically speaking, nineteenth-century) sense. It is the nature of the skeptical method to partake of all and to subscribe wholly to none; and the great skeptic fittingly rests content,

While Tories call me Whig, and Whigs Tory.

Syracuse University

XII

HUME: SCEPTIC AND TORY?

By Marjorie Grene

Boswell's report of his last interview with Hume,[1] as well as Hume's statement in *My Own Life*,[2] indicate in the philosopher's own mind a sense of sympathy with the Stuart as against the Parliamentary cause in the history of the seventeenth century—a sympathy developed in the course of studying the period in order to compose the *History*. It has been suggested that this presumptive Tory leaning, dogmatic as it seems in Hume's own formulation, especially in *My Own Life*, needs somehow to be reconciled with the general sceptical position that appears in other parts of Hume's writings. One way of effecting such reconciliation is to show, as Mr. E. C. Mossner did in his recent article in this journal, that Hume's Tory leaning was not as strong as Hume in *My Own Life*, presumably for reasons of policy, said it was.[3] But an alternative solution to this apparent problem is, I think, equally possible. Hume's basic philosophic position may, it is true, be said to be consistent with his professed "Tory" sympathy if that sympathy be reduced to a "leaning" rather than a dogmatic assertion of partisan views, so that the moderate and hesitant philosopher takes his place beyond party lines as an objective spectator in some broadly liberal, non-partisan sense. But it may be insisted with equal force that Hume's philosophic position entails a Tory leaning in a somewhat more positive way: that is, that a man of Hume's position, in a study of seventeenth-century history, would naturally be led more and more by his own fundamental premises to a view very definitely on the Tory rather than the Whig, or at any rate the Roundhead, side of the dispute. There is good evidence, e.g., from the abovementioned conversation with Boswell, or from Hume's late revisions of the *Dialogues*,[4] that Hume did not in his later years essen-

[1] *Dialogues Concerning Natural Religion*, ed. Norman Kemp Smith (Oxford, 1935), 97–100.

[2] *Essays, Moral, Political, and Literary*, ed. Green and Grose (London, 1889), I, 11.

[3] Mossner, Ernest Campbell: "Was Hume a Tory Historian? Facts and Reconsiderations," in this journal II, 2 (1941), 225–235, *passim*. Mr. Mossner's general interpretation of Hume as historian ["An Apology for David Hume, Historian," *PMLA*, LVI (1941), 657–690] seems to me entirely sound; what I am suggesting here is an alternative view of the narrower political question based on a different emphasis but not, I think, on a radical difference in interpretation.

[4] See Norman Kemp Smith's introduction to the dialogues (*op. cit.*).

tially alter his fundamental philosophic views. There is also good evidence, in *My Own Life* and the Boswell interview, that as he grew more intimately acquainted with the history of the Civil Wars, he did emphasize increasingly the Stuart side of the case; in fact, he felt himself to have vindicated the first James and Charles so completely that they would never be attacked again. From these two well-established facts one may fairly infer, as an hypothesis plausible enough for serious consideration, that Hume's Tory leaning developed not inconsistently with and perhaps even as a positive outcome of his general philosophic views.

Certainly Hume is not exclusively a Tory in the most extreme eighteenth-century or Jacobite sense, nor in what he considers the somewhat earlier sense of a defender of passive obedience. Certainly there is always in his statement of political theory and his accounts of political practice a peculiar duality of emphasis; a tension between the two poles of liberty and authority, neither of which can be entirely renounced. That does not necessarily indicate, however, that Hume's leaning to the Stuart side in his historical view is a mere appendage, expressive of a personal liking for James and Charles I, to a thoroughly Whig political philosophy. It is rather an indication that, in politics conspicuously, but actually in the whole of his philosophy, Hume's basic distinctions are almost always of degree. Although, as I shall try to show, Hume's philosophic views do indicate at least in history a definite Tory leaning that is not merely a personal weakness intruding on Whig principles, every such leaning is for Hume just a leaning, not a complete or radical decision; it corresponds in the sphere of moral and political judgment to the logical status a probable inference can have in the field of causal generalization. For that reason his Tory sympathies can always be toned down in the interest of substituting good-humored politeness for angry factionalism. For kindness was Hume's besetting virtue; in fact his "scepticism" as well as his politics is rather the offspring than the source of that fundamental trait. To be sure, such a basic temper does in good part eliminate dogmatism from the philosophy of its possessor; but it does not eliminate an emphasis one way rather than another on moral, political and scientific issues.

The notion that Hume's views in various subsidiary fields are consistent with and in fact demanded by his fundamental sceptical position in the *Treatise* needs further exposition in several directions: with regard to Books II and III of the *Treatise,* to the views presented in the various *Essays* on politics and aesthetics, to the arguments on natural religion in the *Dialogues* and *History of Natural Religion,* and even with regard to the application of the methods of the first book of the *Treatise* to itself. To treat the *History,* whose subject matter seems the most remote from general epistemological considerations, independently of the other, more obviously integrated portions of Hume's writings, is, in a way, to take the last of a chain of inferences before the intervening ones. But if a case can be made out for the connection here, perhaps the case for the integral connection of other, more obviously associated parts of Hume's thought will be strengthened.

The thesis here proposed, that Hume's scepticism underlies his Tory leaning, depends, first, on the interpretation of the crucial terms "sceptic" and "Tory" as they apply to Hume, and secondly, on tracing Hume's metaphysical scepticism through his general moral philosophy (which follows, as he presents it, from his fundamental position) to his particular political bias in the *History.*

In order to connect Hume's sceptical philosophy with his views as an historian it is first essential to establish just what "scepticism" means as applied to Hume. The problem indeed exists because of the conventional notion that a sceptic is one who is chary of "positive" opinions on any subject—and correlatively, one who is especially chary of reactionary opinions, which to the liberal critic, seem more opinionated than any others. But Hume's mitigated scepticism involves, as we all know, an affirmative as well as a negative position.[5] To put it very briefly, the cornerstone of Hume's scepticism is the reduction of all cognitive and moral judgment to perception: perception transformed and transfigured, no doubt, by the laws of association—but those laws themselves are just statements of the patterns in which perceptions, by their own inexplicable chemistry, do generally happen to group themselves. Such a reduction, minimizing the role of "reason" as a faculty of demonstration, making belief sensation and inference custom, is certainly "sceptical." But such a sceptical reduction does not forbid a reasonable though calm adherence to opinions on all sorts of subjects: reasonable because well grounded in a broad foundation of experience vividly retained. In fact, in its analysis of gen-

[5] See, for example, R. W. Church, *Hume's Theory of the Understanding* (Ithaca, 1935), *passim;* especially the treatment of the natural relations and their significance for Hume's system.

eral rules and their self-correcting nature, in its careful distinction between knowledge, proofs, probabilities of cause and chance, and unphilosophical probabilities, and in its enumeration of simple, workable rules for causal inference,[6] Hume's exposition provides in his view an ample basis for natural, moral and political philosophy.[7]

For what Hume means by the "Tory side" the obvious text to consult is his own, in the essays *Of Parties in General* and *Of the Parties of Great Britain.*[8]

In differentiating between Whig and Tory Hume points out three stages which bear on his attitude toward present and past. There is first the distinction between Roundhead and Cavalier, of which Hume says:

> The hopes of success being nearly equal on both sides, *interest* had no general influence in this contest: so that ROUNDHEAD and CAVALIER were merely parties of principle, neither of which disowned either monarchy or liberty; but the former party inclined most to the republican part of our government, the latter to the monarchical. In this respect, they may be considered as court and country party, inflamed into a civil war, by an unhappy concurrence of circumstances, and by the turbulent spirit of the age. The commonwealth's men, and the partisans of absolute power, lay concealed in both parties, and formed but an inconsiderable part of them.[9]

Secondly, there is the distinction between Whig and Tory prior to the Revolution. It is here that the "absurd principles" of passive obedience and indefeasible right make their appearance, though only briefly. But with the Revolution the true nature of the Tories appeared, as against their fantastic avowals of absolutism in the preceding period: "The Tories, as men, were enemies to oppression; and also, as Englishmen, they were enemies to arbitrary power."[10] They are not entirely happy about the "set-

---

[6] *Treatise,* Book I, Part III, sec. XIII; sec. I and XI–XIII; sec. XV.

[7] The close connection of Hume's system of the passions and of morals with the causal logic of Book I is repeatedly emphasized in Books II and III. See for example Book II, Part I, sec. IV, V and XI. The account of the passions results from the same principles (i.e., of perceptions and their associations; see sec. IV) and is analogous in its content (sec. XI) to the analysis of the understanding in the first book.

[8] *Essays,* I, 127–144.

[9] *Ibid.,* 137. Hume here calls the decision between the two sides a very difficult and uncertain one. One senses here, as against the *History*, the difference in emphasis to which the passage in *My Own Life* doubtless refers: a shift, again, of degree not of kind, which a closer acquaintance with the major figures of the civil wars could easily occasion.

tlement in the Protestant line," partly out of affection, partly out of principle. But they showed by their conduct at the Revolution once for all that, though they love monarchy, they love liberty as well. Thus in Hume's terms, the two parties may be contrasted in their personal sympathies, and also in their principles—not radically, to be sure, but in the ordering and emphasis of their abstract allegiance:

A TORY, therefore, since the *Revolution*, may be defined, in a few words, to be *a lover of monarchy, though without abandoning liberty, and a partisan of the family of Stuart:* as a WHIG may be defined to be *a lover of liberty, though without renouncing monarchy, and a friend to the settlement in the Protestant line.*[11]

It is to be noted, moreover, that Hume here distinguishes Tories from Jacobites, in terms of his own century: a Tory does not necessarily advocate either the Roman Catholic cause, or the violent restoration of the Stuarts.[12] Hence, the issue of Stuarts or Hanoverians is—with significant application to Hume himself—rather complicated for partisans on the eighteenth-century scene.

In order to determine the relation between Hume's basic sceptical view and his Tory sympathies, it is necessary to keep in mind just what kind of moral judgments Hume the sceptic could allow Hume the historian to make. It is the essence of Hume's philosophy to derive all the types of human experience from their simplest elements. So, just as the more and the less vivid impressions arising from sensation are sufficient to account for all our cognitive judgments, the calmer and the more violent passions, distinguished in terms of degrees of intensity, are adequate to explain human emotion, together with patterns of association similar to those operative in the other field. This analysis of the passions Hume feels to be not only consistent with but closely analogous to and therefore confirmatory of his analysis of knowledge in the *Treatise*, Book I. And on the basis of this unified treatment of thought and emotion, it is possible to explain the nature and origin of moral judgments, still in terms of "perception" as the psychological material for all aspects of human life. The central question of ethical theory is put clearly and explicitly in terms of this principle: whether it is by impressions or by ideas (the two basic types of perception) that we distinguish between vice and virtue. The

[10] *Ibid.*, 138.

[11] *Ibid.*, 139.

[12] *Ibid.*, 141 (from editions A to P).

answer, of course, is that our judgments of right and wrong depend on a moral sense, occurring "when a character is considered in general, without reference to our particular interest"—a kind of consideration which in turn depends for its possibility upon the "calm determination" of the passions. Such judgments, or better, feelings are divided into four groups: "For we reap a pleasure from the view of a character, which is naturally fitted to be useful to others, or to the person himself, or which is agreeable to others, or to the person himself."[13] And in his account of the four types Hume places greatest emphasis on the "gentler affections" or "social virtues"; benevolence, generosity, etc., as opposed to the more energetic characters like courage and ambition which may be good or bad depending on circumstances.

Hume's analysis of the moral sense explains in general how the historian can pass moral judgment. Moral judgments depend at their very core on the only kind of impartiality possible to any man, a wider range of imagination than the pressure of interest usually permits. The partiality of an historian should be just such an impartial partiality, determined by a wide, disinterested view, in which sympathy in the literal sense dominates the imagination, instead of the narrower vision of the self-interested office-seeker or violently impassioned zealot. Such impartiality, like the probabilism of the mitigated sceptic, of which it is the practical corollary, allows and even demands positive moral judgment: judgment not positive in the sense of "dogmatical" but nevertheless definite enough.

In contrast to the natural virtues, the virtue of justice rests remotely on considerations of interest as well as sympathy.[14] The most general social conventions first of all, and the institution of government secondly, depend ultimately for their existence on the end of private advantage they originally served. But by the operation of custom and general rules, political institutions have come to rely for their sanction on a consideration of public rather than private interest. So when public interest is flagrantly violated the conventions themselves and the judgments based on them would

[13] *Treatise,* Book III, Part III, Sec. I (ed. Selby-Bigge, second edition, Oxford, 1896), 591.
[14] *Ibid.,* Book III, Part II, Sec. I and *passim.* Though the distinction between natural and conventional is toned down in the *Enquiry* the situation described there is fundamentally the same.

presumably collapse;[15] and here Hume denies emphatically the doctrine of passive obedience—though, as we shall see in the concrete
context of the history, with a peculiar twist that restricts the practical importance of the right to revolution far more stringently
than the doctrine, for instance, of Paine or Locke. But against
such general considerations, one must—remembering the all-em-
bracing rôle of perception or feeling in this sceptical system—place
in the balance several other factors which influence allegiance and
counteract the tendency to question government's authority when
it acts against the public interest.

Where the public good does not evidently demand a change, it is certain
that the concurrence of all those titles, *original contract, long possession,
present possession, succession,* and *positive laws,* forms the strongest title to
sovereignty, and is justly regarded as sacred and inviolable.[16]

So factors of custom have, as one might expect, a powerful influence on the judgment, or rather the sentiment, of allegiance; and
where long inheritance or law is lacking, other elements, like present possession, exert some influence. Partly summing up and
partly supplementing all these considerations in a given case, moreover, there is the general tenor of public opinion which forms an
important weight on the delicate scale of political judgments.[17]   In
short, here as everywhere, and more than for the natural virtues,
those feelings we call judgments result, when they are reliable,
from the self-correcting nature of general rules which teach us by
experience how to let various factors take their just weight to bring
about a calm and reasoned rather than a hot and hasty choice.
Against the abstract considerations of public interest and the right
of subjects to maintain such interests against tyrannical rulers,
these influential psychological factors must in most cases be
weighed, and the decision made in terms of the resulting balance
of many values and many feelings.

In the light of this theory of moral judgment, closely integrated
as it is with his basic sceptical position, what particular political
judgments would Hume be likely to draw (a) in studying the history of the preceding century and (b) in looking at the events of
his own time and the more recent past?

[15] *Ibid.,* Book III, Part II, Sec. IX, 550–553.

[16] *Ibid.,* Book III, Part II, Sec. X, 562.

[17] This is partly implicit in Hume's treatment of the preceding five factors,
partly in his statement (Book III, Part II, Sec. VIII, 546) of the peculiar authority
of opinion in moral matters.

First, on the conflict between Cavaliers and Roundheads, what would the judgments of Hume the moralist be? The political virtues take the center of the stage in this historical controversy. Here there is at first sight on the side of the Roundheads as against the Cavaliers a principle of liberty essential to social and political institutions. Certainly, as we saw above, Hume denies the principle of passive obedience and insists on the right of subjects to resist extreme oppression. Against that abstract principle, however, there are at least two important factors in favor of the Stuarts.

The question was not one of absolute monarchy or liberty, but of the balance of the two; and as the history of the Commonwealth showed it was in fact the presumptive seekers after extreme liberty who actually brought the nation, as Hume seems to think is usually the case, to the extremest tyranny instead.[18] Liberty is all very well, and all very necessary in the abstract as a basis for political conventions; but as the essay on the British Government suggests,[19] too much liberty, as it may occur in republican governments, more frequently turns into an extreme of despotism (the despotism of a man of ill-breeding like Cromwell!) than does an excess, within a balanced government, of monarchical authority. The British constitution is blessed in having monarchy better mixed with liberty than the French, Hume thinks—but blessed too in having the balance of the mixture somewhat to the monarchical rather than the popular side. So, despite instances like the Star Chamber or the ship money, the question of public interest is not automatically decided in favor of the Commonwealth men as against the Cavaliers.

In fact, the *Treatise,* the *Political Essays,* and the *History* concur in sustaining, within the continual polarity of Hume's political view, an emphasis on the dangers of liberty rather than its converse. Hume is against passive obedience, proud of British free speech, etc.; but he is extremely conscious of the dangers of a fanatical zeal for liberty—of the fury of the mob when roused to an overkeen consciousness of its rights. A Nero or a Caligula deserves rebellion and perhaps even punishment on the part of his

[18] "The slavery into which the nation, from the too eager pursuit of liberty, has fallen." *History of England,* ed. Porter and Coates, 5 vols., following Hume's last corrections (Philadelphia, no year), IV, 545; cf. 549.

[19] *Whether the British Government Inclines More to Absolute Monarchy, or to a Republic. Essays,* I, 122–6.

subjects, but in the case of Charles I, a prince sometimes rash or weak but on the whole virtuous and well-intentioned, there is for Hume no question of justifying such extremes.[20]

There are two passages in the *History*, the second of which is paralleled in the *Treatise*, which bear most significantly on the question of Hume's emphasis here. In his account of Charles's trial Hume relates how the Parliament introduced for their own purposes "a principle noble in itself and which seems specious, but is belied by all history and experience, *that the people are the origin of all just power.*"[21] Surely for Hume the philosopher, as for Hume the objective and impartial historian, a principle belied by all history and experience is no principle at all, but a superstitious illusion to be dispelled by judicious consideration of past and present. But can Hume the liberal philosopher deny the very keystone of liberalism, the central expression of those laws of nature which, indeed, in Hume's view, men and not gods have made for their own interest, but which are nevertheless basic to organized society? No; the abstract principle of liberty stands for Hume, despite this striking denial of an empirical foundation: practically, because it would not be the part of a gentleman and a humanitarian to deny it; intellectually, because there is in Hume's system no apparatus for its denial—no superstate or supersovereign to sanction a source of power other than the human beings who compose society and whose interests necessitate the foundation of the state. And it is of course a principle jointly acknowledged, in Hume's view, by Whig and Tory in his own day.

But the principle is singularly attenuated in its practical application, not only indirectly in the above denial of its historical validation, but more pointedly in the treatment of men's basic right of revolution both in the *History* and in the *Treatise*. In both these works Hume insists generally that while extreme tyranny provokes, and justifies, rebellion, there is no need to tell every one about it— when the case is extreme enough, the rebellion will come of itself; and in the meantime one had better hush up this provocative (though undeniable) principle.[22] Why? Because the end of gov-

[20] *History*, IV, 492.

[21] *Ibid.*, IV, 480.

[22] *Ibid.*, IV, 491: "Government is instituted in order to restrain the fury and injustice of the people, and being always founded on opinion, not on force, it is dangerous to weaken, by these speculations (i.e., on the right to revolution) the reverence which the multitude owe to authority, and to instruct them beforehand that the

ernment is (at least, according to the statement of the *History*) to restrain mob violence (a lesson easily learned from the Civil Wars); and mob violence would be only encouraged by a universal consciousness of universal rights. Such is in the main the tenor of Hume's argument, in general in the *Treatise* (Bk. III, Pt. II, sec. X) and in particular in the discussion relative to Charles I's execution in the *History* (Ch. LIX).

This is at first sight an amazing statement on the part of a signally mild and humane philosopher, whose trust in human benevolence is proverbial. Philosophically the situation here is similar to that in the first book of the *Treatise* with respect to causal inference and the general causal principle. Intellectually, there is no thoroughgoing, "rational" validation for a causal law; but it is demanded practically and practically sanctioned by custom and imagination. Here, conversely, there is no intellectual, rational justification for a *denial* of the libertarian principle and the right to revolution; but practical need demands its public denial or at any rate its concealment in most circumstances. As with knowledge Hume's intellectual doubt gives way to his practical naturalism, so here the intellectual liberalism which the latter in turn demands (because it offers no alternative view of the *raison d'être* of organized society) gives way for practical purposes to a much more qualified and conservative view of political education. In neither case does the one principle cancel the other; but where practice and experience, or in short perception, is the test of truth and of values, it does significantly balance and perhaps even outweigh the abstract generality to which, as pole to pole, it is at once related and opposed.

Compare Hume's view here with Locke's position in the *Second Treatise of Civil Government*. Both stress the libertarian basis for civil society, deny passive obedience, and thus suggest the view of political society as a commonwealth of free men. Both mention the unruliness of the passions as an important fact relative to the need for and end of political organization. But in Locke, the friend of Shaftesbury, and in Hume, the acknowledged partisan of

---

case can ever happen when they may be freed from their duty of allegiance. Or should it be found impossible to restrain the license of human disquisitions, it must be acknowledged that the doctrine of obedience ought alone to be *inculcated* and that the exceptions, which are rare, ought seldom or never to be mentioned in popular reasonings and discourses." Cf. *Treatise*, Book III, Part II, Sec. X, 555–6 and 563–4.

the Stuarts, the emphasis on these two concomitant elements is significantly at variance. For Locke it is the commonwealth of free men with their parliamentary rights and liberties that is continually, practically as well as abstractly, of importance; the *motif* of the passions enters as an explanatory factor relative to the account of the organization of society with its apparent limitation on men's native liberties. For Hume, liberty is basic, it is true; the end of the state is the maintenance of these liberties, but *through* the continual control and suppression of the violent passions, and especially the prevention of mob violence—a means so necessary and so important that it can on occasion be called the end of political institutions: "government is instituted in order to restrain the fury and injustice of the people."[23]

Let us look carefully, in the light of these general considerations, at Hume's treatment of Charles I's trial and execution. Hume's general consideration in the *History* of the right of subjects to depose, judge and execute their sovereign,[24] coming after his continual stress on the unjust conduct of the Parliamentarians and the nobility and virtue of the wronged king, may look ambiguous and inconclusive. But it is clearly consistent with the closely parallel passage in the *Treatise* and its ambiguity consists, not in a hesitation on Hume's part as to whether the deposition (perhaps even execution) of sovereigns is *ever* permissible—clearly it sometimes is; nor in a hesitation as to whether the treatment of Charles was just—clearly it was not. It arises rather from the duality inherent in Hume's political theory: a duality which, however, does not prevent a strong and consistent emphasis on one of the two elements involved. Liberty is necessary to government; but the zealous pursuit of liberty often leads—and in the case of the Civil Wars, did lead—to the extremest slavery, and hence to the negation of the public good on which alone society is ultimately based. The right of revolution is necessary to government; but its untoward exercise often leads—and in the case of the Civil Wars did lead—to the violation of honored and honorable persons, the arbitrary overthrow of ancient institutions, and the chaotic play of violence against violence, the avoidance of which is among the primary constituents of that basic "public good."

Consequently, in terms of the heavier emphasis on monarchy than on liberty (while retaining a belief in both), Hume's own

[23] See note 21 above (p. 341).
[24] *History*, IV, 491; see note 22 above (pp. 341–2).

position, with regard to the events of the seventeenth century, fits his own definition of Tory.

In addition to the primary factors of public interest which enter into such problems of allegiance as those facing partisans in the period of the Civil Wars, there are, as we noticed above, a group of other factors centering chiefly in phenomena of popular custom and of public opinion, which need likewise to be taken into account in a cool and reasoned evaluation of the various parties' claims. "Where the public good does not evidently demand a change," Hume says, the questions of original contract, long possession, present possession, succession, and positive laws all enter into account. Where these secondary factors concur, there is no difficulty in deciding the issue; vexed questions arise—as in any causal inference—only through a conflict in the influences impelling our judgment one way and another. With regard to Charles I, as we have seen, the public good was not so grossly violated as clearly to demand a change. On the other hand, the influence of "original contract" in this case is rather hard to see; but in his initial description of these elements in political judgment Hume isolates the first as a factor sometimes occurring in some states, and mentions long possession in particular as a sort of alternative to it.[25] The five are, after all, not abstract canons of right, but lines of psychological and associative influence, and it is only in a few cases (as for instance later in the constitutions of the North American states or revolutionary France) that the consciousness of a contractual relation plays an important part in the imagination of a people. Usually they have been governed so long that their judgments on political matters have come to feel as natural as their judgments on the natural virtues—and the question of a voluntary and contractual foundation of the state is not one that plays an important part in forming their opinions. It is for that reason perhaps that Hume with his eye always on the psychological basis for his moral theory hesitates to make universal and necessary the social contract theory of political origins.[26]

The other four factors, however, certainly do concur in this instance. Long possession, present possession, succession, and positive law are all on the Cavalier side, with no contrary pressure from the remaining principle. Long possession, in particular, combined with positive law, provides a strong source of authority

[25] *Treatise,* Book III, Part II, Sec. X, 554–5.
[26] *Ibid.,* Book III, Part II, Sec. VIII, 541–2.

for the supporters of the king.[27]   In fact that is the point made by
Hume himself in the letter to Mrs. Macaulay quoted by Mr. Mossner
in the above-mentioned article:

> For as I look upon all kinds of subdivision of power, from the monarchy
> of France to the freest democracy of some Swiss cantons, to be equally legal,
> if established by custom and authority; I cannot but think, that the mixed
> monarchy of England, such as it was left by Queen Elizabeth, was a lawful
> form of government, and carried obligations to obedience and allegiance; at
> least it must be acknowledged, that the princes and ministers who supported
> that form, tho' somewhat arbitrarily, could not incur much blame on that
> account; and that there is more reason to make an apology for their antago-
> nists than for them.[28]

To be sure, in Hume's own day, the well-established possession of
the crown by the House of Hanover is sufficient to preclude, in
Hume's view, a need for violent restoration of the Stuarts.   But
at the same time long possession and legality were, a century
earlier, very definitely strong enough forces to put the burden of
proof on the Parliamentarians—who in the violence and fanaticism
of their behavior furnished no very persuasive argument on the
other side.   Granted that history and true philosophy teach us
according to Hume "to regard the controversies in politics as incapable of any decision in most cases, and as entirely subordinate
to the interests of peace and liberty."[29]   Still the concurrence of
all the subordinate principles, he goes on to say, "forms the strongest title to sovereignty, and is justly regarded as sacred and inviolable."[30]   They did concur in the case of Charles I; and his title
and his person were therefore to be respected accordingly.   (Not
to mention, of course, that the interest of peace and even, as it
turned out, of liberty, too, might well have been better served by
the Royalists than the Cromwellians.)   In short, however specious
the abstract principles sponsored by the Roundheads, their concrete

[27] See for example in the *History* (IV, 454) on the king's hopes for a reasonable
settlement: "A people without government and without liberty, a Parliament without authority, an army without a legal master; distractions everywhere, terrors, op-
pressions, convulsions; from this scene of confusion, which could not long continue,
all men, he hoped, would be brought to reflect on that ancient government under
which they and their ancestors had so long enjoyed happiness and tranquillity."

[28] Mossner, *op. cit.*, 234–5.   From *European Magazine and London Review*,
(November, 1793), 33.

[29] See *Treatise,* Book III, Part II, Sec. X, 562.

[30] *Loc. cit.*

and psychological claims to allegiance certainly did not suffice to justify the impeachment, let alone the murder (for as such Hume saw it) of their lawful sovereign, and within a brief space the overthrow in all but the semblance of the parliamentary institutions in defense of which, ostensibly, they had condemned their king. Here, again, the sympathy with established authority in general and the Stuart family in particular prevails.

But the subordinate principles of long possession, etc., have a further importance: their introduction suggests a reason for Hume's reactionary view of political education and for his view that peace and the maintenance of order are at least as basic an end of government as liberty itself. For here once more is the omnipresent principle of custom with its influence on imagination and hence on the intensity and direction of human passions. Interest is the foundation of states; and the fair principles of liberty are the dictate of interest. But with long custom that basis is forgotten: custom makes subjection and allegiance feel as natural as any extra-political sentiment. And custom, that great guide of human life, cannot be lightly overturned—nor should it be, for its overthrow lets loose a chaos of violent passions unchecked by general rules. Calm reflection, combined with a distant view, can operate only in the gentle and sheltered atmosphere of an orderly society: and liberty itself, always present as the foundation of the state, is in the extremest danger when custom, in its dual form of inherited rule and civil law, breaks down and "the madness of the people" and "the furies of fanaticism"[31] are let loose.

Looked at another way, finally, the subordinate principles sum up to a statement of factors forming and influencing public opinion. And taking them in that sense, their weight is once more on the Royalist side. For, whatever abstract sanction the principle of liberty might have given the Roundheads (had that principle been genuinely involved as an issue, as by the time of the institution of the Commonwealth it certainly was not), against that abstract consideration there would stand the very concrete and effective factor of the present issuance of political habit into public sentiment. The Commonwealth was a real tyranny in the sense that no one or only a very few men wanted it, and only the stupor of exhaustion after long civil war made its initiation possible at all.[32]

[31] *History,* IV, 493.
[32] See the account of the stupor and astonishment of the people at the events leading up to the king's death (486); their reaction to it (488). Compare the ac-

One may conclude that Hume's moral judgment, that is, his disinterested judgment—such judgment as his sceptical position allows and in fact demands—would incline him to the Tory side in his view of the Civil Wars.

With regard to the contemporary scene, Hume's position is different. His Stuart sympathies (though short of Jacobitism) might remain; as would his preference for a good safe balance of monarchy first with liberty second. He would certainly not accept the notion of passive obedience; but, as he himself says, that goes only with a part of the Pre-Revolution Tory notion,[33] and even there, is more talk than genuine belief. So his view might still be found to fit fairly well his own definition of Tory with regard to his own time. But despite that sympathy he professedly disapproves of Jacobites:[34] for he would not sympathize with the Catholic cause as it grows more openly equated with that of the Stuart family, nor would he desire a violent renunciation of the *status quo* so long as the *status quo* is fairly comfortable for most of the people he cares about. He would not, like Hobbes, accept any *status quo*, even the Commonwealth: it was too uncomfortable for every one. But the Protestant succession is, first of all, Protestant (an advantage where Protestantism wears a less positively religious front than the Roman church—the reversal of the seventeenth-century situation); and secondly, fairly secure by Hume's time. So there is, despite the agreeable character of the Stuarts and even the legitimacy of their claim, no particular reason to upset the present settlement. If that is to be a Whig, or at least less of a Tory, then Hume is, if not a Whig, at least less of a Tory in contemporary politics than in his historical view. A sense of the delicacy and uncertainty of political decisions, a liking for calmness and good-nature, as it makes him outspoken against the fanaticism of the Roundheads, blunts the edge of his partiality in respect to his own times, when the side of greater religious bigotry seems to have shifted, when the peaceful present compels allegiance, and when the demands of politeness and a philosophical disposition prevent the adherence to what is now a revolutionary cause. It is this side of his peculiarly double-edged position that appears in the essay

---

count of the authority behind the Commonwealth (497) and the account of the Restoration, *passim*.

[33] *Essays*, I, 137–8.
[34] *Ibid.*, I, 143–4.

on the Protestant succession,[35] in the note on the Revolution in the *Treatise*,[36] and in the latter part of the paragraph from the letter to Mrs. Macaulay quoted above:

I grant, that the cause of liberty, which you, Madame, with the Pyms and Hampdens, have adopted, is noble and generous; but most of the partizans of that cause, in the last century, disgraced it, by their violence, and also by their cant, hypocrisy, and bigotry, which, more than the principles of civil liberty, seem to have been the motive of all their actions. Had those principles always appeared in the amiable light which they receive from your person and writings, it would have been impossible to resist them; and however much inclined to indulgence toward the first James and Charles, I should have been the first to condemn those monarchs for not yielding to them.[37]

As against the legality of the English constitution prior to the Civil Wars, as against his disapproval of violence and cant, perceptible as the prime motives in the seventeenth-century Parliamentary party, as against an indulgence, in contrast, to the first James and Charles, Hume stresses the fair character of liberty (a principle admitted both by Whigs and Tories, according to his definitions, though with unequal emphasis), and professes to admire Whig principles when they are placed in ''so amiable a light''; that, is, when they are transferred from affiliation with violence and fanaticism to the politer and more moderate surroundings of Hume's own world. The mildness and complacency of Hume's disposition involve, philosophically, a serious emphasis on the importance of the public peace and on the correlative sanctity of well-established custom. That emphasis issues, in practical terms, in a genuine sympathy with a conservative politics in general and in particular with the Stuart side of the historical dispute; and in an equally genuine approval of a convenient settlement approved at its outset by the moderates of both political parties and guaranteeing, by the manner of its allegiance to liberty, not the violent upheavals consequent on the libertarian avowals of ''the Pyms and Hamdens,'' but an agreeably well-ordered existence in a decent, moderate and enlightened state.

The University of Chicago.

[35] *Ibid.,* I, 470–480.
[36] *Treatise,* Book III, Part II, Sec. X, 563–6.
[37] See note 28 above.

PART FOUR

HUME'S CRITIQUE OF EMPIRE AND THE AMERICAN CRISIS

XIII

HUME ON PROPERTY, COMMERCE, AND EMPIRE IN THE GOOD SOCIETY: THE ROLE OF HISTORICAL NECESSITY

By Corey Venning

If David Hume held an ultimate political value he described it only as the public happiness.[1] What can be inferred from his more specific political statements about his conception of the ingredients of public happiness, and the institutions and instrumental values that advance his conception? This question may usefully be approached through examination of his writings on property, commerce, and empire, and the connections among them.

Hume's central philosophical position is famous for its emphasis on the essential role of experience in the conduct of human affairs: "Custom is the great guide of human life."[2] True to this conviction, he relied on the historical experience of Europe, and more particularly of England, in the formulation of his fundamental political views.[3] Furthermore, he made a strong theoretical case for the position that, given man's nature and situation, the future will resemble the past, that history provides us with illustrations of the probable consequences of actions taken under various circumstantial conditions; that it in effect illuminates the limiting cases for human social organization and behavior.[4]

This is not to say that Hume thought history, given the state of the art of political reasoning, could yield insights that would permit one "to fix many general truths in politics."[5] Nor was he monistic in his conception of human nature. The empiricist Hume emphasized the variety of human types, and the multiplicity and plurality of human values and satisfactions, both individual and social.[6] It follows that "we must not ... expect that ... uniformity of human actions should be carried to such a length that all men, in the same circumstances, will always act precisely in the same manner. . . . All causes are not conjoined to their

---

[1]David Hume, *An Enquiry Concerning the Principles of Morals, Hume's Moral and Political Philosophy*, ed. Henry D. Aiken (New York, 1948), V, 207–21.

[2]Hume, *A Treatise of Human Nature, David Hume: A Treatise of Human Nature, Book I: Of the Understanding*, ed. D. G. C. Macnabb (Cleveland, 1962), 133–40; *David Hume: An Inquiry Concerning Human Understanding*, ed. Charles W. Hendel (New York, 1955), 58.

[3]"That Politics May Be Reduced to a Science," *Essays, Moral, Political and Literary, by David Hume*, ed. T. H. Green and T. H. Grose (London, 1882), I, 98–108.

[4]*An Inquiry Concerning Human Understanding, op. cit.*, 92–96.

[5]"Of Civil Liberty," *Essays, op. cit.*, I, 156.

[6]"The Epicurean," "The Stoic," "The Platonist," "The Sceptic," *ibid.*, I, 197–231.

effects in a like uniformity."[7] The concept of historical necessity must therefore be carefully interpreted and conclusions based on it treated with some diffidence.

Survival and happiness (however the latter may be defined) must nonetheless be posited as universal human goals. That which conduces to the fulfillment of goals has *utility*. History, in providing a record of man's experience, indicates why certain "habits and customs," formalized in institutions, are—allowing of course for variation in circumstances—preferred to others. They are preferred because in the eyes of their practitioners they have superior utility for realization of the two basic goals and the varied instrumental values which they are perceived to entail.[8]

Society itself originates in utility. It is the only effective means whereby man can compensate for the imbalance between his weakness, on the one hand, and the extent and exigency of his needs and desires, on the other.[9] But some degree of stability and order is necessary for the continuation of society. That which strengthens a society and its ordered relationships, and which conduces to realization of other important ends, has utility for that society.

Security of property is eminently of this character, for social stability and order, and therefore society itself, depend on it. Hume's argument runs as follows: three "species of goods" comprise the basic equipment with which each man faces the world. Hume believed that the individual is secure in the first of these, his mental capacities. The second, the individual's physical powers, can be "ravished from us," but the ravisher cannot then appropriate them to his own advantage.[10] Only the third basic good—"such possessions as we have acquired by our industry and good fortune"—can be so appropriated; furthermore, these possessions are always in short supply. Property is therefore the original and great problem for society, the solution of which is essential to society's continuation. Property thus becomes the matrix of development of notions of justice and the conventions that taken together form a society's laws.[11]

In response to this original great problem political society is established. Its purpose is the administration of justice,[12] that is, the

---

[7] *An Inquiry Concerning Human Understanding, op. cit.,* 95–96.

[8] Hume's emphasis on utility would seem adequately to resolve the question raised by Robert Lyon: "For Hume the justification of a belief lay not in its origin in experience, but in its consequences. But he never worked out, in any of his writings, how the criterion of true belief was to be established in terms of its consequences." "Notes on Hume's Philosophy of Political Economy," *JHI,* **31** (1970), 445–46.

[9] *Treatise,* Bk. III, *op. cit.,* 58–63.

[10] Hume does not discuss slavery in this connection; cf. n. 13, below.

[11] *Treatise,* Bk. III, *op. cit.,* 58–63.

[12] "Of the Origin of Government," *Essays, op. cit.,* I, 113.

maintenance of conditions under which individuals can live together in cooperative relations, and thus better assure their survival and well being than each could hope to do alone. Hume thought Locke had overstated the role of property when he made it the foundation of all government, but agreed that the question of property rights "is of moment in all matters of government."[13]

Property rights, then, must be secure, but they can never be sacred. They are regulated by such rules as are adopted by and suitable to the particular society in question; such rules are not immutable. *In extremis,* specific property rights—or for that matter any other rules of law and justice—are and should be jettisoned, if that is the price of survival of society.[14]

Outside such rare and extreme cases, Hume regards security of property as the *sine qua non* of the strength of the state, of liberty, which implies limited government, and of the stability of society itself. By "property" he means the possessions of the members of society, private property. In his praises and defenses of legitimate authority, in his expansive views of the extent of legitimate royal powers and prerogative in England up to 1688, there is not the slightest hint that the property of Englishmen is ultimately the property of the English sovereign, ultimately open to invasion and disposal by the sovereign for purposes of state as he or she sees fit.[15] Correspondingly, the thought of socialization of land and other wealth—"so monstrous a situation as that of making the public the chief or sole proprietor of land"—occasioned a polemic couched in terms far warmer than Hume's usual even-tempered style. Such a socialization, which would follow destruction of the middle class, would mark the onset of "a degree of despotism,

[13]"Of the First Principles of Government," *ibid.,* I, 111. Green and Grose indicate that Hume's reference was to Harrington, not Locke, and refer to Hume's discussion of Harrington's asserted capacity to make accurate political predictions (*ibid.,* I, 122). Hendel's preference for Locke as Hume's referent seems better justified in the context of Hume's remark. See Locke, *Second Treatise of Government,* Ch. IX, and *David Hume's Political Essays,* ed. Charles W. Hendel (New York, 1953). Locke held that the person of an individual, and his labor, are part of his property. Hume seems to have placed these items in his first and second categories of basic goods (mental and bodily capacities). This difference in the definition of property as between Locke and Hume may explain the contrast in their views of the relationship of property to government. But we are left with a question: certainly the labor of the body, and even that of the mind, can be appropriated by others. If Hume did not regard it as property, how could he hold that the individual is secure in possession of the first and second basic "species of goods"?

[14]Hume, *An Enquiry Concerning the Principles of Morals,* Aiken, *op. cit.,* III, 187–90, 195.

[15]Hume, *The History of England, from the Invasion of Julius Caesar to the Revolution in 1688; A new edition, with the author's last corrections and improvements,* 8 vols. (London, 1778; reprinted New York, 1885, in 6 vols.), vols. V–VI, *passim;* see esp. V, Note E.

which no oriental monarch has ever yet attained."[16] Though he emphasized that the liberty of its owner to transfer property is essential to
the idea of property itself, Hume also thought a prevalence of rapid and
wholesale exchanges is socially dangerous, because it inevitably results
in a general loss of sense of stake in possessions, and could conceivably
eventuate in such extensive concentration of property as to resemble or
even constitute socialization.[17]

Moreover, Hume affirmed that individuals are happiest, and the
state best served, in circumstances of general prosperity, in which each
enjoys the fruits of his own labors, and where wealth and therefore
property are widely distributed throughout the society.[18] This does not
mean that equality of economic condition is desirable or even possible;
inequalities in this respect inevitably arise on the increase in numbers
and emergence from savagery of a people.[19] But it is the existence of
classes as such that Hume regards as inevitable. Their specific relationships and personnel do not concern him. He can reflect with equanimity on the likelihood that "in 500 years, the posterity of those now in
the coaches, and of those upon the boxes, will probably have changed
places, without affecting the public by these revolutions."[20]

Thus Hume was no egalitarian. But he thought *radical* inequality—
utter incapacity of the weaker to resist the stronger—renders irrelevant
any conceptions of property rights of the inferior, or for that matter
conceptions of society or justice as regards relations between superior
and inferior. In such cases (which Hume implies are probably
hypothetical as among human beings), only sentiments of mercy on the
part of the stronger, and not considerations of justice or arrangements
that can be called social, can be present.[21] Some element of equality,
some degree of capacity to resist, is necessary to the institution of
private property and to liberty itself. For, as noted above, security of
property includes the liberty to acquire and transfer it, and its security
from wholesale and general invasion by the state or by others.

Property, then, is in Hume's view basic to society, and its security is
necessary to the existence of a free, prosperous, and happy citizenry.
Like Burke, he saw large individual holdings of private wealth as on the
whole socially beneficial; like him, he apparently did not anticipate and

[16]"Of Public Credit," *Essays, op. cit.*, I, 369.   [17]*Ibid.*, I, 367.
[18]"Of Commerce," *ibid.*, I, 296-97.   [19]"Of Interest," *ibid.*, I, 322.
[20]"Of Public Credit," *ibid.*, I, 367. Cf. Hume's comment on Wat Tyler's rebellion:
"There were two verses at that time in the mouths of all the common people, which, in
spite of prejudice, one cannot but regard with some degree of approbation:

'When Adam delv'd and Eve span,
Where then was the gentleman?'"

(*History, op. cit.*, II, 230n.)
[21]"Of Justice," *Essays, op. cit.*, II, 185.

would not have welcomed the enormous concentrations of wealth and economic power that capitalism would create in later times. He emphatically disliked the idea of property as simply a counter in wholesale speculative games; some metaexpediential connection between property and its holder is implied. Nor is property primarily a means of congealing a particular class structure and fixing personnel within it. Though property rights may be altered, and even invaded in dire circumstances, there is no ultimate general right of the state to appropriate it; property, to conduce to both individual happiness and the "public happiness," must be regarded as belonging to, and must be controlled by, private owners.

Similar considerations apply to commerce. That Hume was an enthusiastic proponent of mercantile activity is evident from his *History of England.* From his approbation of Athelstan,

regarded as one of the ablest and most active of those ancient princes . . . [who] passed a remarkable law, which was calculated for the encouragement of commerce, and which it required some liberality of mind in that age to have devised: that a merchant, who had made three long sea-voyages on his own account, should be admitted to the rank of a Thane or Gentleman,[22]

through the whole stately progress of English dynasties and reigns, up to the observation that "the commerce and riches of England did never, during any period, increase so fast as from the restoration to the revolution,"[23] Hume never neglects, in his *History,* to inform his readers of the state of the English economy, with special reference to commerce and navigation.[24] He seems to have discovered a happy general coincidence between reigns, policies, and principles which he could praise, and encouragement and expansion through them of domestic and foreign trade. History amply supported, in the case of England, a view of commerce as conducive to public happiness.[25]

Hume's theoretical statement of the role of commerce centers on its facilitation of exchange of goods among producers, and the realization thereby of the advantages of division of labor and consequent increase in total production and consumption. Not only are material necessities more adequately provided for than would otherwise be the case; they can be provided for a larger population, and ever-increasing human and material resources become available for application to "the finer arts . . . commonly denominated the arts of *luxury,* [which] add to the happiness of the state; since they afford to many the opportunity of receiving enjoyments, with which they would otherwise have been unac-

---

[22] *History, op. cit.,* I, 88.   [23] *Ibid.,* VI, 324.
[24] See especially the Appendices to the chapters describing events during each of the dynasties through the Tudors, and the reign of James I (*ibid., passim*).
[25] E.g., *ibid.,* II, 219-23.

quainted."[26] In short, commerce encourages economic development and therefore human happiness., For this, Hume unstintingly praises commerce and holds merchants—"one of the most useful races of men"—in high regard.[27]

Contrast situations in which commerce is not respected or energetically undertaken. Here manufacturing fails to develop, and "indolence and poverty" prevail, regardless of the possible natural richness of the land. Commerce flourishes in situations of political liberty. Absolute government is harmful to commerce, Hume thought, "not because commerce is there less secure, but because it is less honour[ed]."[28] Both domestic and foreign commerce thrive best where the parties to it are prosperous and active, and can deal with one another on a basis of some equality.[29]

Material gain is thus not the only impetus to or benefit of commercial activity. Material well being is of course prerequisite to enjoyment of the "innocent luxuries" and intellectual and cultural refinements which distinguish a people of advanced civilization from those of more barbaric times and circumstances. But there is something else: as a purposeful activity, commerce provides an important outlet for man's need for "liveliness," and an important means of satisfying his urge to "action," thus giving scope to two of the basic "ingredients of human happiness" which Hume, pluralist as he was in his views of human nature, nonetheless believed are present in some degree in most individuals.[30]

All these advantages refer not to state power but to individual (and *en large,* presumably also social) happiness and fulfillment. Hume by no means disregards or questions the importance of a flourishing commerce for the power of a state, or the opportunities for conflict between public and private interests over allocation of the wealth derived from it. He observes that public and private demands compete for resources: "The one can never be satisfied, but at the expense of the other."[31] He admits that surpluses produced as a result of efficiencies realized through commercial expansion can be taken by the sovereign and used to enhance his own glory or the power and extent of his dominions, and that this has been a common policy of rulers whenever their political and constitutional situations permitted it.[32] But he is of the opinion that, unusual cases such as those of Sparta and the early Roman re-

[26] "Of Commerce," in *Essays, op. cit.,* I, 289. By "state," Hume here obviously refers to the members of the society in question, notwithstanding the accuracy of Aiken's general observation that "[o]ne of the most important of Hume's contributions to social and political theory is his insistence that a sharp distinction be made between society and the state . . ." (*op. cit.,* xliii).

[27] "Of Interest," *Essays, op. cit.,* I, 324.

[28] "Of Civil Liberty," *ibid.,* I, 160; "Of Commerce," *ibid.,* I, 293.

[29] "Of the Jealousy of Trade," *ibid.,* I, 345–48.

[30] "The Epicurean," "The Stoic," "The Platonist," "The Sceptic," *ibid.,* 197–231.

[31] "Of Commerce," *ibid.,* I, 290.   [32] *Ibid.,* I, 289–92.

public possibly excepted, the wise statesman will be content with the increment to state power that accrues naturally, as it were, in the course of economic development: "It is his best policy to comply with the common bent of mankind, and give it all the improvements of which it is susceptible."[33] Hume's reservations about the soundness of mercantilist theory and practice—which posits foreign commerce (preferably on less than equal terms among the parties) not primarily for the benefit of the members of society but for the enrichment and enhanced power of the state itself—are well known. His general views on the relationships among security of property, a flourishing commerce, and state power, are perhaps best summarized in the following remarks:

> The greatness of a state, and the happiness of its subjects, however independent soever they may be supposed in some respects, are commonly allowed to be inseparable with regard to commerce; and as private men receive greater security, in their possession of their trade and riches, from the power of the public, so the public becomes powerful in proportion to the opulence and extensive commerce of private men ... [though] there may be some circumstances, where the commerce and riches and luxury of individuals, instead of adding strength to the public, will serve only to thin its armies and diminish its authority among the neighboring nations.[34]

What might be some of these circumstances, in which individual riches and luxury work to the weakening of the state? Not luxury in itself; according to Hume, those who attribute Rome's decline to excessive luxury are mistaken. Rome's decline "proceeded from an ill modeled government, and the unlimited extent of conquests."[35] Conquest, then, can be a source of weakness and even ultimate destruction *for the victorious state.* And, as Hume certainly knew from his study of history, conquest is the typical (though not the only) route to empire.

With regard to comprehensive forms of political organization the conservative and historically-oriented student of politics may well conclude that the highest stage and crowning achievement of a great people will be the establishment under its aegis of some form of universal empire. History indicates that the typical progress of such peoples has been from tribe or nation, through participation as a major actor in a balance of power, to hegemony and at last imperium over the whole civilization or political universe to which that people belongs. At critical points in this progress, the imperial consequences of the policies adopted may be clearly understood and enthusiastically embraced by protagonists and supporters of such policies; on the other hand, their real nature may be masked, such policies being perceived as a means of discharging some variety of mission or political responsibility, or even simply as necessary to national security. On occasion imperial status has been the result of a number of discrete and incremental decisions

---

[33] *Idem.;* cf. n.53, below.   [34] *Ibid.,* I, 288–89.
[35] "Of Refinement in the Arts," *ibid.,* I, 305.

and outcomes none of which, alone or in itself, would constitute action directed toward or eventuating in the establishment of empire. In the latter cases, what is happening is usually earlier and better understood by those who are becoming imperialized than by those who set their state on the path of imperial rule.

The achievement of imperial status has been and to some extent remains in our own day the explicit or implicit criterion of greatness in a state or a people.[36] It is also held that if a people to whom empire is accessible does not grasp it, some rival will do so, and succeed—there is always a rival, until empire is complete. It is logically implicit in this view that other political and social values and activities must be judged by the standard of whether and to what extent, and in what manner, their pursuit and attainment conduce to national greatness defined as achievement and maintenance of imperial status.[37]

Did Hume's historical orientation lead him to a similar opinion? He believed that the "great uniformity among the actions of men, in all nations and ages," produces a "constant and regular conjunction of similar events,"[38] and that this uniformity is rooted in man's discovery, through experience, of utility in certain institutions and activities. Did he then conclude that the high incidence of universal empire implies its utility and its inevitable appearance at some mature stage in any political universe whose development has not been somehow arrested?

Hume heartily approved of at least one type of imperial policy, exemplified by British colonization of North America. He regarded the inception of this colonization as the outstanding event of the reign of James I, one which by Hume's own time had produced

colonies established on the noblest footing that has been known in any age or nation. . . . Peopled gradually from England by the necessitous and indigent, who at home increased neither wealth nor populousness, the colonies which were planted . . . have prompted the navigation, encouraged the industry, and even perhaps multiplied the inhabitants of their mother country. The spirit of independency, which was reviving in England, here shone forth in its full lustre,

[36] Thus, e.g., C. L. Sulzberger: "If one looks back across Asia's endless centuries one finds that China has often been great but India never—except under [foreign] conquerors" (*New York Times,* Feb. 22, 1967); also, e.g., George Liska, *Imperial America* (Baltimore, 1967) and *War and Order: Reflections on Vietnam and History* (Baltimore, 1968); James L. Payne, *The American Threat: the Fear of War as an Instrument of Foreign Policy* (Chicago, 1970), esp. chs. 8 and 10; and the voluminous literature of the debate over the extent of American responsibility for creation and maintenance of order in the world and opposition to challenges to that order.

[37] This exceedingly compressed delineation of empire is of course subject to important qualifications. These qualifications, notably including the apparent exception of modern Europe and its overseas empires, are examined in another study by the present author. See also Richard Koebner, *Empire* (Cambridge, 1961), Koebner and Helmut Dan Schmidt, *Imperialism: the Story and Significance of a Political Word, 1840-1960* (Cambridge, 1965), and W. H. McNeill, *The Rise of the West: A History of the Human Community* (Chicago, 1961), 834-41.

[38] *An Inquiry Concerning Human Understanding, op. cit.,* 92.

and received new accession from the aspiring character of those who, being discontented with the established church and monarchy, had sought for freedom amidst those savage deserts.[39]

Hume discounted fears that the American colonies would wax strong and populous at the expense of the mother country, and would one day detach themselves and become England's rivals.[40]

Not all colonization is beneficial, however. The Spaniards, in contrast to the British, exploited rather than cultivated their colonies. As a result, "they were tempted to depopulate their own country, as well as that which they had conquered: and added the vice of sloth to those of avidity and barbarity."[41] In Hume's view the two cases point to the lesson that where an energetic people enjoy liberty, security of property, and encouragement of commerce, and where colonies and their people are full members of the larger society and its body politic—there the blessings of liberty and refinement simply expand into a larger frame. Where such qualities are absent, where colonies are merely objects of exploitation, then not only will the colonies be miserable, but the mother country itself will eventually become weakened and impoverished.[42]

So much for colonial expansion. Hume's remarks about it do not touch on the question of the inevitability of expansion *per se,* though they do shed light on his conception of a good society. What of the classic form of empire, in which a vigorous and ascendant state, through conquest or by other means, comes to rule the political universe in which it is situated?

Hume well knew the prevalence of universal empire in history, and the honor accorded conquerors, whose glory most people consider to be "the most sublime kind of merit." It even dazzles the thoughtful into admiration.[43] Hume found an example of this phenomenon in Cromwell—hardly one of his favorite English rulers—whose

[39] *History, op. cit.,* IV, 369.
[40] *Ibid.,* IV, 371. The quoted remarks were written before the Seven Years' War, and at a time when the American colonists themselves were content to be Englishmen. Conscious as he was of the workings of contingency in human affairs and versed as he was in history, Hume may at some time have pondered the Hellenic colonial experience. If he did so, his reflections are not recorded in his published works.   [41] *Ibid.,* IV, 369.
[42] Cf. Hume's opinion that in general, commerce is most beneficial when both (or all) parties are prosperous and energetic ("Of the Jealousy of Trade," *Essays, op. cit.,* I, 345–48). Hume did not give much attention to the fate of indigenous inhabitants of colonies, or their right, if any, to maintain their own sociocultural forms undisturbed. He did favorably compare the treatment of peoples conquered by an absolute monarch to that which they may expect on being subordinated to a free state ("That Politics May be Reduced to a Science," *ibid.,* I, 101–03). Their property rights in the colonized territory would presumably be erased either by contract or by conquest (*A Treatise of Human Nature,* Bk. III, *op. cit.,* 117). There may also be present that element of radical inequality, as between colonist and colonized, which renders questions of right and property irrelevant to the situation. See p.83, above.
[43] *A Treatise of Human Nature,* Bk. III, *op. cit.,* 153.

boast [was] that he would render the name of an Englishman as much feared
and revered as ever was that of a Roman; and as his countrymen found some
reality in these pretensions, their national vanity being gratified, made them
bear with more patience all the indignities and calamities under which they labored.[44]

Hume, then, was aware not only of the reality of heroic glory, but also
of the uses to which it lends itself.

He regarded conquest as an example of acquisition of property by
right of present possession, strengthened in this case by "the notions of
glory which we ascribe to conquerors."[45] He did not question this right,
or even discuss conquest and empire in terms of justice. Justice, after
all, presupposes a degree of equality of the parties. Conquest affirms,
for the time being at least, the absence of equality.

But national vanity, the dazzling glory of conquering heroes, the
rights and wrongs of imperial situations—these carried limited weight
with Hume. Vast empires, he thought, are destructive of property,
commerce, liberty, the arts and sciences, and eventually of themselves.
Hume reasons that since the "ancient nobility" will not remain permanently away from their homeland, and in any case must be closely attached to the imperial court, where their ambitions may be curbed, the
defense of these vast domains must eventually devolve on mercenaries.
Mercenaries serve the highest bidder, be he legitimate ruler or not—
and always serve themselves first and foremost.[46] The exigencies of
inevitable and probably continuous wars against rebels and intruders
destroys security of property and ruins commerce. Eventually the ruler
becomes absolute.[47] The arts and sciences—so valuable both as sources
of morale and progress and as impetus for the development and exercise of human energies—require a "spirit of emulation," and cease to
flourish where "none has courage to resist the torrent of popular
opinion."[48] Thus is human variety and individuality, and liberty along
with it, lost in a languid egalitarian ocean. And at last "the melancholy
fate of the Roman emperors . . . is renewed over and over again, till the
final dissolution of the monarchy."[49] Perhaps the empire falls before
peoples like "the German nations, who . . . broke the Roman chains,
and restored liberty to mankind. . . ."[50] In short, "enormous monarchies are probably destructive to human nature; in their progress, in
their continuance, and even in their downfall, which never can be very
distant from their establishment."[51]

[44] *History, op. cit.,* V, 366.
[45] *A Treatise of Human Nature,* Bk. III, *op. cit.,* 117.
[46] "Of the Balance of Power," *Essays, op. cit.,* I, 355.
[47] "Of Public Credit," *ibid.,* I, 368–69.
[48] "Of the Rise and Progress of the Arts and Sciences," *ibid.,* I, 183.
[49] "Of the Balance of Power," *ibid.,* I, 356.   [50] *History, op. cit.,* IV, 299.
[51] "Of the Balance of Power," *Essays, op. cit.,* I, 355. Hume found something of a
problem in the extreme longevity of the Chinese empire, and found his answer in

No institution destructive of human nature can be said to have utility, or to be characteristic of a good society or of a people's greatness. Hume's *dislike* of universal empire is obvious. But "it is not certain that an opinion is false because of its dangerous circumstances."[52] That something is repugnant does not prove that it can be avoided. Hume, with his respect for habit and experience as guides to human conduct, would not have proposed or supported institutions or organizational arrangements he viewed as at best evanescent. Did he then think that (perhaps like death, which is also inevitable, but—at least from the point of view of the individual concerned—cannot normally be said to have much utility) it is the historically inevitable conclusion to the story of great races of men? If he entertained any thoughts on this point, Hume did not record them. But, given the role of empire in world history, it remains a fundamental point in any consideration of basic questions of macropolitical organization. It is inconceivable that so thorough a student as Hume, one as concerned as he with human nature, society, and politics, and one who was among the most knowledgeable historians of his time, would simply never have thought about the question or made any implicit assumptions about it.

It may be possible, by comparing what Hume did say about universal empire with his opinions about other macrosystemic arrangements, and by examining his preferences among them, to infer something about his thought or assumptions about the inevitability of universal empire. In this connection it may also be useful to summarize certain of his conclusions with regard to other institutions, in this case property and commerce.

Hume thought both individual and sociopolitical interests are best served when a large portion of the members of a society are also property holders; he believed the concentration of property in a few hands—and above all, in one hand only (be it ruler or "public")—to be the acme of social inutility and misfortune. He did not think such concentration is inevitable. (It must be noted here that only in certain cases of imperial despotism has such concentration in one hand been even theoretically the case.)

China's isolation and its security behind its "famous wall." Because of these factors, he thought, "military discipline has always been much neglected amongst them; and their standing forces are mere militia, of the worst kind; and unfit to suppress any general insurrection in countries so populous" ("Of the Rise and Progress of the Arts and Sciences," *ibid.*, I, 183n.). The reader is left to wonder whether China had had the unbelievable luck not to experience general insurrection, or whether (as is actually the case) such insurrections had in fact occurred from time to time, but either had suffered the fate of Wat Tyler's rebellion in England (which was not suppressed wholly or even primarily by "standing forces"), or the rebels had successfully toppled one dynasty, only to replace it with another which had then gone on to reproduce the governmental forms of its predecessor.

[52] *An Inquiry Concerning Human Understanding, op. cit.,* 96.

He was of the opinion that commerce, whose social utility he saw no need to defend, flourishes where a number of equal and active parties participate in it. He did not even discuss, as commerce, exchanges whose terms are dictated by one of the parties. He certainly never contemplated such a situation as the end product or final stage of either commercial development or of other political or economic processes—except universal empire, which he held discourages commerce, property, and liberty together. Furthermore, in Hume's mind the wealth generated by commerce contributes to state power but is not properly viewed or used *primarily* as an instrument for aggrandizement of the state. This is a far cry indeed from the imperialist idea, in which the riches and efforts of the populace are, and must be, ultimately at the disposal of the state, in which individual happiness and well being are at best incidental to public or sovereign strength or glory,[53] or to the discharge of an imperial responsibility or mission.

Notwithstanding the notorious instability which is in fact a premise of its operation, and the paucity of its claims to moral or other extrapolitical sanction,[54] Hume's preferred system of macropolitical organization remains the balance of power. His formulation of the arguments in its favor, and of the tendencies that endanger it,[55] has become a classic. His great criticism of Charles II centered on the latter's partiality to France which, at a time when Louis XIV was "the undisputed leader of Europe," endangered the European balance.[56] Speaking of his own time, Hume found Britain wanting in its concern for preservation of the balance only to the extent that its overenthusiasm permitted its allies "always [to] reckon upon our force as part of their own; and expecting to carry on war at our expense, [to] refuse all reasonable terms of accommodation." This victory of British enthusiasm over prudence also, and most importantly, threatened Britain with financial and other reverses[57] which, should they become severe

[53]Cf., e.g.,: "All states perpetually struggle against the tendency of citizens to see themselves as the ends to which the political order ought to be the instrument: there is often some grave difficulty in persuading them to take the contrary view . . ."; "Underarmament is . . . a benevolence to taxpayers" (David O. Wilkinson, *Comparative Foreign Relations: Framework and Methods* [Belmont, Calif., 1969], 48, 65).

[54]Empire, on the other hand, has been widely (and in premodern times almost universally) perceived as the normal and even divinely sanctioned order to the world. And, under one or another species of leadership it did persist, at least symbolically, in Western civilization and its predecessors, until very close to our own time: "Die Schlussheit des dreitausendjährigen ägyptens Königtums ist also zugleich die Angangzeit des fast neunzehnhundert-jährigen römischem Kaisertums. Durch fünf Jahrtausende erstreckte sich eine ununterbrochene Kette von aufeinanderfolgenden Herrschern" (Karl Fürst Schwarzenberg, *Adler und Drache: der Weltherrschaftsgedanke* [Vienna, 1958]).

[55]"Of the Balance of Power," *Essays, op. cit.*, I, 348–56.

[56]*History, op. cit.*, IV: 13, 74, 92–93, 228–29.

[57]"Of the Balance of Power," *Essays, op. cit.*, I, 354; "Of Public Credit," *ibid.*, I, 368–69.

enough, might "beget . . . as usual, the opposite extreme, and [render] us totally careless and supine with regard to the fate of Europe."[58]

In all Hume's remarks on the balance of power, the kinds of threats to it that may be expected and have been experienced, and the means of successfully opposing these threats, there is not the slightest implication that Hume thought Europe need eventually become incorporated into an imperial unity, or that Britain should attempt, for whatever reason, to become the leader in such a process and therefore the ruler of Europe. His frame of mind in this respect cannot be attributed to the fact that Europe had escaped effective political unification for over a millennium, that there was no danger of imperium being attempted or realized. He believed that first Austria and now in his own era France, indeed held such aims and, if not successfully countered, might well realize them.[59] And Francophile though Hume was in many respects, if he had thought a universal empire of Europe to be inevitable, he would certainly have wanted to see it accomplished by Britain and not France. In fact, he only feared that Britain might not bring enough prudence to its efforts to combat such tendencies and aims, to overcome the threat of their realization. The idea of Britain itself adopting such an aim was utterly foreign to his thought.

We have seen that Hume emphatically did not regard imperium as a component of public happiness, and that—the historical record notwithstanding—he did not regard universal empire as an inevitable stage in the development of a civilization. Yet all those great civilizations of the past which he used as material for construction of his own political theory had indeed aspired to universal imperium.[60] If, as in the Hellenic case, they had not succeeded in establishing and consolidating imperial power, they lost the political power that had rendered their aspirations possible, fell into subordination to a stronger rival, and relapsed into political insignificance. How can this historical evidence, of which Hume was aware, be theoretically reconciled with his apparent judgment that it need not apply to the Europe of his own time?

The answer lies in the very center of Hume's argument about the uniformity of consequences of uniform causes. This uniformity, though it cannot be demonstrated *a priori*,[61] can indeed be observed and firm conclusions, valid in their own terms, drawn from them.[62] But only causes uniform *in all respects* can be counted on to produce uniform consequences. In politics causes include not only "diversity of

---

[58] "Of the Balance of Power," *ibid.*, I, 354.   [59] *Ibid.*, I, 354–55.

[60] He did not discuss the one apparent exception—the Hindu civilization—in this connection. Speculation about the reasons for the apparent nonconformity of this civilization to the pattern of the others is outside the scope of this study; one may, however, point to certain peculiarities in traditional Hindu social structure and in the religious and political values which underlay and supported it, as well as to a historical (or ahistorical) and political perspective which has been represented as unique among the great premodern civilizations. See McNeill, *op. cit.*, 196–97.

[61] *Treatise*, Bk. I, *op. cit.*, Pt. II, Sect. 2.   [62] *Ibid.*, Pt. III, Sect. 3.

character, prejudices and opinions" of men, but also circumstantial variations which, like the grain of dust which—all unobserved by the observer—stops the movement of a clock, produces a consequence different from those which precede it.[63] Hume was modest in his claims for social science. Given what is firmly known about human nature, some general truths in politics may be fixed, but these general truths are few,[64] and Hume's enumeration of those he believed to have been adequately verified does not include any about inevitable progressions of forms of macropolitical organization.[65]

Hume, then, was historically oriented but he held no grand cyclical or developmental theories about man's political fate. He did not assume that all, or enough, relevant historic-political variables have been or surely can be identified, to permit accurate prediction about such matters. Perhaps he believed that history has not yet revealed the permanently limiting case in human political development—if such a case may indeed be posited. He was at any rate unconvinced that man had yet, or could yet, discern it. Substantively, Hume stands squarely among those who hold that, in general, personal and not collective values do and should motivate individual human action, and that domestic and not external objectives are the proper ultimate objectives of political action directed at the ultimate political value of public happiness. Public happiness—insofar as it can be said to be realizable—is realizable *within* a society, and does not depend on a people's domination over others. He regarded security of property and a flourishing commerce as values to be sought and protected, primarily to the benefit and happiness of human persons and only secondarily to the power and glory of the state. As such, they can be realized and yield their benefits only in environments marked by political liberty and diversity, to which universal empire is inimical. He judged foreign policy by the standard of the extent to which it conduces to the security of society and the furtherance of its values, not by the standard of the extent to which it conduces to expanded power of the state within the macropolitical system. Security within that system is a necessary condition of attainment of personal and domestic social values. It may on occasion require abatement of their pursuit. But it does not, in itself, override them. Hume gave no indication of belief either that nature, as history illuminates it, impels, or that conceptions of responsibility, mission, or national glory need or ought to impel, great states to follow those of their predecessors which have chosen the noble, glorious, and fatal path to universal empire.

Loyola University of Chicago.

[63]*An Inquiry Concerning Human Understanding, op. cit.,* 95–96.
[64]"Of Civil Liberty," *Essays, op. cit.,* I, 156.
[65]"That Politics May be Reduced to a Science," *ibid.,* I, 98–109.

XIV

DAVID HUME AND AMERICA

By John M. Werner

The transformation in thought and loyalties that turned thirteen British provinces into one nation has been observed from numerous viewpoints; likewise, the impact of David Hume upon his age also has been elucidated. One question, however remains to be answered: to what extent, if any, did the writings of the man who destroyed the Lockean concept of the social contract theory work an influence upon Americans of the Revolutionary generation, immersed as they were in whig ideology? The uncertainty inherent in this question is that such "influence" is exceedingly difficult to determine. American writers frequently cited several authorities on one point, making it almost impossible to isolate any individual's exact contribution to their thought. As Charles Hendel has aptly pointed out:

American statesmen ... were engaged upon their great task of establishing a republic that would endure. There were grave fears and predictions at the time that the new commonwealth would not last. The men who drew up the [various] resolutions, those who spoke at the Federal Convention, as well as the citizens and country gentlemen who had made a Revolution and were now seeking to govern themselves had little time to document their words and identify the sources of their opinion or inspiration. They were constantly referring to the "experience" of the British Constitution, and quite often in the very phrases of Hume, as when Madison spoke of "the republican principle."[1]

And while it is a truism that the formation of the United States did not take place in an intellectual or political vacuum, it is equally true that not every British or Continental intellectual work crossed the Atlantic; David Hume's writings were no exception. The best compromise that can be achieved, therefore, is to attempt to ascertain which of Hume's works were available to the Americans and what use they made of them.

The philosopher's life spanned the gap nicely between the era when one generation of Americans was fighting loyally for the Crown during the War of the Spanish Succession to the time when the next generation of Americans would take up arms against the Crown. This same period saw the last attempts at Scottish independence crushed by the English. Although he was not an active participant in either the

[1] Bernard Bailyn, *The Ideological Origins of the American Revolution* (Cambridge, Mass., 1967), 26–28; Charles Hendel, ed., *David Hume's Political Essays* (New York, 1953), xlv, xlvii, lvii.

American or the Scottish upheavals, David Hume was affected by both, as is evidenced in some of his later writings.

These years, while unhappy politically, saw Scotland's greatest outpouring of intellectual endeavor. It is referred to accurately as the "Scottish Enlightenment"; David Hume had, of course, been an integral part of it. Indeed, one historian has observed that this epoch could be referred to as "the age of Hume." Another, a well-known intellectual historian, acknowledges Hume as the greatest British philosopher of the eighteenth century.[2] David Hume's ideas mark a turning point in the history of thought in that he abandoned most of the philosophical conceptions of the previous century.

Hume was an empirical philosopher in the tradition of Locke and Berkeley, but, unhampered by theological scruples, Hume was able to draw empiricism out to its logical conclusion—skepticism. What Hume was trying to do was to show that the structure of reality could not be entered merely by rational insight. Hume says that all human knowledge rests on two things: impressions and ideas. Impressions are received by the senses; the ideas corresponding to these impressions are connected in accordance with the causal principle. Any attempt to find some reality underlying these impressions is useless. Reality can be found only in a continuously changing aggregate of feelings bound together by a psychological or social force known as custom. Custom thus replaces *a priori* reason as the subjective basis of beliefs about causation in external and human nature. Hume of course realized that such absolute skepticism was not practical since he had used reasoning to come to the conclusion that all reasoning is absurd. As one modern philosopher has stated, Hume's real problem "was so to use scepticism as to undermine theology and metaphysics, but safeguard science and secular morality." J. A. Passmore has concluded, "Hume's great achievement ... lies in his contribution to a ... conception of science, in which speculation, not security, is the key note...." The ultimate impression Hume drew from his philosophy was that one must, of necessity, rely solely on experience. Only experience could accurately decide questions of morality or politics.[3] The concept of experience was an open sesame

[2]W. L. Taylor, *Frances Hutcheson and David Hume as Predecessors of Adam Smith* (Durham, 1965), 5; P. Hume Brown, "Scotland in the Eighteenth Century," *The Scottish Historical Review*, VI (July 1909), 348; Lawrence Henry Gipson, *The Coming of the Revolution* (New York, 1954), 7; Caroline Robbins, *The Eighteenth-Century Commonwealthman: Studies in the Transmission, Development and Circumstances of English Liberal Thought from the Restoration of Charles II Until the War with the Thirteen Colonies* (Cambridge, Mass., 1959), 380.

[3]Stuart N. Hampshire, "Hume's Place in Philosophy," in D. F. Pears, ed., *David Hume: A Symposium* (London, 1963), 4; C. R. Morris, *Locke Berkeley Hume* (London, 1931), 129, 143; Sir Leslie Stephen, *History of English Thought in the Eigh-*

to the Americans; Patrick Henry referred to experience as a lamp by which the past illuminated the future. Hume's philosophy as a formal system of metaphysical speculation was, however, not well known in America. Americans, concerned with establishing their rights as Englishmen and later their rights to independence, were more concerned with political and historical writings; when Hume moved into these fields the Americans became acquainted with him. Indeed, during his lifetime, Hume enjoyed his greatest earnings and reputation among all peoples as an essayist and historian, not as a philosopher.[4]

Hume regarded history as an essential study, calling it "the greatest mistress of wisdom." He was the first of the British philosophical historians, although his friends William Robertson and Edward Gibbon soon followed, writing history from the same perspective. These men believed history was an intellectual exercise aimed at social analysis; and furthermore, they felt that philosophy and history complemented each other. History traced the development of the human mind. This same human mind provided the materials from which the philosopher derived the principles of thinking and conduct.[5] The close connection between philosophy and history is emphasized in a passage from the *Enquiry Concerning Human Understanding:*

Its [history's] chief Use is only to discover the constant and universal Principles of human Nature, by shewing Men in all Varieties of Circumstances and Situations, and furnishing us with Materials, from which we may form our Observations, and become acquainted with the regular Springs of human Action and Behaviour. These Records of Wars, Intrigues, Factions, and Revolutions, are so many Collections of Experiments, by which the Politician or moral Philosopher fixes the Principles of his science; in the same Manner as the Physician or natural Philosopher becomes acquainted with the Nature of Plants, Minerals, and other external Objects, by the Experiments, which he forms concerning them.[6]

teenth Century, 2 vols. (New York, 1962), I, 1, 36–37; D. G. C. MacNabb, *David Hume: His Theory of Knowledge and Morality* (New York, 1966²), 5–6; J. A. Passmore, *Hume's Intentions* (Cambridge, 1952), 154; Carmin Mascia, *A History of Philosophy* (Paterson, 1957), 326. For a different view of Hume's relationship to Locke and Berkeley, see Norman Kemp Smith, *The Philosophy of David Hume* (London, 1949), 78–85.

⁴H. Trevor Colbourn, *The Lamp of Experience: Whig History and the Intellectual Origins of the American Revolution* (Chapel Hill, 1965), xi; Pears, ed., *David Hume: A Symposium*, 6. Hume himself moved from an interest in so-called "pure" philosophy toward a larger conception in which a genuine grasp of human nature would be combined with an intelligent direction of all human endeavors. In short, Hume anticipated modern social scientists.

⁵Colbourn, *Lamp of Experience*, 5; Ernest C. Mossner, *The Life of David Hume* (Austin, 1954), 301.

⁶David Hume, *An Enquiry Concerning Human Understanding and Other Essays*, ed. Ernest C. Mossner (New York, 1963), 86.

Read in a day when the intense passions surrounding the appella-
tions and policies of whig and tory have disappeared, Hume's *History
of England* seems remarkably free from political bias; unfortunately,
in its early life very few men viewed it in this light. Gavin Hamilton
said it was "neither whig nor tory but truely imparshal [sic]."
Hamilton was also the first publisher of the *History*, which vitiates
somewhat his cold-eyed objectivity. Hume, in *My Own Life*, said the
History had caused him to be "assailed by ... [both] Whig and
Tory...." A modern writer agrees. John Stewart says Hume's *History*
comforted neither whig nor tory and both sides denounced him. In
amount of sheer venom, the whigs triumphed; they detested the *History*. Some, like Bishop William Warburton, even labelled it "Jacobite." Horace Walpole came much closer to a perceptive evaluation
of the work: "Where others abuse the Stuarts, he [Hume] laughs at
them."[7]

There most certainly are passages in the *History* that seem to indicate a definite partiality toward one side or the other. Discussing the
reign of Charles I, Hume claimed the king was genuinely sincere in
calling his first parliament. Parliament repaid this sincerity by voting
him the niggardly sum of £112,000 to prosecute a war and run the government. According to Hume, this was a cruel mockery rather than a
serious attempt to support Charles. Hume tempered his support of
Charles by remarking that the monarch's later attempts to raise money
by various schemes would be regarded even in the most absolute government as "irregular and unequal." And further, the king's general
principles were "altogether incompatible with a limited government."
At the conclusion of his *History*, Hume reviewed the reigns of the
four Stuart kings and observed that the Revolution of 1688 had been
advantageous to the nation and since that time Britain had enjoyed not
perfect liberty but at least the best known to mankind. Hume then took
strenuous exception to the whig writers who pictured the Stuarts as
complete devils; as Hume saw it, this was inaccurate and bad history.[8] His own balanced analysis comes much closer to modern historical methods. While we admire this quality in Hume's *History*,
many men of the eighteenth century did not; the Americans were no
exception.

[7] H. Trevor Colbourn, "John Dickinson, Historical Revolutionary," *The Pennsylvania Magazine of History and Biography*, LXXXIII (1959), 282n.; John B. Stewart,
The Moral and Political Philosophy of David Hume (New York and London, 1963), 1,
9; Mossner, *Life of David Hume*, 303, 310; Hume, "My Own Life," in Mossner, ed.,
An Enquiry Concerning Human Understanding, 5. Earl Marischal Keith once wrote
to Hume: "To the highflyers you are ... a sad whig, to the whigs an hidden Jacobite,
and to reasonable men *le bon David*, a Lover of truth." Quoted in V. C. Chappell, ed.,
Hume (New York, 1966), 34.

[8] Hume, *The History of England from the Invasion of Julius Caesar to the Abdica-
tion of James the Second, 1688*, 6 vols. (Boston, 1850 edition), V, 3, 21, 43; VI, 363-66.

The practical Americans preferred to take their philosophy in historical doses rather than in undiluted abstract treatises; accordingly, Hume's *History* was more familiar to them than most of his other works. Although English editions of *The History of England* were rather common in America, the work's unfortunate tory reputation probably limited somewhat its popularity with whiggish-minded Americans. In 1771, Robert Bell, a colonist who had become very successful in the reprint trade, was unable to secure support for an American edition of the *History*.[9] Probably, many Americans were being influenced by the notoriety surrounding the work instead of specific content. In summarizing the reign of James I, Hume had written:

What chiefly renders the reign of James memorable is the commencement of the English colonies in America, colonies established on the noblest footing that has been known in any age or nation.... The spirit of independency, which was reviving in England, here shone forth in its full luster and received new accession from the aspiring character of those who, being discontented with the established church and monarch, had sought for freedom amidst those savage deserts....[10]

It is true, however, that elsewhere Hume did make statements which failed to endear him to some individuals on this side of the water. Like the Austrian eagle, Hume seems to be looking two ways at once. His reference to Puritan "cant, hypocrisy, and bigotry" would not have been read with equanimity by many New Englanders. The eminent Massachusetts theologian Jonathan Edwards averred that he was "glad of an opportunity to read such corrupt books, especially when written by men of considerable genius." Elsewhere, Hume's observations on the English civil wars were bound to be distasteful to a people busily engaged in their own revolution in government: "the sacred boundaries of the laws being once violated, nothing remained to confine the wild projects of zeal and ambition"; and again, "it is seldom that the people gain anything by revolutions in government; because the new government, jealous and insecure, must commonly be supported with more expense and severity than the old...." Hume also carried his assault upon the notion of the original contract over into his historical writing when he observed, "that the people are the origin of all just power . . . is belied by all history and experience."[11]

[9]Charles Evans, *American Bibliography: A Chronological Dictionary of all Books, Pamphlets, and Periodical Publications printed in the United States of America from the Genesis of printing in 1639 down to and including the year 1820* (New York, 1941), IV, sec. 11984; Colbourn, *Lamp of Experience*, 19.

[10]Hume, *History of England*, 6 vols. (New York, 1885 edition), IV, 369.

[11]Charles Hendel, *Hume's Political Essays*, lv; Peter Gay, *A Loss of Mastery: Puritan Historians In Colonial America* (New York, 1968), 91; Hume, *History of England* (1885 edition), V, 219, 248, 370.

The dichotomy in *The History* is more apparent than real; in these passages Hume was not addressing himself to the question of the American colonies and their relationship to the mother country. At the time, these great issues had yet to be raised. What Hume was doing in his *History* was simply using the past to illustrate what he assumed to be the eternal verities of his earlier philosophical and political writings. It is well to remember that for eighteenth-century man, politics, even more than philosophy, walked hand-in-hand with history. Since this was true, Hume's political essays were almost as well known to the Americans as was his *History*.[12]

According to Hume, a state is a relationship combining individual liberty and authority. A good state is one which maintains a proper balance between these two elements. A government represents the authority in a state. Hume sees four major principles by which governments should be bound so as not to transgress their authority. First, subjects should obey their proper governors. The emphasis here is on the word "proper." A government can only expect obedience when it is the properly constituted authority. Secondly, the government is to do its job. The government has no independent purpose, goal, or commission of its own; rather it exists only to advance the common purpose of all its subjects. Hume's third principle relates to government activity: the government is to be neutral, equal, and impartial in its penalties, judgments, positive laws, and activities. Finally, the government is to govern in as calculable a manner as possible. This means that the people should know with a reasonable degree of certainty what the government will do in any given set of circumstances. In the essay "That Politics May be Reduced to a Science," Hume observed "that tho free governments have been commonly the most happy for those who partake of their freedom, yet they are the most ruinous and oppressive to their provinces."[13] Americans could agree easily with this as the imagined English oppression was an obvious case in point.

These premises, in addition to other aspects of Hume's political thought—a belief that a form of government may be changed when the good of society demands it; a strong emphasis on freedom of the press; a non-hereditary second chamber for the legislature—seem to indicate that Hume would prove to be an able spokesman for the colonial cause.[14] He was just this in many cases; the pity is that more

[12]Stewart, *Moral and Political Philosophy of David Hume*, 1; Hendel, *Hume's Political Essays*, viii, xxvii.

[13]Stewart, *Moral and Political Philosophy of David Hume*. This summary of Hume's political thought was gleaned by Stewart from all of Hume's works. Hendel, *Hume's Political Essays*, 15.

[14]Robbins, *The Eighteenth-Century Commonwealthman*, 217; Hume, *Essays and Treatises on Several Subjects* (London, 1758), 6.

of the American leadership could not overcome their narrow political prejudices and rely on Hume more often.

David Hume was, of course, more than a writer; he was a man with definite political responses which have been too often ignored. Hume was a peaceful man who never made a public attempt to vindicate himself in the face of opponents' onslaughts. Hume styled himself a political moderate; his view of *things* corresponded more to whig principles, while his view of *persons* conformed to tory prejudices.[15] By the time it became obvious that a serious crisis was brewing in America, Hume had ceased writing for publication. His correspondence, nevertheless, reveals his feelings regarding America.

In a letter to the Earl of Hertford written on February 27, 1766, Hume announced his pleasure at the repeal of the Stamp Act. But in another letter written to the Earl in May of the same year, Hume was concerned because the Americans (relying on Pitt's speech in parliament on their behalf) now seemed anxious to push their demands much further than originally intended. Hume said if reports from America were true only Pitt seemed capable either of getting the Americans to submit peaceably to his authority or subduing them by his vigor. Hume added that in any case he no longer felt repeal of the Stamp Act would suffice.[16]

Hume's opinion toward America changed rapidly. In 1768 Hume said he longed to see America totally in revolt. He offered this same wish again in a letter to William Strahan the following year. By late winter, 1771, Hume could see nothing but ruin ahead for the British nation and did not think the union with America would last much longer.[17] In another letter to Strahan written in 1774, Hume reminisced over some repartee with a lord:

I remember, one day, at Lord Bathurst's, the Company, among whom, was his Son, the present Chancellor, were speaking of American Affairs; and some of them mention'd former Acts of Authority exercised over the Colonies. I observed to them, that Nations, as well as Individuals, had their different Ages, which challeng'd a different Treatment. For Instance, My Lord, said I to the old Peer, you have sometimes no doubt, given your Son a Whipping; and I doubt not, but it was well merited and did him much good: Yet you will not think proper at present to employ the Birch: The Colonies are no longer in their Infancy. But yet, I say to you, they are still in their Nonage;

---

[15]Mossner, *Life of David Hume*, 311.

[16]David Hume to the Earl of Hertford, Feb. 27, 1766, and May 8, 1766, J. Y. T. Greig, ed., *The Letters of David Hume*, 2 vols. (Oxford, 1932), II, 22, 42–43. Hereafter cited as *Hume's Letters*.

[17]Hume to Sir Gilbert Elliott of Minto, July 22, 1768, *Hume's Letters*, II, 184; Hume to William Strahan, Oct. 25, 1769, and Mar. 1, 1771, *Hume's Letters*, II, 209, 237.

and Dr. Franklyn's [sic] wishes to emancipate them too soon from their mother country.[18]

Hume did not give any indication what year the above exchange took place; but apparently by 1775, he felt the colonies had attained their majority. In that year he declared himself to be an American in his principles and wished the government would leave the colonists alone either to govern or misgovern themselves as best they could.[19] In another 1775 letter Hume advanced the argument that exclusive rights to the American trade were not worth fighting over because even if America's ports were thrown open to the ships of all nations, Britain would still get a great preponderance of the American trade. Warming up to the subject, Hume continued:

We hear that some of the ministers have proposed in Council that both fleet and army be withdrawn from America and these colonists be left entirely to themselves. I wish I had been a member of His Majesty's Cabinet Council that I might have seconded this opinion. I should have said that this measure only anticipates the necessary course of events a few years.

In this same letter, Hume described vividly the futility of trying to subdue so vast a country, and concluded, "Let us therefore lay aside all anger, shake hands, and part friends. Or, if we retain our anger, let it be only against ourselves for our past folly. . . ."[20] Hume again talked of this futility a few weeks later, and in addition, pictured the anarchy and confusion he foresaw descending upon Britain as the result of the American conflict. Hume adopted a rather patronizing attitude when he wrote to a martial-minded relative early in 1776: the colonies could not be subdued unless they divided, but this was a distinct possibility.[21]

It is obvious from his correspondence that Hume sympathized with the American cause, and it is equally obvious that he was appalled at English conduct. Hume's attitude toward England was complex but significant; it was a product of a psychology which marshalled pride against the contemporary anti-Scottish prejudice.[22] There are numerous instances in Hume's letters where this contempt for the English is expressed. In a letter to Sir Gilbert Elliot, Hume remarked:

I fancy the Ministry will remain; tho surely their late Remissness or Ignorance or Pusillanimity ought to make them ashamed to show their Faces. . . . These

[18]Hume to William Strahan, Mar. 1, 1774, *Hume's Letters*, II, 287–88.

[19]Hume to Baron Mure of Caldwell, Oct. 27, 1775, *Hume's Letters*, II, 302–03.

[20]Hume to William Strahan, Oct. 26, 1775, *Hume's Letters*, II, 300–01; Dalphy I. Fagerstrom, "Scottish Opinion and the American Revolution," *The William and Mary Quarterly*, 3d series, XI (1954), 259.

[21]Hume to William Strahan, Nov. 13, 1775, *Hume's Letters*, II, 304–05; Hume to John Home, Feb. 8, 1776, *Hume's Letters*, II, 307–08.

[22]John Clive and Bernard Bailyn, "England's Cultural Provinces: Scotland and America," *The William and Mary Quarterly*, 3d series, XI (1954), 212.

are fine doings in America. O! how I long to see America and the East Indies revolted totally & finally, the Revenue reduc'd to half, public Credit fully discredited by Bankruptcy, the third of London in Ruins. . . .[23]

Hume made an identical wish to Strahan in 1769 and in addition said he has had the misfortune to write in "the Language of the most stupid and factious Barbarians in the World. . . ."[24]

In October 1775, Baron Mure of Caldwell wrote Hume asking him to draft a petition to the King from the freeholders of Renfrewshire, Scotland, recommending forcible measures against the colonists. Such petitions were fairly common at this time. Hume's reply stated that he could not draft such a petition, but if the loyal residents of the County of Renfrew felt compelled to intervene in public affairs they should advise the King to clean out the "insolent rascals" in London. Hume said this would be a more worthy ambition for them than attacking people in another hemisphere. After all, Hume quizzed, how could any government expect to maintain its authority at a distance of 3000 miles when it could not even make itself respected at home? A letter written only two months before his death expressed Hume's indignation that the Earl of Sandwich, First Lord of the Admiralty, and some other lords along with several prostitutes took off for two weeks and travelled sixty miles from London to enjoy the trouting season. All this occurred, in Hume's words, while the fate of the British Empire was being decided in the New World.[25]

As a Scotsman, David Hume could and did commiserate with the Americans in their struggle. And, as noted, in his political and historical writings Hume had furnished arguments which the Americans, through their knack for judicious editing, could turn into excellent propaganda for their cause. American theorists were not slaves to the thoughts of any man or group of men. They searched the writings of many individuals, particularly British political thinkers, for advantageous ideas. They did spurn a few—Hobbes, Filmer, and the Levellers and Diggers of the seventeenth century; however, they generally refused to let a man's reputation either repel or overawe them completely. Thus they eagerly quoted Blackstone when he paid homage to natural law and disregarded Locke when he remarked on the supremacy of parliament.[26] David Hume fitted into this tradition very well; he was neither ignored completely nor accepted completely in North America.

[23] Hume to Sir Gilbert Elliot, July 22, 1768, Hume's Letters, II, 184.
[24] Hume to William Strahan, Oct. 25, 1769, Hume's Letters, II, 209.
[25] Hume to Baron Mure, Oct. 27, 1775, Hume's Letters, II, 302-03; Hume to William Strahan, May 10, 1776, Hume's Letters, II, 319.
[26] Clinton Rossiter, Seedtime of the Republic: the Origin of the American Tradition of Political Liberty (New York, 1953), 356-57.

The most conspicuous example of attachment was that which existed between Hume and Benjamin Franklin. Apparently they became acquainted during Franklin's visit to London in 1757, and, in 1760, Franklin visited Hume at Edinburgh. This same year Franklin wrote Hume a letter which illustrates the deep regard Franklin had for Hume:

> I am not a little pleas'd to hear of your Change of Sentiments in some particulars relating to America; because I think it of Importance to our general Welfare that the People of this Nation should have right Notions of us, and I know of no one that has it more in his Power to rectify their Notions, than Mr. Hume. I have lately read with great Pleasure, as I do every thing of yours, the excellent Essay on the *Jealousy of Commerce*. I think it cannot but have a good Effect in promoting a certain Interest too little thought of by selfish Man, and scarce ever mention'd, so that we hardly have a Name for it; I mean the *Interest of Humanity*, or common Good of Mankind. But I hope particularly from that Essay, an Abatement of the Jealousy that reigns here of the Commerce of the Colonies, at least so far as such Abatement may be reasonable.[27]

In 1762 Franklin sent Hume a monograph describing his lightning rod to be read before the Philosophical Society of Edinburgh. Franklin returned to Great Britain in 1771, and again visited the Scot at his home. The next year Hume wrote Franklin saying that he was glad to hear that the Philadelphian had once again arrived safely in London. This letter of February 7, 1772, was the last of their correspondence (at least the last extant), but in a 1774 letter to Adam Smith, Hume related the shock he felt at Franklin's having been accused before the Privy Council of misusing his position as Deputy Post-Master General of America. Hume seemed to believe that Franklin had gone too far in this instance. If Franklin was aware of a cooling off on the part of his friend, he did not let it influence his regard for Hume as a political theorist. During the Philadelphia Convention of 1787, delegate Franklin suggested that no high officer in any of the three branches of government should receive a salary. This was one of the suggestions Hume had made in his emendation of Harrington's *Oceana*.[28]

[27] L. Jesse Lemisch, ed., *Benjamin Franklin: The Autobiography and Other Writings* (New York, 1961), 154; Franklin to Hume, Sept. 27, 1760, Leonard W. Labaree, ed., *The Papers of Benjamin Franklin* (New Haven and London, 1966), IX, 229. Franklin had his titles mixed up here. He was referring to "Of the Jealousy of Trade," contained in the 1758 edition of *Essays and Treatises on Several Subjects*, and not "Of Commerce," printed in the 1752 edition of *Political Discourses*. For evidence that respect and admiration between the two men was mutual, see Hume to Franklin, May 10, 1762, *Papers of Franklin*, X, 81–82, in which Hume says that "America has sent us many good things, Gold, Silver, Sugar, Tobacco, Indigo &c.: But you are the first Philosopher, and indeed the first Great Man of Letters for whom we are beholden to her...."

[28] Franklin to Hume, Jan. 21, 1762, *Papers of Franklin*, X, 17–23, 80–84; R. Klibansky and Ernest C. Mossner, eds., *New Letters of David Hume* (Oxford, 1954),

Other Americans of the Revolutionary generation relied on Hume to help support their position in various controversies. In 1773, Charles Carroll of Carrollton clashed in a newspaper debate with Daniel Dulany, Jr. over the question of whether a colonial governor had the right to set crown officers' fees within a colony or whether this right should be reserved to the colonial assembly. Dulany, one of the governor's councilors and entitled to these fees, sided with the governor. Carroll became the Maryland Assembly's champion. The debate was carried on in the *Maryland Gazette* from February to July, 1773, with both men relying extensively on history to support their arguments. One of Carroll's chief authorities was David Hume's *History of England*, which he cited frequently. It was generally conceded that Carroll carried the field in this clash between the "First Citizen" (Carroll) and "Antilon" (Dulany). Dulany resorted to some personal attacks on Carroll concerning Carroll's Roman Catholic faith and also was bitterly critical of Carroll's use of Hume's *History* as a source. Dulany said this *History* was nothing more than "a studied apology for the Stuarts."[29] It was unfortunate that Dulany had not read Hume with more care, for Dulany's concern with popular limits on sovereignty and his abhorrence of turbulence, disorder, and disobedience to law were views very similar to those of Hume.

Soon after Carroll had called Hume as an expert witness to the correctness of his cause, Josiah Quincy, Jr. made a similar demand. Early in 1774, the "intolerable" Boston Port Bill was under consideration in parliament. The younger Quincy defended the colonial position in his memorable tract, *Observations on . . . the Boston Port Bill*. At one point, Quincy takes up the question of a free militia versus a standing army and cites Hume to strengthen his position:

When the sword is in the hands of a single person—as in our constitution— *he will always* (says the ingenious Hume) neglect to discipline the militia, in order to have a pretext for keeping up a standing army. 'Tis evident (says the same great character) that this is a mortal distemper of which it must at last *inevitably perish*.[30]

There would appear to be very little relationship between a radical republican like Thomas Paine and a conservative figure like David Hume; however, an examination of some of the political thought expressed in *Common Sense* indicates that Paine read Hume's political

---

194; *Hume's Letters*, II, 286; John M. Burton, *Life and Correspondence of David Hume*, 2 vols. (Edinburgh, 1846), I, 361; Hendel, ed., *Hume's Political Essays*, liii-liv.

[29]Colbourn, *Lamp of Experience*, 138–42; *Maryland Gazette* (Annapolis), Feb. 4, 11, 18, Apr. 8, May 6, and July 1, 1773.

[30]Josiah Quincy, Jr., *Observations on the Act of Parliament, commonly called the Boston Port Bill; with Thoughts on Civil Society and Standing Armies* (Boston and London, 1774), 38.

essays very closely. Paine's explanation of the origin of government and
the different ways of acquiring monarchies is identical with Hume's as
expressed in the essays "Of the Original Contract" and "Of the Origin
of Government." Paine had said that government originated and rose
because of the inability of moral virtue to govern the world. Hume
showed that he believed in a similar rise of government by asserting
that human nature was incapable of sustaining original perfection.
Paine noted how a man like William the Conqueror ("a French bastard
landing with armed banditti") could usurp the throne and how through
succeeding generations this usurpation could become sanctified until
some of his successors believed they ruled by divine right. Hume had
earlier concluded similarly:

When a new government is established, by whatever means, the people are
commonly dissatisfied with it, and pay obedience more from fear and necessity, than from any idea of allegiance or of moral obligation. . . . Time, by degrees, removes all these difficulties, and accustoms the nation to regard, as
their lawful or native princes, that family, whom, at first, they regarded as
usurpers or foreign conquerors.[31]

Furthermore, Paine's examination of the republican and monarchical
elements existing in the English constitution is nothing more than an
elaboration of the question raised by Hume in his essay, "Whether the
British Government inclines more to absolute monarchy, or to a Republic?"[32]

Unfortunately, Hume had another sort of influence upon Americans, an influence marked by racial prejudice. In an appended note to
his essay "Of National Characters" Hume had written:

I am apt to suspect the Negroes to be naturally inferior to the whites. There
scarcely ever was a civilized nation of that complexion, nor even any individual eminent either in action or speculation. No ingenious manufactures
among them, no arts, no sciences. On the other hand, the most rude and bar-
barous of the whites, such as the ancient GERMANS, the present TARTARS,
have still something eminent about them, in their valour, form of government, or some other particular. Such a uniform and constant difference could
not happen, in so many countries and ages, if nature had not made an original
distinction between these breeds of men. Not to mention our colonies, there
are NEGROE slaves dispersed all over EUROPE, of whom none ever discovered any symptoms of ingenuity; though low people, without education,
will start up amongst us, and distinguish themselves in every profession. In
JAMAICA, indeed, they talk of one Negroe as a man of parts and learning;

[31]Nelson F. Adkins, ed., *Thomas Paine: Common Sense and Other Political
Writings* (New York, 1953), 15–16; Hume, *Essays*, 8, 10.
[32]Felix Gilbert, "The English Background of American Isolationalism in the
Eighteenth Century," *The William and Mary Quarterly*, 3d series, I (1944), 156.

but it is likely he is admired for slender accomplishments, like a parrot, who speaks a few words plainly.[33]

This note is not consistent with Hume's usual respect for the dignity of man. Ernest Mossner observes correctly that Hume doubtless was making an unwarranted generalization based on myths and hearsay.[34]

A dogmatic statement of this nature from a famous man of letters was picked up eagerly by American proslavery writers. In 1773, an anonymous pamphlet was published entitled *Personal Slavery Established.* The author must have had a copy of Hume's essay at his elbow as he wrote, "There never was a civilized nation of any other complexion than *white;* nor ever any individual eminent either in action or speculation that was not rather inclining to the *fair.*" In the same year, Richard Nisbet published *Slavery Not Forbidden by Scripture* and like the anonymous author of *Personal Slavery Established,* relied upon Hume for part of his argument in defense of slavery. Perhaps the most fitting conclusion to this unsavory episode was furnished in 1791 when James McHenry of Baltimore wrote the introduction to Benjamin Banneker's first almanac. McHenry said that Banneker's attainments were a "striking contradiction to Mr. *Hume's* doctrine, that the Negroes are naturally inferior to the whites...."[35] Had the philosopher still been alive, he might have hastened to add his "Amen."

Hume's influence was present not only in the writings of Americans; it was felt also in their deliberative bodies. In 1780, the Committee on Finance in the Continental Congress, seeking to make themselves knowledgeable in all matters pertaining to finance, delved thoroughly into Hume's economic essays. And in the Federal Convention of 1787, Alexander Hamilton spoke out against a proposal to attach legal penalties against corruption on the part of office-holders. Hamilton insisted that this was unnecessary by referring to Hume. The New Yorker said: "Hume's opinion of the British Constitution confirms the remark, that there is always a body of firm patriots, who often shake a corrupt administration."[36]

---

[33] Hume, "Of National Characters," *An Enquiry Concerning Human Understanding and Other Essays,* 221–22.

[34] Mossner, ed., in *ibid.,* 222.

[35] Winthrop D. Jordan, *White Over Black: American Attitudes Toward the Negro, 1550–1812* (Baltimore, 1969), 304–07, 450.

[36] Edmund Cody Burnett, *The Continental Congress* (New York, 1964 edition), 479; Hendel, ed., *Hume's Political Essays,* lix; Max Farrand, ed., *The Records of the Federal Convention of 1787,* 4 vols., (New Haven and London, 1966 edition), I, 381. Vernon L. Parrington in *Main Currents in American Thought: The Colonial Mind, 1620–1800* (New York, 1954 edition), I, 301, 303, says that Hume was one of the major influences upon the formation of Hamilton's thought, and that it may well have been

Hamilton called Hume "a writer equally solid and ingenious," and carried his reliance upon the Scot over into the fight for ratification of the new constitution. Hamilton more or less summarized the arguments advanced in the *Federalist Papers* in his conclusion to "Federalist No. 85," the last in the series. Hamilton presented his readers with some "judicious reflections" from one of Hume's essays entitled "Of The Rise and Progress of the Arts and Sciences":

To balance a large state or society [says he], whether monarchical or republican, on general laws, is a work of so great difficulty that no human genius, however comprehensive, is able, by the mere dint of reason and reflection, to effect it. The judgements of many must unite in the work; experience must guide their labor; time must bring it to perfection, and the feeling of inconveniences must correct the mistakes which they *inevitably* fall into in their first trials and experiments.[37]

Hume perhaps had his most penetrating influence upon America through the person of James Madison. The late Douglass G. Adair has shown in a convincing manner that, at the time of the Constitutional Convention, Madison was a disciple of Hume. In 1913, Charles A. Beard had confidently asserted that Madison's *Federalist* No. 10 was "a masterly statement of the theory of economic determinism in politics." Adair challenged this interpretation in his Ph.D. dissertation and in two ingenious essays, "The Tenth Federalist Revisited" and "That Politics May be Reduced To a Science." According to Adair, the tenth *Federalist* is "eighteenth-century political theory directed toward an eighteenth-century problem...."[38] The problem was whether republicanism could be adopted effectively by an area as large as the United States. Most men, relying on theorists like Montesquieu, felt that it could not be. It was believed that the far-flung sections of a large geographical area could be united and held together only by a great leader who because of the lure of power usually ended up as an absolute monarch. However, in a 1752 essay called the "Idea of a Perfect Commonwealth," David Hume speculated that it would be possible to set up an extended republic in a large area. It would be much more difficult to establish a republic in a large area

---

from the great Scottish skeptic that Hamilton derived his own "cynical psychology." For numerous specific examples of Hamilton's indebtedness to Hume, see Harold C. Syrett, ed., *The Papers of Alexander Hamilton* (New York and London, 1961–), I, 94–95, 100; II, 595, 608; III, 77, 705; VI, 53; X, 8, 241–42, 255–57, 267, 280, 313.

[37]C. Hendel, ed., *Hume's Political Essays*, lix; Syrett, ed., *Papers of Hamilton*, IV, 216, 720–21; Alexander Hamilton, James Madison, John Jay, *The Federalist Papers*, with an Introduction by Clinton Rossiter (New York, 1961), 526–27.

[38]Charles A. Beard, *An Economic Interpretation of the Constitution of the United States* (New York, 1965 edition), 15; Douglass G. Adair, "The Tenth Federalist Revisited," *The William and Mary Quarterly*, 3d series, VIII (1951), 67.

than in a small area, but once established, its very largeness would help protect against and control the disintegrating effects of economic, religious, and political factions—the endemic plague of small republics. Adair demonstrates that Madison was familiar with Hume's essays and that the Virginian realized that here in America all of Hume's theoretical foundations for a stable, large republic were already present. Madison believed that if the opposing economic interests of a large territory could be combined with a federal system of thirteen semi-sovereign states and a system of indirect elections which would help refine pure democracy, it would be possible to establish a stable republic in this country. This, then, was Madison's answer to the problem, an answer which obviated any need for a system of mixed government for the new United States.[39] In short, in *Federalist* No. 10, Madison was restating Humean political theory rather than anticipating Marxian economic doctrine.

Other American notables—men such as Samuel Adams, John Dickinson, Charles Lee, George Washington, John Randolph of Roanoke, Benjamin Rush, and Robert Carter of Nomini Hall—had read Hume's *History* and political writings or at least had them in their libraries. Samuel Adams relied on Hume in part, to help support his polemics; John Randolph, in an 1818 letter, said that he had been "bred in the school of Hobbs and Bayle, and Shaftesbury and Bolingbroke, and Hume and Voltaire and Gibbon [and had] cultivated the skeptical philosophy since boyhood." Benjamin Rush had met Hume while studying medicine at Edinburgh, and in later life made favorable references to the *History*. John Dickinson called him, "this great man whose political speculations are so much admired." The erratic Charles Lee, however, was not an admirer. Lee wrote an ironical tract in 1770 directed toward Hume and titled "Epistle." The "Epistle" subtly held Hume up to ridicule for the way he had supposedly whitewashed the House of Stuart in his *History*.[40] Unhappily, Hume

[39] Douglass G. Adair, "The Intellectual Origins of Jeffersonian Democracy: Republicanism, the Class Struggle and the Virtuous Farmer," Unpublished Ph.D. dissertation (Yale University, 1943), 220 ff.; Adair, " 'That Politics May Be Reduced To A Science': David Hume, James Madison, and the Tenth *Federalist*," *The Huntington Library Quarterly*, XX, (1957), 343–60.

[40] Claude Van Tyne, *The Causes of the War of Independence: being the first volume of a history of the founding of the American Republic* (Boston and New York, 1922), 344; Colbourn, *Lamp of Experience*, 76, 216; Harry A. Cushing, ed., *The Writings of Samuel Adams*, 4 vols. (New York and London, 1906), II, 189, 325; John Randolph to Dr. John Brockenbrough, Sept. 25, 1818, Russell Kirk, *John Randolph of Roanoke: A Study in American Politics* (Chicago, 1964), 223; John A. Schutz and Douglass Adair, eds., *The Spur of Fame: Dialogues of John Adams and Benjamin Rush, 1805–1813* (San Marino, 1966), 12, 67, 169; Parrington, *Main Currents*, I, 228, 242; Edward Robins, "Charles Lee–Stormy Petrel of The Revolution," *The Pennsylvania Magazine of History and Biography*, XLV (1921), 71–73.

had made other American adversaries, two men much more influential than Charles Lee.

John Adams and Thomas Jefferson execrated Hume's work, particularly *The History of England*. Prior to the 1800's, however, there was little in the writings of either man to indicate what was to become deep animosity in later years. Indeed, in 1790, Jefferson admitted in a letter to Thomas Mann Randolph that several of Hume's political essays were good. Jefferson ended on this cryptic note, never mentioning specifically the ones he liked. His library catalogue furnishes only the information that Jefferson did have some of Hume's essays but does not say which ones.[41]

With Adams also, the picture is one of early attraction followed by alienation in later years. In a clash with William Brattle in 1772 over the issue of salaries for Superior Court judges in Massachusetts, Adams buttressed his stand by reference to British historians (Hume among them), as well as the traditional common law authorities. In his *Defense of the Constitutions of Government of the United States* published in 1787 and 1788, Adams did attack Hume briefly for the supposed unicameralism advocated in "Idea of a Perfect Commonwealth" but, in another section, Adams revealed that he was not yet estranged completely when he wrote that the legislator must presuppose mankind's natural political badness. This is one of Hume's political maxims.[42] Yet it does seem odd that Adams, a consummate political theorist, should have referred to Hume's writings so seldom.

By the second decade of the nineteenth century it was obvious that the two old revolutionaries, Adams and Jefferson, had no use for the man who had once longed to see America totally in revolt. It is also evident that if it had been possible, they would have expunged all traces of Humean influence. Referring to the *History*, Adams, in an 1816 letter to Jefferson, called Hume a "conceited Scotchman," and said that Americans were too intelligent to be talked out of their freedom, even by such impressive names as Locke or Hume. In another 1816 letter to Jefferson, Adams said that Hume's *History of England* had greatly increased the tories at the expense of the whigs. Adams referred to this *History* as "the bane of Great Britain" adding

[41]Thomas Jefferson to Thomas Mann Randolph, May 30, 1790, Albert E. Bergh, ed., *The Writings of Thomas Jefferson*, 20 vols. (Washington, 1907), VIII, 32. Hereafter cited as *Jefferson's Writings*; E. Millicent Sowerby, ed., *Catalogue of the Library of Thomas Jefferson* (Washington, 1952).

[42]L. Kinvin Wroth and Hiller B. Zobel, eds., *Legal Papers of John Adams*, 4 vols. in *The Adams Papers* series, Lyman H. Butterfield, ed. (Cambridge, Mass., 1965), I, lxxxix; Correa M. Walsh, *The Political Science of John Adams: A Study in the Theory of Mixed Government and the Bicameral System* (New York and London, 1915), 16 and n., 40n.

that it had completely forced out all the honest histories written by men like Paul de Rapin-Thoyras, Gilbert Burnet, and John Oldmixon. These men were representative of the whig writers Hume criticized severely in his conclusion to the reigns of the Stuarts. Hume called their compositions worthless both as to style and content.[43]

Imbued as he was with whig political principles, Thomas Jefferson could not let such derogatory remarks go unchallenged. Among Hume's American critics, Jefferson was most sustained in his denunciation. Jefferson said that Hume's *History* had done more to undermine the principles of the English Constitution than the largest standing army ever could hope to have achieved. And in another letter:

What the patriots of the last age dreaded & deprecated from a standing army, and what could not have been achieved for the crown by any standing army, but with torrents of blood, one man, by the magic of his pen, has effected covertly, insensibly, peaceably; and has made voluntary converts of the best men of the present age to the parricide opinions of the worst of the last. . . .[44]

Responding to a letter from Major John Cartwright in 1824, Jefferson called Hume the "great apostle of Toryism," a "degenerate son of science," and a "traitor to his fellow men." In a letter to William Duane in 1810, Jefferson admitted that he had been an enthusiastic reader of Hume's *History* when a young man and then had to spend a great deal of time in research and reflection to "eradicate the tory poison" which it had instilled into his mind.[45]

In other letters Jefferson did admit that Hume had an elegant style even if it was biased. As an antidote to Hume, Jefferson constantly recommended a history written by another Briton, John Baxter, Baxter's *History*, according to Jefferson, was really just Hume's *History* with the offensive parts deleted. The last entry in Jefferson's *Commonplace Book* was a satire upon some of Hume's writings. Jefferson first

[43]John Adams to Thomas Jefferson, Dec. 25, 1816, Charles Francis Adams, ed., *The Works of John Adams, Second President of the United States,* 10 vols. (Boston, 1851), IV, 466–67, X, 82; Adams to Jefferson, Dec. 16, 1816, *Jefferson's Writings,* XV, 91–92; Hume, *History of England,* (1885 edition), VI, 320. It is interesting to note that Locke as well as Hume, had fallen from Adams' favor with the passage of years. In his *Thoughts on Government,* published in 1776, Adams had praised Locke highly.

[44]Jefferson to John Adams, Nov. 25, 1816, *Jefferson's Writings,* XV, 81; Lester J. Cappon, ed., *The Adams-Jefferson Letters: The Complete Correspondence Between Thomas Jefferson and Abigail and John Adams,* 2 vols. (Chapel Hill, 1959), 498; Jefferson to Matthew Carey, Nov. 22, 1818, Sowerby, ed. *Catalogue of Jefferson,* I, 176–77, 178–79.

[45]Jefferson to John Cartwright, June 5, 1824, Philip S. Foner, *Basic Writings of Thomas Jefferson* (New York, 1944), 788; Jefferson to William Duane, Aug. 12, 1810, *Jefferson's Writings,* XII, 406–07; Adrienne Koch, *The Philosophy of Thomas Jefferson* (Gloucester, 1957), 126.

quoted Hume on some terrible punishments handed out formerly by English courts. Hume stated that considering the general character of the age, these punishments were not that inhuman. Jefferson next used a statement of Hume's out of context and asked if all men will not eventually come to agree with Hume that an absolute monarchy is not such a terrible thing.[46]

It is ironic that Hume, who had expressed approval of the American experiment and who had sided emotionally with them in their struggle, should have suffered so much abuse for his *History of England* from some Americans such as the younger Dulany, Jefferson, and John Adams. Considering the harsh nature of their criticism of this work, it is questionable whether any of Hume's writings exerted substantial influence upon these men. To be sure, not all Americans detested Hume and for these men the Scot's political and historical works were available in both private and public libraries.[47] Charles Carroll, Benjamin Franklin, Alexander Hamilton, James Madison, Josiah Quincy, Jr., and Thomas Paine, among others, were inspired by Hume and borrowed from his thoughts on politics, economics, and history.

Even the Americans who read only Hume's *History* were exposed to the philosophical and political thought it contained, and the majority of the American leadership had read at least this much. Because of this familiarity, and because he was referred to frequently, it can be maintained with a degree of assurance that David Hume's writings were of importance in the intellectual formation of the United States.

Western Illinois University.

[46] Jefferson to H. G. Spafford, Mar. 17, 1814, Samuel E. Forman, ed., *The Life and Writings of Thomas Jefferson* (Indianapolis, 1900); Jefferson to John Norvall, June 14, 1807, Paul L. Ford, ed., *The Writings of Thomas Jefferson*, 10 vols. (New York and London, 1898), 72; Jefferson to George Washington Lewis, Oct. 25, 1825, *Jefferson's Writings*, XVI, 124–28; Gilbert Chinard, *The Commonplace Book of Thomas Jefferson: A Repertory of His Ideas on Government* (Baltimore and Paris, 1926), 374–76.

[47] Colbourn, *Lamp of Experience*, Appendix II.